CU01335243

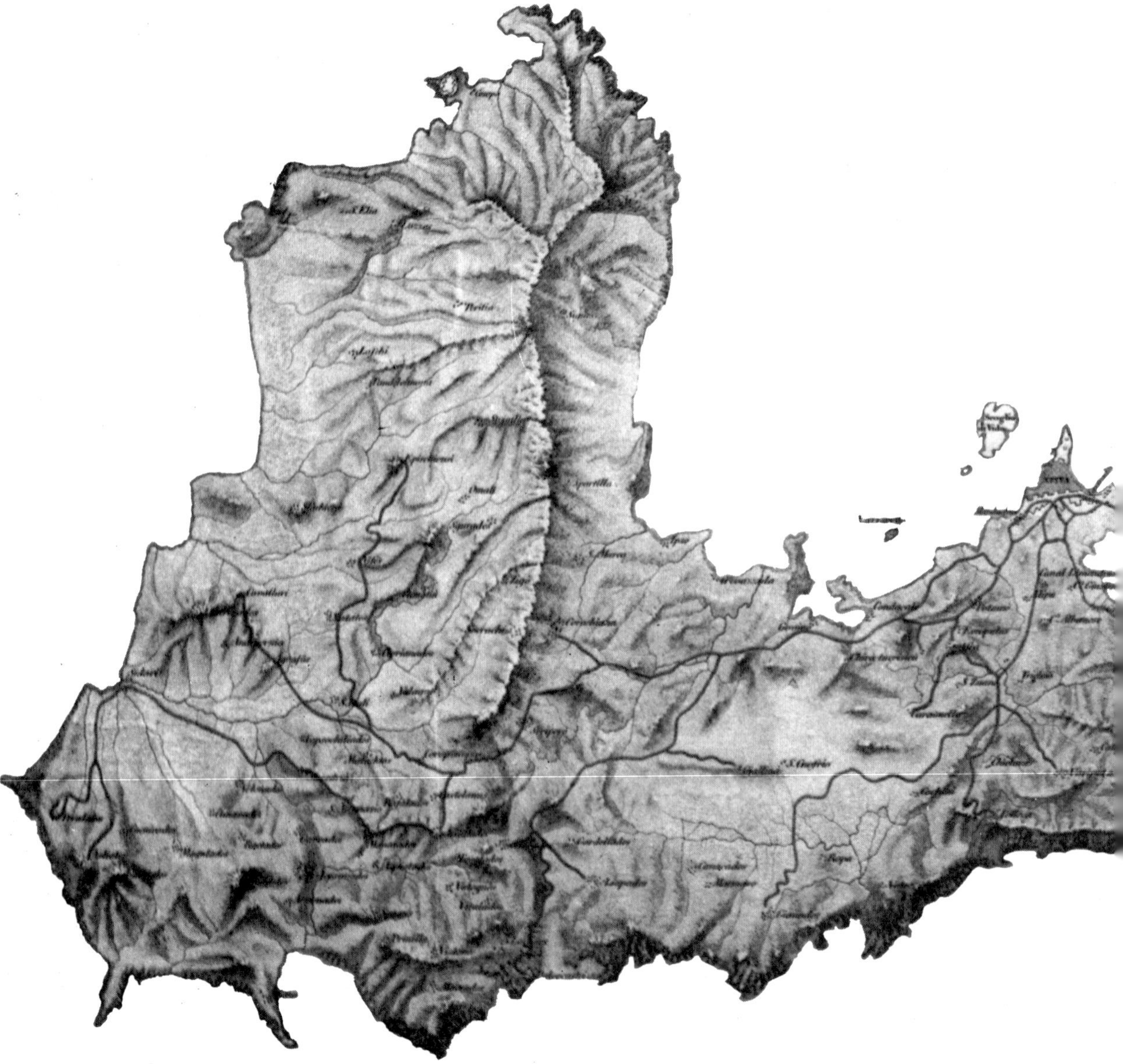

THE CORFU YEARS

Dear Monty,
Happy Birthday
Many thanks
All love
Yours
Theodore & Trish
Corfu 1988.

EDWARD LEAR

The Corfu Years

A CHRONICLE
PRESENTED THROUGH HIS LETTERS
AND
JOURNALS

EDITED AND INTRODUCED
BY
PHILIP SHERRARD

DENISE HARVEY & COMPANY
ATHENS – DEDHAM

First published in 1988 by
Denise Harvey & Company
Lambrou Fotiadi 6, 116 36 Athens, Greece
and
The Sanctuary, Dedham, Essex, England

© Denise Harvey & Company
The Corfu Years is the tenth publication in
THE ROMIOSYNI SERIES

Phototypeset by Fotron S.A.
Colour separation and montage by Memigraph
Printed in Greece by Veskouki Bros.
Bound by Zervini Bros.

British Library Cataloguing in Publication Data

Lear, Edward, *1812–1888*
Edward Lear, the Corfu years;
a chronicle presented through his letters & journals.
(The Romiosyni series; 10).
1. Greece. Corfu. Description & travel, 1855–1864
I. Title II. Sherrard, Philip III. Series 914.95'5

ISBN 0-907978-25-8

CONTENTS

Introduction

    The Place 9

    The Person 20

Acknowledgements 35

Textual Note 36

The Text 37

Appendix 1: Lear as Landscape Painter 229

Appendix 2: The New Barbarism 237

Notes 238

Map of Corfu 246–7

To Marie Aspioti, M.B.E.
who loves her island so well

INTRODUCTION

THE PLACE

When Edward Lear first visited Corfu in April 1848, the island had already been under British rule for thirty-three years: it was in 1815, through the Treaty of Paris, that Corfu and the other Ionian Islands became 'a single, free, and independent state under the exclusive protection of His Britannic Majesty'. But this conversion to British rule was only yet another variation in the pattern of the island's history of domination by foreign powers. The most influential of these powers where the general character of the island — and indeed of all the Ionian Islands — was concerned was undoubtedly Venice. The Ionian Islands came under the control of Venice as the result of the 4th Crusade (1204), and three years later (1207) Corfu, Paxos and the adjacent islands were transferred to 10 Venetian nobles, whose obligation it was to be responsible for the defence of the islands and to pay the Venetian Republic an annual tribute of 500 gold pieces.

Although this period of indirect Venetian rule was interrupted when in 1267 Corfu was added to the dominions of Charles of Anjou, King of Naples, the island again reverted to the Venetians in 1387, and in 1402 Venice's rights of direct suzerainty were explicitly formalized. The Doge guaranteed the observation of all the Corfiotes' traditional privileges, confirmed all fiefs and titles of nobility, and merely stipulated that justice should be represented by both Greek and Venetian laws. In return, the Corfu community surrendered its time-honoured exemption from taxes and tolls, provided that the walls of the city were repaired. The Republic's promise to defend Corfu and never to dispose of it was enshrined in the Golden Bull, charter of the island's liberties which remained in force for the four hundred odd years of Venetian rule that was to follow.

Since the main purpose of the Venetians in occupying Corfu was to use it as a base from which to promote their control of the major maritime trade-routes from Europe to the Levant, they had inevitably turned the town itself into a kind of extended fortress, with an Arsenal for their galleys. Originally the town was confined to the Citadel, a high triangular promontory jutting out into the channel of Corfu and bathed naturally on two of its sides by the sea, while on the third side it was separated by the Venetians from the rest of the island by a canal straddled by a wooden bridge (now replaced by a fixed bridge some 60 metres in length). The Citadel, about 500 metres long by 200 metres wide, forms a kind of platform surmounted by two upthrusting peaks of rock, each of which was crowned with a fort, and enclosed with walls and bastions. At the base of the Citadel, and cut off from it by the canal, runs the Esplanade, once the exercise-ground of the garrison but subsequently becoming the chief strolling-ground of the Corfiotes. Opposite the bridge over the canal lies a small square, and it was from here that the main town gradually spread, southwards along the Bay of Garítsa, and north-west to Mandoúki, the resort of fishermen and

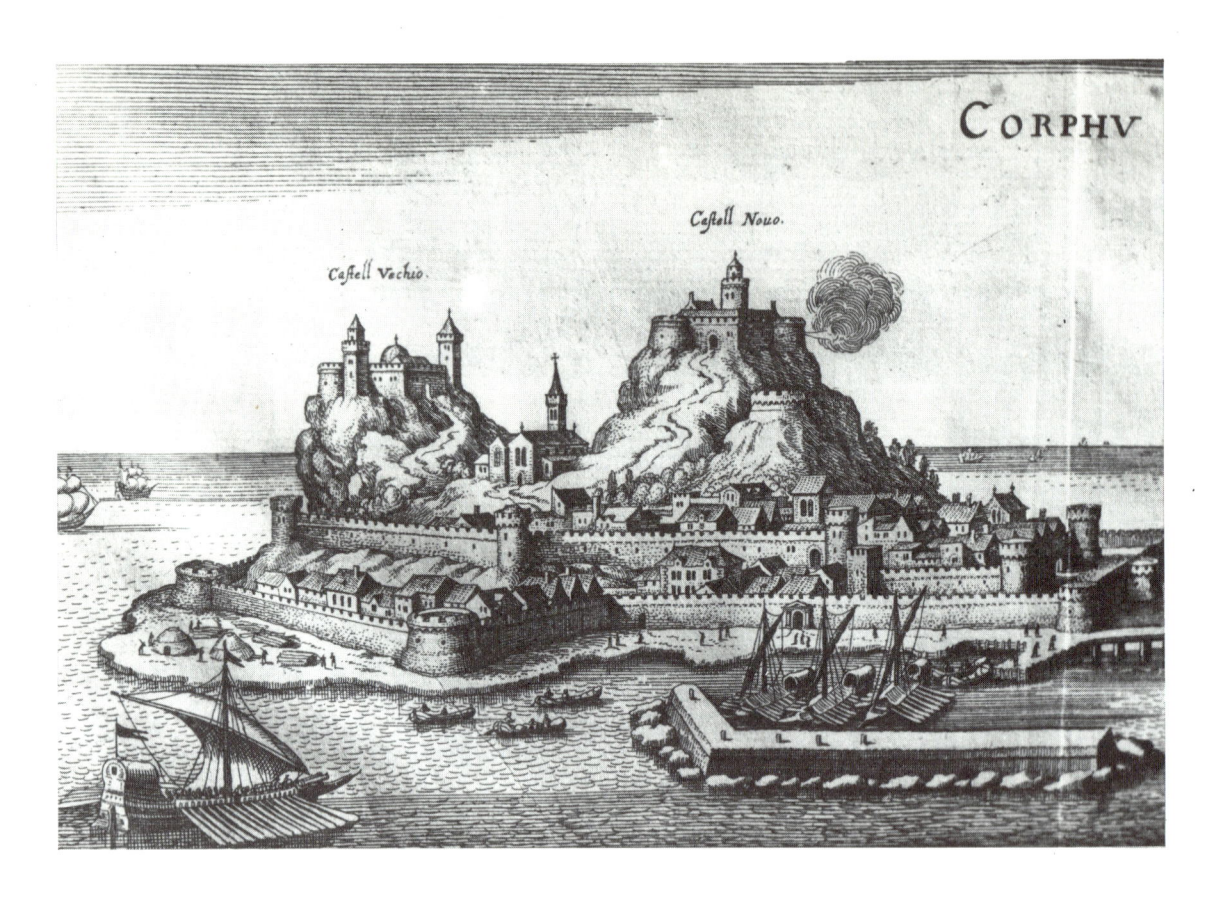

The early Citadel with the castellated dwelling-houses around its base.

free-lance pirates, the whole area being enclosed on the landward side by ramparts. Beyond the ramparts, on dominating heights like Mt Abraham and San Rocco, other forts were built, to complete the embattled complex.

Although Venetian domination of the island came to an end in 1797, and was followed by brief periods of French and of Russo-Turkish occupation before it was taken over by the British in 1815, the structure of 19th century Corfiote society, as well as the conditions of land tenure and the habits of the people, were, as I have indicated, largely determined by the centuries of Venetian sovereignty. The Orthodox Church — perhaps the most important element in this structure — had not been persecuted, although this did not lessen its hostility towards the Roman Church. In fact, many Roman Catholics converted to Orthodoxy, often as a result of mixed marriages, and by 1775, it is said, only two noble families in Corfu still adhered to the Church of Rome. Long before this — in 1457 — an event had taken place which provided the focus for what was to become and still continues to be the crowning manifestation of the island's religious life: the relics of St Spirídon were brought from Constantinople to Corfu. The church built to house them — the richest in Corfu and possessing the

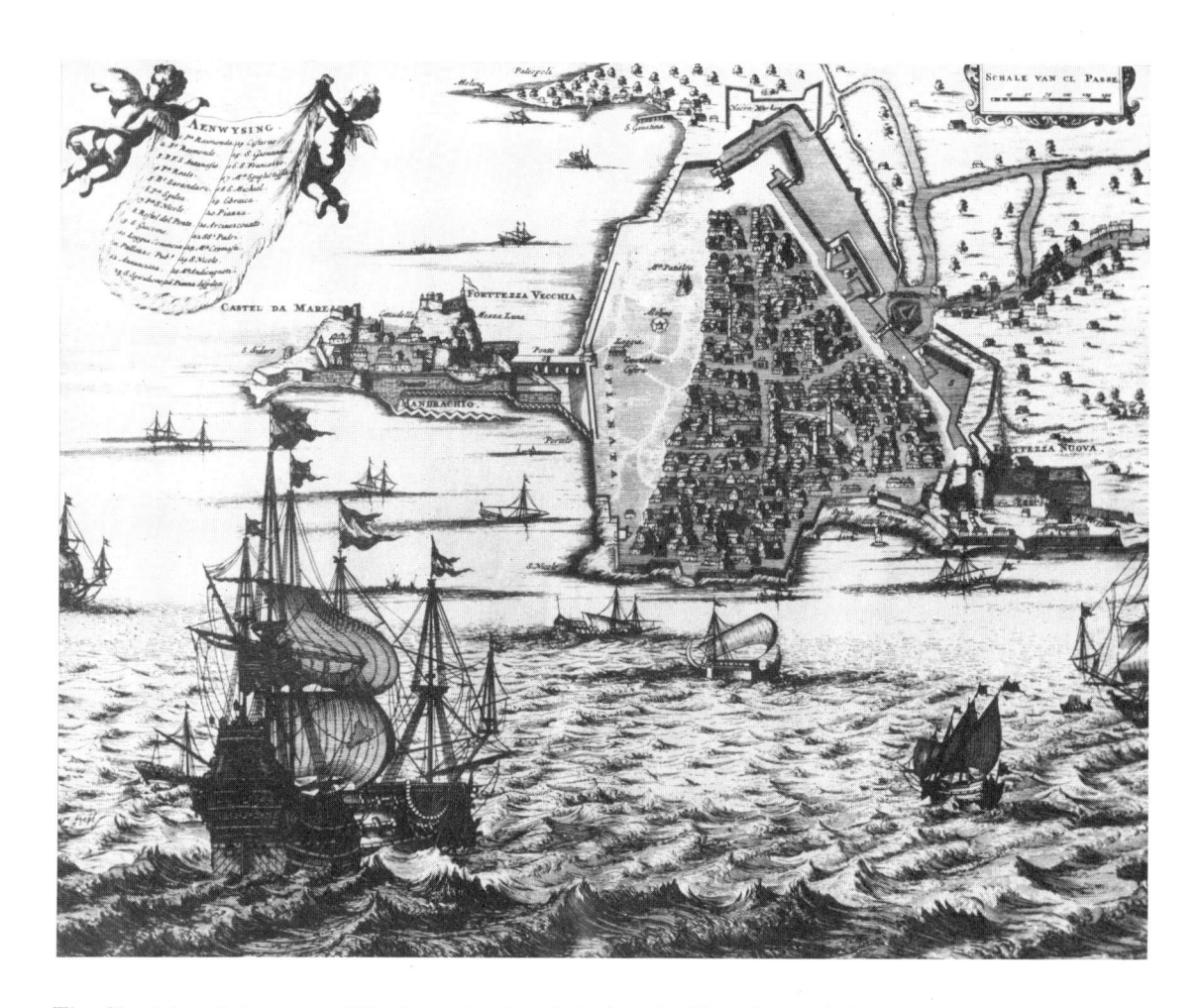

The Citadel and the town of Corfu as developed during the Venetian period.

highest campanile — was begun in 1589; and the saint himself was honoured in four annual processions: that on Palm Sunday, on Easter Saturday, on 11th August, and on the first Sunday in November.

If the Greek Orthodox faith retained its ascendancy under Venetian rule, the Greek language suffered an eclipse. Italian became the language of justice, of commerce and of the administration generally. An Ionian who wished to prosper had to use the language of his rulers, and this meant that, except for the clergy, the educated and better-off members of Corfiote society spoke Italian, not Greek, among themselves, and many of them were educated in Italy. Only the peasants still spoke in their native language. It is symptomatic of this predominance of the Italian language — and culture — that the first national poet of modern Greece, Dionýsios Solomós (1798–1857)[1] — who although born on the neighbouring island of Zakinthos (Zantë)

[1] Lear knew Solomós's poetry — or at least he bought of volume of his poems: see his journal for 1 May 1862.

settled in 1828 in Corfu — wrote most of his early poetry and many of the preliminary sketches of his later poetry in Italian. Nor did this state of affairs substantially change under the British Protectorate. For although the first British Lord High Commissioner decreed in 1817 that Greek should be the language of the law and of the government, thirty years elapsed before the decree became in any way effective. For their part, of course, very few British officials possessed even a working knowledge of Greek or Italian, a fact which only exacerbated their already inbuilt incapacity to regard any culture other than their own as worthy of sympathy or interest.

The Republic of Venice maintained its hegemony largely through the landowning class in the island, eliciting the support of this class by the creation of a large number of Counts; and the island's administration was largely in the hands of this local aristocracy. This aristocracy, although shorn of most of its administrative authority, was likewise sustained by the British; for in 1818 the Prince Regent instituted the Order of St Michael and St George 'for natives of the Ionian Islands and of the Island of Malta' and for His Majesty's subjects holding 'posts of confidence in the Mediterranean'.

The landowning class had already begun to build country houses for its members as far back as the 16th century, and this practice was continued under British rule. It also contrived to keep the peasants in a considerable state of depression, in which they were little more than serfs of the local barons, with no political status. The Venetians, it is true, had encouraged the planting of olive trees, but they refused to allow the development of local industries which might compete with their own. The other main produce was the currants, a lucrative source of trade for the Levant Company founded under Elizabeth I for the purpose of gaining a monopoly of trade in Turkish and Venetian ports in the East Mediterranean.

Again, this state of affairs was not substantially changed under the British Protectorate. For although the British attempted to put the judiciary on a sound footing, and built roads and aqueducts and so on, they did little or nothing to alleviate the lot of the peasantry, and on the other hand decreased the participation of the local educated and aristocratic class in the effective power of government. By virtue of the constitution approved in 1817 and in force for the next thirty years — it was largely the work of the first Lord High Commissioner, General Sir Thomas Maitland, and bears the stamp of his authoritarian mind — all effective power was virtually in the hands of the Lord High Commissioner: he, with little or no check from the English parliament, wielded all executive powers, controlled police, posts, sanitation, could declare emergencies, arrest, imprison or exile without trial, determine foreign policy and the military establishments, and directly, or through the use of his veto, control the membership of the Ionian Senate and the Ionian Assembly (freedom to election to which was in any case virtually confined to the municipalities). Most of the important posts — Treasurer, Garrison General, Chief of Police, Principal Secretaries, members of the Supreme Judicial Bench — were all held by Englishmen. Both the British garrison and the civilian officials remained largely aloof from the local population.

One colourful exception to this authoritarian insularity was the eminent Philhellene, Frederick North, Earl of Guilford. He had been received into the Orthodox Church in 1791 when staying in Corfu, was a friend of Capodístrias, the first President of independent Greece, and had subsequently returned to Corfu and founded a small university, the College of Fort St George, of which in 1824 he became the first Chancellor. There were four faculties — theology, jurisprudence, medicine and philosophy — and by 1827, the year of North's death, the library contained some 21,000 volumes. A future rector of this institution was to be George Bowen, at whose invitation Lear first came to Corfu, but whose subsequent behaviour as Secretary to the Lord High Commissioner was to evoke some of the most bitter invective in all Lear's writing. The university survived, though on a reduced scale, until the final years of the Protectorate, but after the cession of Corfu to Greece in 1864 it was closed down. North took his role as an educator of the Greeks with great seriousness: a fellow-Philhellene describes visiting him in his old palace in Corfu, a maze of intricate endless corridors, where he sat before a blazing fire, surrounded by papers and books, dressed as Socrates: 'his mantle pendant from his shoulder by a golden clasp, and his head bound by a fillet embroidered with the olive and the owl of Athens.' The students of his academy wore a tunic and a chlamys, bound their hair like Hermes, and sported red leather buskins reaching to the knee. Its teaching staff included such distinguished personages as the Greek poet Andreas Kalvos.

Other cultural institutions established during this period included the Philological Society of Corfu, founded in 1836 and subsequently transformed into the still-existing Reading Society, and the Society of the Friends of Learning, founded in

The seat of the Corfu Reading Society, drawn by Lear, 9 May 1857.

1845 for the purpose of discussing literary, artistic and scientific topics. Finally, in 1851, the Ionian Association was founded, chiefly for the purpose of promoting agricultural and industrial projects. Long prior to these ventures was the theatre, built in the merchants' loggia in 1693.

The architecture of the town at the time of Lear's sojourn was also mainly, though by no means exclusively, Venetian. An English visitor residing there some few years prior to Lear's first visit comments on 'the strange architecture of this strange-looking city': 'It is neither Norman nor Gothic, neither ancient nor modern, but an odd jumble of all. Here are a few houses from Strada Mercante, the high narrow pointed windows, the short thick pillars of the balconies, the porticoes supporting broad stone terraces, remind one of Venice; then follows a lofty, straight, unadorned campanile, towering over all the buildings in the vicinity; this, and the smaller church with painted gable ends, tricked out with Chinese-looking bells, are surely of French origin, and strongly contrast with the well in the square: — the well, whose broad flat steps seem made on purpose for gossiping, and whose heavy stone work, covered with quaint tracery, savours strongly of Moorish origin . . .'.[2]

After landing by boat and passing through the Custom House you would enter first into a maze of narrow streets, crowded bazaars full of fruit and vegetable stalls, arcades, gloomy recesses, houses of rich Greeks side by side with houses fallen into ruin, churches (there were 36 Orthodox churches and 5 Latin churches), shops loaded with the most odd assortment of articles: old books, old crockery, millinery, mirrors, photographs and soda water, modern jewellery, canes, hats, umbrellas, nightcaps — in fact you would enter into a kind of polyglot, multi-racial architectural and human compound to which all the countries of Europe and some of North Africa had contributed. From this you would only escape when you emerged on to the Esplanade fronting the Citadel, at one end of which stood the residency of the Lord High Commissioner, the Palace of St Michael and St George, whose colonnade connects by two gates to — on the left — the garrison, library and reading rooms and — on the right — a corresponding structure forming another wing. Two statues, an obelisk, and a little circular temple added to the Esplanade's adornment.

As for the population of the city and its suburbs, this in Lear's time was as varied and colourful as its architecture. In 1860 it was estimated to number some 17,500 people, divided into three main groups. About one third were Jews, distinguished by their blue dresses if not by their physiognomy, living in a Ghetto — the Hebraica — neither dirtier, more noisy nor more crowded than other quarters of the city, and apparently acting chiefly as porters: 'Thus,' notes a visitor[3] during the years of Lear's residence, 'one is constantly liable, in passing along the narrow streets of the town, to meet a procession of good-natured sons of Israel — one, entirely buried under a huge chest of drawers — another, fantastically covered with a chair — a third, yawning under a bedstead — and a fourth, decorated with pots, pans, glass and crockery.' A

---

[2] See Frances Maclellen, *Sketches of Corfu* (London, 1835).
[3] D. T. Ansted, in his *The Ionian Islands in the Year 1863* (London, 1863).

Street-scene in the town of Corfu.

second third of the population was made up of Turks, Maltese, Italians, Albanians, Dalmatians and many other races — 'all, indeed,' the same visitor comments, 'of that mongrel class for which the shores of the Mediterranean have been notorious from times immemorial; these are, as it were, the camp-followers of the English garrison' and 'do no credit to anybody'. The final third was made up of Greeks, who included among their number the more wealthy and better educated section of the population, descendents of the Venetian-sponsored aristocracy, landowners, traders and merchants. Of course, this urban Greek community was but a small part of the Greek population of the island: the peasants were virtually all Greeks.

Superimposed on this local hotchpotch were the administrators and officials of the British Protectorate, headed by the Lord High Commissioner and his immediate entourage, complemented by the officers and men of the garrison, and attended by wives, children, nannies, servants, desultory relatives, sporadic guests and inevitable hangers-on. I shall have something to say about the dominant cast and character of this British community in the second part of this Introduction. All it is necesary to add here is that when not engaged in their official duties, its members strove to pass their time in a seemingly endless succession of organized frivolity and distraction: picnics,

Corfu Garrison cricket-match on the Esplanade.

teaparties, balls, dinners, card-playing, horseback paperchases, yachting trips, hunting, mock military antics, church bazaars, cricket, and anything else that could be devised, all compounded as they were with the prittle-prattle of gossip, the titivation of scandal or romance, the bustles, topboots, sidewhiskers and protocols of fashion and gentility, and the unmuted purr of imperial self-satisfaction. But whatever else it might do, one thing this self-engrossed British society would not do, and that was to demean itself by any attempt to understand the people over whom it exercised its unsolicited guardianship: as one British observer[4] succinctly put it, between the British and the Greeks 'no love . . . is lost: they hold us in utter contempt, and we look on them as removed but one degree from donkeys.'

The town, as I noted, was enclosed on its landward side by ramparts, and beyond these ramparts one entered a totally different world. 'When we have passed through the ramparts that enclose the town of Corfu,' writes the observer from whom I have just quoted, 'novelty greets us at every step . . . You presently lose sight of all traces of man, his industry and ingenuity; and in a few minutes may wander in a solitude as

[4] Frances Maclellen, in her *Sketches of Corfu*, op. cit.

profound as though not a creature existed in the island but yourself. Now and then you may just distinguish a little white church like a Swiss chalet, peeping through the olives on the summit of a distant hill . . . ; they are opened only once in a year, on the saint's days to whom they are dedicated; therefore you need not fear interruption; and if you do occasionally pass an Albanian in his shaggy capote, guarding his goats and sheep along the ledges of the precipices, or a dark graceful girl with a pitcher on her head, wending slowly along the narrow pathway that leads from the fountain to the valley, they are both in perfect harmony with the scene . . .'

In perfect harmony also with the scene was the incredible richness of the flora: irises, virginia stock, asphodels, whole fields of lupins, marigolds as plentiful as daisies, cyclamen, anemones, crocus, snowdrops, clematis, arbutus, myrtle, cherry trees, coronilla, orange trees, vineyards, banana, pomegranate and fig trees, and the two most emblematic of all, the cypress and the olive, its silvery gray-green relieved here as nowhere else in Greece by the emerald-coloured sward of grass growing beneath it. The Venetians gave ten gold pieces for every grove of a hundred olive trees planted, until when they left, it is said, the islanders possessed nearly two million trees.

The British of course had set no deadline for the termination of their Protectorate, but in the event their departure was precipitated by circumstances they could not have foreseen when in 1815 they took the islands over. The outbreak of the Greek war of Independence in 1821, and the establishment of the modern Greek state in 1830, could not but have repercussions in Corfu and in the Ionian Islands generally; and the call for union — *enosis* — with the newly-founded state grew in intensity as the years went by. The British could not persistently ignore such a demand, but at first they felt they could temper if not assuage it through the introduction of constitutional reforms. Impetus in this direction was greatly stimulated in 1848 — the year of Lear's first visit — by the series of revolts in the name of liberal doctrines which broke out in several European cities, and even, in the summer of 1849, in Kefaloniá. The political temperature began to rise. The Lord High Commissioner, Lord Seaton, reacted, as one observer put it, by hurrying 'the wandering Ionians through more political changes in ten days than England had undergone since the reign of Queen Elizabeth'.[5] His successor, Sir Henry Ward, the seventh High Commissioner, continued the process. The press was made free, the franchise was extended, and members of the Assembly were to be freely elected. But the powers of the High Commissioner remained: he still nominated his own executive council and designated the Senate; and this of course meant that the popularly elected Assembly had no effective power. The reforms fundamentally left things where they always had been.

As a result, hostility to the British grew, and with it grew civil agitation. In any case, those who demanded union with Greece were not going to be fobbed off with constitutional reforms, however radical, and did all they could to thwart their implementation. In addition to this the Greek language had, in 1852, at last

[5] See Michael Pratt, *Britain's Greek Empire* (London, 1978), p. 133.

Corfu from the south, by General Sir Arthur Herbert, 1861.

superseded Italian and English as the official language, and this meant that the British administration had to conduct official business largely through Greek-speaking subordinates. In the face of the mounting perplexities the eighth High Commissioner, Sir John Young, in 1857 secretly recommended to the Colonial Secretary that Corfu and Paxos should, with the consent of their inhabitants, be declared Crown Colonies, and that the five remaining Ionian Islands should be ceded to Greece. That Young could make such a proposal adequately demonstrates how far the British were from realizing the strength of the Corfiotes' call for union with Greece. Even the great Gladstone — in 1858 appointed High Commissioner Extraordinary and in 1859 High Commissioner — was totally stymied by it in his attempt to introduce yet more reforms, and returned to London 'disgusted with Greeks in general, and the Ionians in particular'.

The truth of the matter seems to be that the British Protectorate had singularly failed to gain or deserve the respect and confidence of the Corfiotes or of the other Ionian islanders. As one independent contemporary observer put it: 'All tourists write of the ever-blue Ionian sky, of the mild climate of the islands, that makes everything glistening and fragrant, and awakens ardent desire; but they know nothing of the inhabitants of these islands, nothing of their deplorable circumstances, of their mental depression, of their social and material misery. They might ask, "Is there not floating here the tricolour of a free state? Is she not upheld and protected by the claws of the English leopard; ennobled by being called under the protectorate of the most civilized nation in the world?" Englishmen, however, care for nothing but their military

Corfu from the north, by General Sir Arthur Herbert, 1861.

establishment; they say they have no wish to interfere with the management of internal affairs; it appears to me, however, worthy of a civilized nation to exercise some influence on the civilization of a country over which they have allowed the flag of their power and their ambition to float. The eyes of the Ionians, weary of the English Protectorate, are ever directed towards the kingdom of Greece, with which they would wish to be incorporated . . . On these islands, which might well be termed fortunate, in virtue of their happy climate and their fruitful soil, the children remain without instruction, the adults without civilization, the courts of justice without respect — tourists, sir, spoil all.'[6]

Under the tenth and final High Commissioner, Colonel Sir Henry Storks, things went from bad to worse, and only an unexpected event prevented the total breakdown of British rule in the Islands and gave a brief respite. In 1862, King Otho of Greece abdicated and the Greeks offered the vacant throne to Prince Alfred, the second son of Queen Victoria, later Duke of Edinburgh. Alfred had visited Corfu in 1859 and had made an excellent impression. It was hoped that if he became king of Greece he would bring the Ionian Islands with him. But although the Greek people, by popular suffrage, voted overwhelmingly in his favour, Alfred was prevented from accepting the offer by protocols to Treaties signed in 1832 whereby no prince of the reigning families of Britain, France and Russia could sit on the throne of Greece. Nevertheless, Lord Palmerston, now prime-minister, realized that he could play the card of the cession of the Ionian Islands to Greece in order to persuade the Greeks to choose a monarch

[6] See L. A. Frankl, *The Jews in the East*, trans. P. Beaton (London, 1859), p. 8.

favourable to British interests. In December 1862 the cabinet decided to adopt this scheme as official policy, and the Greeks were duly informed. By offering the throne to Prince William of Denmark (whose sister, Princess Alexandra, had married the Prince of Wales) the Greeks fulfilled their side of the bargain, Prince William becoming George the First, King of the Hellenes, in 1863. It now only remained for the British to fulfil theirs.

They took over a year in doing so, and even when the cession was finally approved it was with the proviso that both Corfu and Paxos were to be neutralized and the massive fortifications of Corfu were to be demolished: only the famous Citadel was to be left intact. This last condition was one the Corfiotes particularly resented, for the Ionians had contributed substantially to the defences during the Protectorate, not to mention the Venetian and French contribution prior to this. Nevertheless, in February 1864 the work of demolition began, a sad postscript to British rule; and a few months later, on June 2nd 1864, the tenth and last Lord High Commissioner embarked on Her Majesty's ship *Malborough*, the British colours on the remaining forts were lowered, and the Protectorate was at an end. Four days later the young king of the Hellenes landed in Corfu to the salute of guns and the pealing of bells, and proceeded to the church of St Spirídon to celebrate a Te Deum. But this event Lear was not to witness: on Monday, 4th April 1864, he had left Corfu on the first stage of his journey to Crete and, except for fleeting visits in 1866 and 1877, he was never to return.

THE PERSON

It was, then, to this island of Corfu that Lear came in 1848, invited, as we noted, by George Bowen, Rector of the University, whom he had met a few months previously in Rome; and it was to be this island that, especially from 1855 onwards, was to serve as his main base until its cession to Greece, although his sojourn on it was by no means uninterrupted and amounted in all to only some months over three years.[7] Lear when he arrived was approaching his 36th birthday, and already the main lines of his life and the main features of his character were well in evidence, however more pronounced they were to become as the years went by. What were these lines and these features? Who was he, this man, and what image of him emerges as we read his letters, his journals and his poems, and listen to the testimony of his friends?

---

[7] The actual dates of Lear's stays in Corfu (except for 4 or 5 days in June 1849 and a brief stop-over in April 1866) and in the Ionian islands generally are as follows:
>   April – May 1848.
>   December 1855 – May 1857, with a break in August – October 1856 for a visit to Mt Athos etc.
>   December 1857 – March 1858.
>   June – August 1858.
>   November 1861 – May 1862.
>   November 1862 – June 1863.
>   January – April 1864.
>   September 1877.

The external course of Lear's life is well charted[8] and does not contain in it anything exceptionally sensational or dramatic. He was born in 1812 in a small village on the outskirts of London, a village becoming fashionable for those who had made good in the city. Lear's father had made good in this way, as a stockbroker, and had bought an elegant Georgian house to house his wife Ann and their rapidly growing family — Lear himself was the 20th out of 21 children, though many of them died in infancy. But a few years after his birth, when he was four years old, Lear's father ran into debt, the family was forced to move (though the house was not actually sold), and to ease the strain on his mother Lear was put in the charge of his sister Ann, the eldest of the children, 22 years older than Lear himself. It was shortly after this — though I am not implying that there is a direct connection — that Lear had his first attack of epilepsy — an illness that never left him and that he was to call 'the demon'. He sometimes had several attacks a day, but he seems to have had warning of them, so he could always withdraw if in company. In fact, he managed to keep his affliction entirely to himself. 'It is wonderful', he wrote in his diary some few years before he died, 'that these fits have never been discovered — except that partly apprehending them beforehand, I go into my room'. At about the age of seven, the fits themselves were followed by acute attacks of depression — what Lear was to call 'the Morbids'. There is no question that Lear's demon and the Morbids, however heroically endured, were a deep source of sorrow and suffering for him throughout his life.

Lear's education was virtually the sole responsibility of his sister Ann. Except possibly for a short spell when he was 11, Lear had absolutely no formal education: he went neither to school nor to university, and had no qualified tutor. Years later, when he was 47, he expresses his enormous thankfulness for this: 'I am almost thanking God', he writes, 'that I was never educated, for it seems to me that 999 [out of a 1000] of those who are so, expensively and laboriously, have lost all before they arrive at my age — & remain like Swift's Stulbrugge — out & dry for life, making no use of their earlier-gained treasures: whereas I seem to be on the threshold of knowledge . . .'. What Ann encouraged him to study, or initiated him into, seems largely to have been classical mythology, the Bible, and the Romantic poets — Wordsworth and Coleridge were still writing when Lear was born, Shelley had just been sent down from Oxford, Keats was still apprenticed to a surgeon, and Byron had published the first two cantos of *Childe Harold*. Ann also taught him painting — mostly, one gathers, the painting of flowers, butterflies and birds. And these pursuits were given a fuller dimension when, at about the age of 11, Lear started visiting another sister, who was married and lived near Arundal, in Sussex, for it was here that he wrote his first poems, and it was from here that he was able to visit the nearby Petworth, where the Earl of Egremont had his fine collection of paintings, above all his collection of paintings by Turner, a painter whose art Lear was to venerate all his life.

At the age of $15\frac{1}{2}$ Lear had to start earning a living. He began doing, he reports,

---

[8] See Angus Davidson, *Edward Lear: Landscape Painter and Nonsense Poet* (London, 1938) and Vivien Noakes, *Edward Lear: The Life of a Wanderer* (London, 1968).

'uncommon queer shop-sketches — selling them for prices varying from ninepence to four shillings: colouring prints, screens, fans; awhile making morbid disease drawings, for hospitals & certain doctors of physic'. He also taught drawing, and then he himself graduated to painting birds. In 1830 — Lear was then 18 — he was given permission to draw parrots in the newly-founded Zoological Gardens in Regent's Park: he moved, thought, looked at and existed among parrots for so long that he felt his soul would be uncomfortable in anything except a parrot. The result of this enterprise was a book, *Illustrations to the Family of Psittacidae, or Parrots*, published in 12 parts. It was Lear's first book, and when the final part was published in 1832 he was just 20 years old, and his reputation as one of the most accomplished craftsmen among early lithographers was made. In addition, these paintings of parrots represent the first positive manifestation of a quality which marked him all his life: his intuitive sympathy with the intelligence of birds and animals.

This achievement in its turn led to a commission which was to change the whole course of Lear's life and to set him within a social context which was to be his for the rest of his days. In 1832 he was asked by Lord Stanley, heir to the 12th Earl of Derby, to stay at the family seat, Knowsley Hall, outside Liverpool, and to draw the animals in his private menagerie, famous throughout Europe. Except for visits to London, and visits to Ireland and the Lake District, Lear was to reside at Knowsley for the next five years, painting the animals, working on other bird books, composing for the delight of the Earl's children and grandchildren many of the limericks that were to go into his first *Book of Nonsense*, published some ten years later, in 1846. But his eyesight was failing, the northern climate aggravated his bronchitis and asthma: 'Hail, Snow, Frost & Desolation', he wrote to a friend. 'I have such a bad cold that I am half blind [and] my eyes are so sadly worse that no bird under an ostrich shall I soon be able to see.' It was time for him to seek out new pastures, more temperate climes; and in the summer of 1837, with help from the Earl and his nephew, he set out for Rome.

Except for one long stay in England between 1849 and 1853, and many short visits there, Lear was to spend the rest of his life abroad, dedicated to the new career he had chosen, that of a Topographical Landscape Painter — or 'dirty landscape painter', as he had been dubbed when on tour in Calabria in 1847: 'I'm a landscape painter, & I desire you like me as sich, or not at all', he wrote to a friend in 1851. He travelled extensively, and often in extreme discomfort — in Italy, Switzerland, Greece, Albania, Egypt, Crete, Palestine, Corsica, India. Everywhere he went he painted his pictures, sketched his sketches, wrote his letters and his journals. He never married. Until the last years of his life he had no home, not even a fixed place of abode, Corfu being the nearest he got to one. The one constant factor in this respect was the kind of society he moved among — the English upper class society to which he had first been introduced at Knowsley and on whose presence at various fashionable or colonial locations in Europe and elsewhere — Rome, Cannes, Nice, Corfu, India — he was dependent for his patronage. Only in his last years, after 1871, did he have his own house, at San Remo, in northern Italy. In fact he built, successively, two houses there. He called the first Villa Emily and the second Villa Tennyson. And it was at the Villa Tennyson that he died on 29th January 1888, a few months before his 76th birthday.

I said that the external course of Lear's life does not contain anything exceptionally sensational or dramatic, any great heights or depths. Given that even in the most restricted, regulated and prosaic life one or two spectacular and horrible things are likely to happen, Lear's life might be said to have been unusually tranquil. He travelled, he came back, he wrote his poems, his letters, his journals, he painted his pictures, and on the surface nothing very much disrupted or ruffled his dedicated and industrious life as a landscape painter. But his inner life was not so even or tranquil. Here there were the most terrible ups and downs and dislocations. One moment, or for a few hours or sometimes days, he was delightfully happy — in the company of friends, or of children (of children particularly), or when his work was going well. Yet a few moments, or hours, or days, later, he would be plunged into the most miserable states of gloom and melancholy and even despair.

> He weeps by the side of the ocean,
> He weeps on the top of the hill . . .

he wrote in a late poem about himself, and it hardly seems an exaggeration.

Time and again in Lear's letters and diaries one comes across phrases like: 'I can go on no more. It makes me almost cry to think of what I suffer.' Or: 'I am in such great sorrow & distress that I am obliged to turn to real friends in the hope of their sending me ever so little a line by post, so that I may feel myself less alone than I am.' Or: 'I am wholly alone . . . & sit at home all day, almost unable to paint from very dejection. It is better you should know this, I think, than that I should sham & tell you I am happy.' Or: 'O! that this blank of life would break into some varied light or shade!' Or: 'Wake, to impatience, blindness and misery. Incapable of deciding whether life can be cured or cursed — I totter giddily, refusing to take any road, yet agonized by staying irresolute.' Or: 'I am doing little, but dimly walking on along the dusky twilight lanes of incomprehensible life.' Or: 'On the whole I do not know if I am living or dead at times.' Such phrases are too frequent — a consistent refrain throughout his life — to be seen merely as the expression of temporary dejection or frustration. They stem from some deep-rooted, seemingly unrootable malaise, from some deep and seemingly incurable wound of the soul.

It is not for nothing, one feels, that Lear was the friend of that prince of melancholia, the poet Tennyson, and that he used to sing, in his little voice, but with intense feeling and individuality, his own settings to music of some of Tennyson's poignant lyrics, accompanying himself on the piano:

> Come not, when I am dead,
>   To drop thy foolish tears upon my grave,
> To trample round my fallen head,
>   And vex the unhappy dust thou wouldst not save.

> There let the wind sweep and the plover cry;
> But thou, go by.

Or, more familiarly:

> Break, break, break,
> At the foot of thy crags, O Sea!
> But the tender grace of a day that is dead
> Will never come back to me.

Or:

> Nightingales warbled without,
> Within was weeping for thee:
> Shadows of three dead men
> Walk'd in the walks with me,
> Shadows of three dead men and thou
> Wast one of the three.

And may it not have been something more than talent and artistic disposition that made Lear choose the profession of topographical landscape painter and that shaped the ambition of his life: to illustrate the scenery of all the countries of southern Europe and the Near East, and later of India and Ceylon? — a programme one would have thought impossibly daunting, yet one that gave him an excuse and a justification for being always on the move, always escaping from something, from perhaps some ultimate shore of darkness or abyss of loneliness where 'nobody answers the bell':

> There was an old man who said 'Well!
> Will nobody answer this bell?
> I have pulled day and night
> Till my hair has grown white,
> But nobody answers this bell.'

Is not comic verse itself — what Lear called his Nonsense — in many ways often more fit than serious poetry to express a tragic view of life? However it may be, there was something in Lear, some hidden and perhaps unrecognised disquiet and unhappiness, that never left him and which neither travel nor work could assuage.

One can at once point to and even identify factors that clearly contributed towards this state. There was first of all most obviously his 'demon', the epilepsy, from which he suffered from early childhood — 'a sorrow so inborn & ingrained, so to speak, was evidently part of what I have been born to suffer — & could not have been so far avoided, willed I never so much to do so', Lear was to write when he was well on in life, as he was also to write, while in India, with reference to the same affliction: 'The . . . misery of some 55 or 56 years of past life ever before me — & ever I have to turn away from too much thought of it, by a decision that it was no fault of my making, but inevitable & [growing] always from my 6th or 7th year — year by year.' This, and the fact that he was short-sighted to a degree and regarded himself as extremely ugly — what he took to be the disproportionate size of his nose became an obsession with him: he wrote several lyrics and one long poem, 'The Dong with the Luminous Nose', on the theme — undoubtedly added to his shyness and pushed him into isolation. 'I feel wonderfully like a spectator, all through my life, of what goes on amongst those I know; very little an actor', he wrote to Tennyson. 'If one were but a chimmey-pot, or a pipkin, or a mackerel, or anything respectable & consistent, there would be some comfort . . .'

Undoubtedly, too, Lear's ingrained affliction and his great self-consciousness about his ungainly physical appearance induced in him a sense that he was unfit to marry, even that no woman would accept him. He thought of marriage and marrying many times, sometimes negatively, sometimes positively. 'No . . . I *don't* mean to marry — never — I should paint less & less well, & the thought of annual infants would drive me wild. If I attain to 65, and have an "establishment" with lots of spoons etc. to offer — I *may* chain myself; but surely not before', he wrote to a friend in 1853. But a few years later, corresponding with the same friend about the possibility of there being, in the Platonic sense, an ideal Edward Lear, he wrote: 'But, hang it, there must be an ideal Mrs Lear to make up the perfect ideal.' 'I wish I was married to a clever good nice fat little Greek girl — & had 25 olive trees, some goats & a house', he writes a few years later, adding: 'But the above girl, happily for herself, likes somebody else.' At the age of 60, he is again thinking, somewhat wistfully and whimsically, of marriage: 'I think of marrying some domestic henbird & then of building a nest in one of my olive trees, whence I should descend at remote intervals during the rest of my life.' And a few years later he laments that his garden at San Remo is 'very much like Paradise — only Adam hath no Eve'. Even in 1887, the year before his death, when he was 74, he is put into a dither at having to decide whether or not to propose to a woman whom he had wished to marry for several years.

It may be too simple to say that what Lear lost through not marrying he more than made up for through friendship. But he did form deep lasting friendships, with both men and women, in a way that few people are privileged enough to experience. He himself was astonished at this and immensely grateful for it. 'I often wonder & wonder how I have made so many certainly real friends as I have', he writes; and again in the same strain: 'I cannot understand how such an asinine beetle as myself could ever have made such friends as I have.' Before going to India in 1873, he sorted out his correspondence — three 'chestfuls or chestfull' of it. His first thought was that 'every created human being capable of writing ever since the invention of letters must have written to me, with few exceptions perhaps, such as the prophet Ezekiel, Mary Queen of Scots, & the Venerable Bede.' Then he reflected that 'either all my friends must be fools or mad, or, on the contrary, if they are not so, there must be more good qualities about this child than he ever gives or has given credit for possessing — else so vast & long continued a mass of kindness in all sorts of shapes could never have happened to him. Seriously, it is one of the greatest puzzles to me, who am sure I am one of the most selfish & cantankerous brutes ever born, that heaps & heaps of letters

— & these letters only the visible signs of endless acts of kindness — from such varieties of persons could ever have been written to me! Out of all', he concludes, 'I kept some specimens of each writer more or less interesting — four hundred & forty-four individuals in all.' On his deathbed, his last words, spoken to his Italian man-servant, were of his friends: 'My good Giuseppe, I feel that I am dying. You will render me a sacred service in telling my friends and relations that my last thought was for them . . . I cannot find words sufficient to thank my good friends for the good they have always done me.' One of the closest of these friends — Franklin Lushington, whom we will encounter frequently in this book — would have been expressing the recognition of all of them when he said that the love Lear's friends had felt for him was 'the best & sweetest of garlands that can in spirit be laid on his tomb'. Like Yeats, Lear could have said that his glory was he had such friends.

At this point I should perhaps make a comment. I have said that Lear's friendships were with both men and women. This is true: his friendship with Emily Tennyson, the wife of the poet, was, for instance, one of the richest and closest of them all. But at the same time it is in friendships with men that Lear manifests the greatest intensity of feeling — or, rather, it is in two instances of his friendships with men that this intensity of feeling attains such a strength that the failure of these men in both instances to respond to his love with an equal intensity and dedication brought Lear to the brink of total breakdown and despair, to the two deepest crises of his life. This has led to the conjecture that Lear was a homosexual and indeed that the root of his perennial malaise lies above all in his suppressed or unrequited homosexuality.

I think that such a conjecture may be misleading — and certainly is misleading if homosexuality is understood with the connotations that it possesses in today's parlance. That Lear keenly felt the lack of a companionship involving heart and soul in the deepest sense is not to be denied — he is not the first or the last to have felt it; and that he thought and desperately hoped that he might find such companionship on the two occasions to which I have referred is also not to be denied. Whether or not this constitutes homosexuality, especially as we understand the word, is entirely another matter; and I think that in assuming it does we are simply projecting on to a form of relationship unfamiliar to our present way of thinking a categorization that explains it in the rather hackneyed terms in which we tend to envisage it. The mystery of the love of what Plato calls the 'philosophical lover' has been part and parcel of our culture at least down to the last century: no one, I think, in 1850 would have called Tennyson a homosexual, with all the overtones that the word has today, because his passionate lament, 'In Memoriam', published in that year, was written in memory of the man who had been his friend. By the same token I think we are misunderstanding or misrepresenting things when we speak of Lear's friendships with men — or at least these two most intense of them — as evidence of a suppressed homosexuality and attribute to this above all his deep unhappiness.

Similarly, I think we are misunderstanding or misrepresenting things when we attribute Lear's unhappiness — relating this to his failure to form a satisfying love-relationship in his adult life — to a kind of arrested development or permanent adolescence, to something in him that refused to grow up. This notion is embellished by another, to the effect that Lear was the victim of the substitute mother-love which he received from his sister Ann, who brought him up, taught him art, fashioned his tastes and generally fostered what has been called, with a condescending if not denigrating bias, his Peter Pantheism. His presumed state of permanent immaturity is, that is to say, the by-product of his inability to escape from his subjection to this substitute mother-love, or to violate its image; and correspondingly this prevented him from forming any alternative mature love-relationship.

This surely is a far too simplified version of things, reflecting a current disposition to propound explanations in over-simplified psychological terms. After all, we have it on high authority that unless we are as little children we will not enter the Kingdom of heaven. But apart from that, what does this growing up or becoming mature really signify in our modern world? Normally it signifies that our thought becomes more materialistic, more abstract, impersonal and analytical, more purely concerned with this-worldly preoccupations and purposes. The imagination — the glorious prerogative of childhood — withers, the sensitivity dries up, the capacity to experience things with spontaneity disappears, and we become enslaved to routine, to our dull, almost mechanical reactions and stock responses, the wonder of our being obscured by the film of familiarity and the beauty of so much about us annihilated for us by the recurrence of impressions blunted by reiteration. We remember Charles Darwin who after poring for years over earthworms was forced to confess that his appreciation of poetry had shrunk to a worm's capacity. 'We become what we behold', as Blake put it. And Ruskin has a passage on the same theme: 'Every archaeologist, every natural philosopher', he writes, 'knows that there is a peculiar rigidity of mind brought on by long devotion to logical and analytical enquiries. Weak men, by giving themselves to such studies, are utterly hardened by them, and become incapable of understanding anything nobler, or even feeling the value of the results to which they lead. But even the best men are in a sort injured by them . . . They gain a peculiar strength, but lose in tenderness, elasticity, and impressibility.' Coleridge knew about the process when he spoke of 'abstruse research' stealing 'from my own nature all the natural man', and of how, on gazing on the beauties of an evening, he can see, but no longer feel, how beautiful they are. And Wordsworth too:

> There was a time when meadow, grove, and stream,
> The earth, and every common sight,
>   To me did seem
>   Apparelled in celestial light,
> The glory and the freshness of a dream.
> It is not now as it hath been of yore.
>   Turn whereso'er I may,
>   By night or day,
> The things which I have seen I now can see no more.

'Shades of the prison-house begin to close / Upon the growing boy' and the celestial light fades into the light of common day. And in *The Excursion* Wordsworth berates the presumptuous littleness of our sophisticated adult minds that, 'Viewing all objects unremittingly / In disconnexion dead and spiritless', wage 'An impious warfare with the very life / Of our own souls!'

This, then, is the price that most of us pay — have to pay — if we are to 'grow up' in our world, a world which, *mutatis mutandis*, is also that of Lear. But for Lear the consequences were aggravated by his own particular circumstances. As we have seen, Lear himself had been spared a formal education. Yet the kind of society in which he lived — that dominantly upper class, even aristocratic society on which he depended for his patronage — had been through the mills of the English educational system. Or at least the male element of it had, and the schools to which this upper class male element went were the most peculiar institutions, almost unimaginable to anyone who has not in some degree experienced them. They were meant to be based on classical ideals. Yet these ideals were interpreted in a most particular manner. They were interpreted, if one may put it like this, in accordance with the Protestant ethos that since the 16th century had been increasing its grip on the English mentality. One of the consequences of Protestantism in England was the weakening, if not the destruction, of the idea of the communion of the saints. The veneration of the saints had as a result ceased to be part and parcel of English religious practice. But if people cease to venerate saints or divinities, they have to find substitutes; and now that in the latter half of the 18th century and the opening decades of the 19th century religious certainties themselves were crumbling into doubts, and the veneration of saints was all but in abeyance, there was a tendency for people — educated people — to transfer their adulation to the great figures of antiquity, particularly of Greek antiquity. In these figures, especially in the Homeric heroes, they thought they saw the prototypes of the Protestant competitive spirit, of the desire to do better than other people: was not Peleus's instruction to his son Achilles 'always to be the champion and to excel over others'?

Moreover, this being the champion and excelling over others was seen as applying to athletics just as much as to book-learning: again, was not Achilles taught to be 'both a speaker of words and a doer of deeds'? Hence the enormous emphasis on sport in the schools and universities of England, so much so that the classical ideal was regarded as consumated in a combination of Greek and athletics. The result of this emphasis on athletics was that in practice the school regimen was based not so much on the Attic model — this was regarded as too concerned with the arts and other effeminate preoccupations, good enough for the French but not for the English — as on the Spartan model; and its aim was to stamp out undue sensibility and to dessicate the inner and imaginative life in order to produce men in whom firmness of character was matched by physical prowess. This type of human being became the norm for the English gentleman, a norm which still persists even today, though what was regarded as its corner-stone — a knowledge of the classics — has largely been displaced.

The consequences of the acceptance and implementation of this norm were not long in manifesting themselves. Already an elder contemporary of Lear, John Stuart Mill, could detect in his mentors 'an undermining of poetry, and of Imagination generally, as an element of human nature'; and was aware how the English character, moulded in the manner we have been describing, makes it 'so seldom possible to derive happiness from the exercise of the sympathies'. And he continues: 'In most other countries the paramount importance of the sympathies as a constituent of human happiness is an axiom, taken for granted rather than needing any formal statement; but most English thinkers almost seem to regard them as necessary evils, required for keeping men's actions benevolent and compassionate.' A few years later Matthew Arnold, son of the famous Dr Arnold so instrumental in shaping the public school ethos, could describe its upper class products, in an unguarded moment, as philistines and barbarians.

This was, perhaps, exaggeration, however pardonable. Members of the English upper class of the 19th century had their virtues, even if they lacked the qualities which might have made them sympathetic as human beings. Their forcefulness, desire to dominate, their quite unassailable conviction of their own superiority, their prudery and self-righteousness were tempered by a sense of justice, of moral duty and of loyal service. They were on the whole good and upright administrators, and as servants of the crown set a standard of non-corruptability which I doubt if any body of civil servants in the modern world can even remotely rival. And as for their conviction about their own superiority *vis à vis* virtually all other peoples of the earth, and certainly *vis à vis* all those subject peoples over whom they ruled in the far-flung dominions of their sovereign, this was no more, though also no less, than quite consistent with the logic of the ideology in which they had been educated. For the very fact that they did rule over these far-flung dominions was in itself proof and verification that they were indeed champions and did excel over all others: had they not been superior they would not have been in the position in which they found themselves.

It is this that in part at least explains how members of this class were almost totally immune to any influence from cultures other than their own, in fact to even the suspicion that cultures other than their own might possess qualities superior to those of their own culture. I doubt if a single member of the English upper class during the 19th century ever seriously doubted the instrinsic supremacy of the English way of life, as exemplified by this class, over every alternative. Lesser breeds not only without the law but also beyond the pale could — and should — learn from him; he had nothing to learn from them. His aesthetic sense stunted or non-existent, and his mind encased in the ignorance of its ineptitude — of its desperate need for understanding and vision — the English upper class gentleman of the 19th century could circumvent the globe without experiencing its natural beauty or showing the slightest interest in the inner — spiritual and artistic — life of the peoples whose labour and lands he exploited.

Lear did not belong to this class. He had never wielded a cricket bat or plied an oar. He was not a champion of anything and had no desire to dominate. He certainly possessed no conviction of his own superiority. He even had serious doubts about his capacity for the profession he had chosen. 'I don't improve as I wish', he wrote in 1851; 'It is true I don't *expect* to improve, because I am aware of my peculiar incapacities for art, mental & physical — but that don't mend the matter, anymore than the knowledge that he is always to be blind delights a man whose eye is poked out.' His whole effort and intent were directed to keeping alive in himself that 'vein of poetry' which, as he confessed to Holman Hunt, he knew he possessed; to keeping alive in himself, that is to say, precisely those qualities — a sense of beauty, a fertility of imagination — least of all cultivated by the upper class Englishman. Above all he was a man of deep feeling and sympathy. As one of his lifelong friends wrote of him when he first met him in Rome in the 1840s: 'Among other qualifications, he is one of those men of real feeling it is so delightful to meet in this cold-hearted world.'

Judged, then, by the norm valid for the English upper class, Lear was virtually a non-starter. Yet here he was pitch-forked into the world of upper class Englishmen, dependent on it for his livelihood, having to conform to its manners and precepts as a condition of being accepted by it, even forming his friendships with its members. Yet he knew it wasn't his world, and that he was at odds with it. Even when first introduced into it, at Knowsley, he had written: 'The uniform apathetic tone assumed by lofty society irks me dreadfully.' And later experience of this society confirmed his first reactions to it. 'Beastly aristocratic idiots' he calls its members at one point; and at another he exclaims: 'Lord! how I hate the bustle & lights & fuss of 'society' . . . Geese, swine, gnats . . . ' When in 1872 he was invited to travel to India as part of the suite of an old friend who had just been appointed Viceroy of India, he wrote: 'There is something antagonistic to my nature in travelling as part of a suite; & indeed, though I am not in the strongest sense of the word Bohemian, I have just so much of that nature as it is perhaps impossible the artistic & poetic beast can be born without. Always accustomed as a boy to go my own ways uncontrolled, I cannot help fearing that I should run rusty & sulky by reason of retinues & routines . . . ' — a foreboding amply confirmed in passages of his journal written when he was actually in India. Tied to the apron-strings of a society that he despised, and upon which he was in a sense parasitical, and which tolerated him not as one of its own kind but as a genial, congenial, amusing diverting oddity, if not as a hanger-on or interloper, well might Lear have exclaimed, with Fulke Greville in another context:

> O wearisome condition of humanity!
> Born under one law, to another bound . . .

As he wrote to Holman Hunt in 1857, after several months of incarceration within the English upper class colonial society at Corfu: 'I have, alas! too present a feeling of the want of all kind of sympathy not to find one of your letters most welcome. Perhaps to irritable natures of my temperament, my unsettled early life makes me more susceptible to what devours me here — isolation & loneliness — & sometimes drives me half crazy with vexation. Really, when anyone tells me, as you do, your own inward thoughts & feelings, it flashes across me that after all I *am* a human being, notwithstanding much of the past year & a half has almost made me come to think otherwise . . . There are hours when I would rather life were abruptly ended — so as not to add weight to weight as my days but too often do.'

If Lear found this upper class world so asphyxiating, so inimical to the vein of poetry within him, why, it may be asked, did he stick to it? Why didn't he cut the apron-strings and flee? The short answer to this is of course that he was dependent on it for his livelihood. It is one of the misfortunes of things that artists also have to keep alive — at least if they are to continue their work. Lear had no private income, and by temperament, health (one must remember his epilepsy) and in many other ways was quite unsuited to earning a living except through his painting. Besides, not to have painted would have been to have denied his vocation. Thus the only solution available to Lear was to try to sell his paintings: to set himself up as a kind of travelling-salesman of his own wares. And the only people who had the money, leisure and predisposition (for whatever reason) to buy such superfluous and non-utilitarian wares as those that Lear was able to offer belonged to this English upper class world.

Hence the only viable way for Lear was that which he followed: to choose a centre which the people of this world had 'colonised' — Rome, Corfu, Nice, San Remo, London — and to open there a gallery, in his own rooms or house, in which he could exhibit his work and to which he could invite the local English society. It was a procedure which he loathed. But what else could he do? And to where, had he wanted to escape, could he have escaped? One cannot see that, being what he was, he had any alternative. True, this being what he was allowed him to accept the patronage and protection of this world rather than choose a way, as others have done, that leads to the madhouse or to prison or penury, which so often seem to be the alternatives to the kind of compromise that Lear opted for. No doubt, too, Lear enjoyed some of its privileges, just as he came to assimilate some of its less attractive features. When in India, for instance, he was asked for his credentials by a Brahmin who thought he intended to visit a Hindu temple, Lear replied: 'I am an English gentleman, & that is enough' — a response typical of the English raj mentality. Typical also of this mentality was Lear's comparative indifference to the inner nature of the life of the peoples among whom he travelled — to their customs, religious beliefs, culture and values: he, too, tended to go about in his carapace of English insularity and to make similar assumptions of superiority with regard to English civilization, morality and manners. What saved him, however, from being merely a typical Englishman abroad was that the way he tended to travel — mostly on foot, or on mule- or horseback — brought him into contact with the most varied types of people and that his own basic humanity more often than not broke through the barriers of artifice, snobbery and presumption which the English erected around themselves.

Yet on another and perhaps deeper level Lear's loneliness, if not the ultimate cause of his malaise, lies in the condition in which any artist or poet finds himself when life and poetry — life and art — have fallen as far apart as they had in the society of 19th century England. In this society poetry and art were virtually the last considerations — as indeed they still are today. Consequently the person for whom they are the first considerations is bound to be at extreme odds with it. Conformity to its standards, its motives and aspirations would be tantamount to surrendering all one holds most dear, including what one recognizes to be the very essence and purpose of one's own life. It would be self-apostasy, a denigration on the part of the artist of what he most truly is. Necessarily, then, the resolve of the artist to be an artist must lead to alienation, to the opening up of a gulf between the artist and society; and the refusal on the part of the artist of the terms and conditions of a recognised social role which he could occupy only provided he gave up his identity as an artist, necessarily leads to exclusion and pain. It was a situation with which, for instance, Keats was familiar: 'I suffer greatly', he wrote, 'by going into parties where from the rules of society and a natural pride I am obliged to smother my Spirit and look like an Idiot — because I feel my impulses given way to would too much amaze them — I live under everlasting restraint — never relieved except when I am composing — so I will write away.' Time and again in Lear's diaries and correspondence one finds him expressing his sense of a similar situation. Like Keats he too found refuge in the endless plying of his craft: 'It is clear to me', he once wrote, '... that *totally unbroken* application to poetical-topographical painting & drawing is my universal panacea for the ills of life.' But unlike Keats, who in the face of this alienation was content to 'look like an Idiot', Lear went one further: he actually played the fool: he wrote his Nonsense.

Nor does this state of affairs appear to have been greatly alleviated in Lear's case by recourse to religion. It was not that Lear was not religious. In his own way he was. But it was an unadorned and unimpassioned kind of religion that appealed to him. He didn't like what one might call religious enthusiasm, or ceremony and ritual, or theologies and confessions. 'But I shall – or should – have a chapel of my own', he wrote. 'Belfast Protestantism, Athanasian creeds, & all kinds of moony miracles should have no entrance there; but a plain worship of God, & a perpetual endeavour at progress.' He possessed an almost pathological dislike of priests and monks. 'For in all ages the Priest has been the advocate of lying', he writes in his journal, 'the promoter of darkness & hatred, the antagonist of light & progress: & enduring & [?gross] as his injuries to his fellow men have ever been, yet he has worked them with impunity, knowing himself to be safe under the never-failing shields of superstition & fanaticism. Nor are the propensities of the priesthood as a body one whit changed or mitigated even in our own day, save by the only safeguard of nations — law & reason.' A visit to Mount Athos provokes similar vituperation: 'But however wondrous & picturesque the exterior & interior of the monasteries, & however abundantly & exquisitely glorious & stupendous the scenery of the mountain, I would not go again to the Ἅγιον Ὄρος for any money, so gloomy, so shockingly unnatural, so lonely, so lying, so unatonably odious seems to me all the atmosphere of such monkery.' He had a belief in what we call the after-life: 'I do not know what your views of future states or material annihilation may be', he writes to a friend in 1875, 'but probably similar to mine — hating dogma about what we really *know* nothing about, yet willing to hope dimly.' And he had an idea of Paradise, but it was for him a place of natural innocence rather than of supernatural illumination — a place of charming landscapes and no noise or bother: 'In the next eggzi stens', he writes to the same friend, 'you & I & My Lady may be able to sit for placid hours under a lotus tree a eating of ice creams & pelican pie, with our feet in a hazure stream & with the birds & beasts of Paradise a sporting around us.' And on another occasion he writes: 'Let me have a park & a beautiful view of sea & hill, mountain & river, valley & plain, with no end of tropical foliage; a few well-behaved cherubs to cook & keep the place clean — & — after I am quite established — say for a million or two years — an angel of a wife.'

With respect to his religious faith, then, Lear was like many other men of his age. It was not that he lacked faith; but it was an immature, tepid kind of faith, not one capable of seeing the world in a grain of sand and eternity in an hour — the relative made numinous by the absolute, the seen by the unseen, the human by the divine, the natural by the supernatural — still less one that could move mountains. If he may be accused of not growing up, it is in terms of spiritual vision that he fails to do so. Though he deeply admired Plato — 'how is it that the thoughts of this wonderful man are kept darkly away from the youths of the age?' he asks on one occasion — and particularly the *Phaedo*, that marvellous plea for the recognition of the immortality of the soul, he never seems to have assimilated or made his own in a living experiential way the metaphysical vision that Plato expounds. The kind of experience of which Gerard Manley Hopkins speaks in the second half of his poem, 'The Leaden Echo and the Golden Echo' — the spontaneous tracing or rendering back of all beauty to God, 'beauty's self and beauty's giver' — was as a consequence something beyond his scope.

This meant that he was left only with the experience of the first half of Hopkins' poem — left only with the despair that the beauty and love of which he had such powerful intimations should be irrevocably lost and unrecapturable. '. . . a keen sense of every kind of beauty', he once wrote, 'is . . . if given in the extreme — always more or less a sorrow to its owner.' 'Tears, idle tears — always' he wrote in his diary at the shattering of his final hopes of achieving the Platonic love-relationship to which he aspired. 'In vain I resolve & re-resolve — gloom contracts & convulses me. But I am gradually getting to see that the past must be past, & buried; yet I can by no means think of anything to put forward as the future.' In default of that deep transfiguring vision which animates Hopkins, the glimpses of some almost unattainable or impossible happiness and perfection can only induce a great unhappiness, a cosmic melancholia: 'a bright blue & green landscape with purple hills, & winding rivers, & unexplored forests, & airy downs, & trees & birds, & all sorts of calm repose, exchanged for a dull plain, horizonless, pathless, & covered with cloud above, while beneath are brambles & weariness', as Lear himself put it. 'Is it better, I wonder, as

A.T. says, "to have loved & lost, than never to have loved at all"?' he wrote to Mrs Tennyson; and he continued: 'I don't know. I think, as I can't help being alone, it is perhaps best to be altogether jellyfish fashion, caring for nobody.'

Yet even if anyone who reads Lear's letters and journals and above all his poems — and I am thinking chiefly of 'The Courtship of the Yonghy-Bonghy-Bo' and 'Incidents in the Life of My Uncle Arly' — cannot but fail to catch the pervasive note of this cosmic melancholy — the note of '*sunt lachrimae rerum*' — it would be wrong to regard Lear as someone who looked on his life as an unmitigated disaster. Even in his own lifetime he acquired a quite unusual status, and he was aware of it, and proud of it. 'It is queer', he wrote to a friend in 1871, after the publication of his *More Nonsense*, '(and you would say so if you saw me) that I am the man as is making some three or four thousand people laugh in England all at one time.' He was duly appreciative of John Ruskin's tribute: 'I don't know of any author to whom I am half so grateful for my idle self as Edward Lear. I shall put him first of my hundred authors.' He was cited in the House of Commons, for a brief period gave drawing lessons to Queen Victoria, Alfred Tennyson, the Poet Laureate, wrote a poem about his travels in Greece —

> Tomohrit, Athos, all things fair,
> With such a pencil, such a pen,
> You shadow forth to distant men,
> I read and feel that I was there . . .

and he was aware that what he called his 'ridiculous life' had 'given much of various sorts of stuff to others' and would continue to do so. Although, as he said, 'the liver has often had a sad time of it', he had the assurance that his life had not been wasted and that now and in time to come it would be 'pleasant to know Mr Lear'. Such a sense of achievement and recognition may not have assuaged his perennial melancholy, but it must surely have deeply tempered it.

This, then, is something of the image — of the life and features — of that remarkable man, Edward Lear. Painter of birds and animals, painter of landscapes, poet, musician, linguist, intrepid traveller, author of several long journals and countless letters — 'volumes of stuff' — heavy drinker — 'O! that t'were possible to drink less!' — 'But never gets tipsy at all'; upset by dogs and sailing-boats, aggrieved by his nose, haunted by his Terrible Demon and his Morbids, lover of flowers and cats and owls — 'How the darling owls did cry' — a whole continent for children and their kin to colonize; gourmet and gourmond — 'his body is perfectly spherical' — concoctor of such gastronomic delicacies as Amblogus Pie and Gasky Patties, wearer of a white waterproof and a runcible hat — (But his shoes were far too tight) — the list of his accomplishments and characteristics is seemingly endless. And it is this image that we encounter, from one angle or another, in one pose or another, in the letters and journals that Lear wrote on Corfu and in the pictures he painted there.

Philip Sherrard

EDITOR'S AND PUBLISHER'S ACKNOWLEDGEMENTS

Where the text of this book is concerned we would like to express our gratitude first of all to Vivien Noakes. With a generosity rare among scholars, she put at our disposal her rich archive of Lear's letters and other material relating to his Corfu years, and subsequently — at a time during which she was extremely preoccupied with editing her selection of Lear's correspondence — responded with a equal generosity to endless petitions for information, enlightenment and verification. For the use of other unpublished material, we are grateful to the Houghton Library, Harvard University (Lear's diaries); Dr Michell (Lear's letters to his sister Ann); the Somerset Record Office (Lear's letters to Chichester Fortescue and Lady Waldegrave); the Department of Manuscripts, The Huntingdon, San Marino, California (Lear's letters to Holman Hunt); Lord Tennyson and the Lincolnshire Library Service (Lear's letters to Emily Tennyson); while for the citations from Lear's letters to William Leake and Nora Decie we are indebted to the Record Office, Hertfordshire County Council and to J. J. Farquharson (descendant of the Decie family) respectively. We would also like to thank members of the staffs of the institutions mentioned above for their courtesy and helpfulness, particularly Susan Gates and Sara Hodson.

For illustrative material and permission to reproduce it we would like to thank The Hon. Sir Steven Runciman, C.H. (pp. 38, 47, 154, 173, 174, 202, 211); the Gennadius Library, Athens (pp. 45, 69, 74, 79, 80, 81, 104, 156, 158, 159, 163, 168, 169, 170, 175, 189, 192, 193, 199, 201); D.E. Johns (pp. 13, 49, 125); the British Embassy, Athens (pp. 18, 19, 40, 41); the British Council, Athens (pp. 42, 77); the Managing Committee of the British School at Athens (p. 167); the Tennyson Research Centre Collection, Lincoln, by courtesy of Lord Tennyson and the Lincolnshire Library Service (p. 94); the Reading Society, Corfu (pp. 2–3, 16, 39, 122, 161, 176); the Houghton Library, Harvard University (pp. 70, 206); the Fine Art Society (pp. 52, 57, 64, 157); J. J. Farquharson (pp. 204, 220); the Whitworth Art Gallery, University of Manchester (p. 62); the Fitzwilliam Museum, Cambridge (p. 50); the Trustees of the British Museum (pp. 76, 99, 127); Spink and Son Ltd (pp. 118, 169, 172); Sotheby's (pp. 43, 60, 75, 82, 103, 152, 166); Christie's (pp. 63, 84, 108, 153, 183); Thomas Agnew & Sons Ltd (p. 105); the Glamorgan Archive Service (p. 227); the Trustees, the Cecil Higgins Art Gallery, Bedford (p. 56); Humphrey Nevill (p. 65); Piero Kourkouméli (pp. 96, 97, 182); the Ashmolean Museum (p. 109); the Radio Times Hulton Picture Library (p. 110); the Courtauld Institute of Art (p. 182); Sheffield Arts Department (p. 132); Liverpool City Libraries (p. 212); the National Portrait Gallery, London (p. 213). We apologize should there be any omission in these acknowledgements.

Much of this material would have remained unknown to us had it not been for the painstaking and persistent researches of Sophie Royde-Smith. Eugene Vanderpool took the photographs of the water-colours in the Gennadius Library, the British Embassy, Athens, the British Council, Athens, and in private collections at Athens. We would be grateful for further information concerning the whereabouts and ownership of other paintings by Lear of Corfu and of the Ionian Islands in general.

Many others have helped us in one form or another; we cannot name them all, but would like to thank Rowena Fowler, editor of *The Cretan Journal* by Edward Lear, the companion volume to this book; Fani-Maria Tsigákou, Derek Johns, George Huxley, Sophia Papageorgiou, Sara Wheeler, Doreen Raptaki, Sheila Conroy, Rhonda Riarchi, Rhonda Parker, Susan Spencer, Elizabeth Panourgiá, Antony Seymour, and in Corfu itself Piero Kourkouméli, Spiro Almános, Maria Psará, Andreas Papadátos, the Kókkali Bros., and Marie Aspióti, M.B.E., to whom we have the privilege of dedicating this book.

TEXTUAL NOTE

The text is taken from Lear's letters to his sister Ann [A.L.], to his friend Chichester Fortescue [C.F.], to Fortescue's wife, Lady Waldegrave [L.W.], to the painter William Holman Hunt [H.H.], Lear's teacher (in so far as he had one), to whom he refers as 'daddy', to Emily Tennyson [E.T.], wife of the Poet Laureate Alfred Tennyson, to Colonel W. M. Leake [W.L.], distinguished geographer, author of *Travels in the Morea* (1830) and *Travels in Northern Greece* (1835), to the 3-month-old Nora Decie [N.D.], daughter of Colonel Richard Decie and his wife, Arabella, who were in Corfu while Lear was there, and from Lear's journal [J.], now in the Houghton Library at Harvard.[1]

Where the editing of the text is concerned, I have by and large simply followed the precedent set by Rowena Fowler when she edited Lear's *The Cretan Journal* (Athens–Dedham, 1984), the companion volume and, in the chronicle of Lear's own life, the immediate sequel to the present book (the entry in Lear's diary which concludes the main part of the text of this book is in fact also the entry with which *The Cretan Journal* opens). That is to say — and here I am virtually quoting verbatim Dr Fowler's own textual note — I have expanded abbreviations and regularized spelling while retaining Lear's intentional misspellings, though sometimes these latter, when they could be mistaken for typographical errors, are followed by *sic* in square brackets. Lear's original punctuation has sometimes been modified, especially where dashes and multiple exclamation marks — to which he was addicted — are concerned.

Incidental words and names in Greek have in the main been replaced by English translations or transliterations (stress marked unless it falls on the first syllable), while dialogue and local terms have been retained, with spelling, accents and breathings regularized, and English translations in square brackets usually added. Place-names have been transliterated in accordance with contemporary Greek usage and pronunciation, except when the accepted English form is so well established that it would be pedantic to change it — 'Corfu' itself is a case in point.[2]

Dates in the text are in accordance with the Gregorian calendar, already adopted in England and in western Europe generally. There is therefore twelve days' difference between these dates and the corresponding dates in Greece, where the Julian calendar was still in use. This explains why, for instance, in Greece Christmas falls, according to the Gregorian calendar, on 6 January. Times mentioned by Lear are within a few minutes of solar time and therefore vary about $1^1/_2$ hours from present day Greek summer time and about $^1/_2$ an hour from present day Greek winter time.

I have kept notes — each signified in the text with an asterisk and listed according to the date of the particular citation to which it relates — to a minimum, identifying people mentioned in the text, for instance, only when they are of consequence in Lear's own life or when their identity is of importance for the understanding of the passage in question.

P.S.

---

[1] Lear's diaries prior to 1858 were destroyed after his death.
[2] The name, Corfu, is in fact a western corruption of the Greek word *korifí (κορυφή* — peak), which denoted the highest peak on the Citadel. The Greek name for both the town and the island as a whole is Kerkyra.

The Corfu Years

The aged & obese Landscape-painter will rejoice to come to H. Excellency tomorrow —

Corfu, 19 May 1848.

APRIL 1848 – MAY 1848

I left Valetta [Malta] in the evening of the 15th at 5 p.m.... The wind was atrociously high, but the sky was bright, when we left the harbour in the war steamer *Volcano*; very soon, as you may suppose, I was in bed — but I dined first, I did — & capitally, & I am sure that it made me less ill. There was amiable Lady & Miss Duncan on board & a Miss Burgoyne, but everybody went to bed. The steamer was most perfectly comfortable. Well, all Sunday, & the night following — Monday 17th — the swell was odious, & I never got up. Monday evening it became still all at once among the Ionian Isles, & a lovely evening we had — full moon. Kefaloniá & Zantë are charming. Next morning, 18th, we were at Patras (a round about voyage, but the mails are so taken) & then, passing Missolónghi, where Lord Byron died, we came to Ithaka, Ulysses' island, & later to Santa Maura [Lefkáda] whence Sappho leaped into the sea. About 3 this morning (19th) we anchored in the beautiful paradise of

19 APRIL
THE UNIVERSITY
CORFU

The Ionian Academy,
the University of Corfu.

Corfu bay, & here I am, in the most perfect library possible, with a bedroom to match, looking out on the calmest of seas, with long lines of wooded hill fringed with cypresses & dotted with villas running down into the water.

These rooms are in the university & belong to my very kind friend Mr Bowen,* whom I dare say you have never heard of before — nor have I known him long; but he, being an intimate of Fortescue,* Wynne, etc. etc., & others of my old friends, & hearing that I was coming to Corfu, wrote to me in the kindest manner & put these rooms & his servant at my disposal, be he here or not. Unfortunately, he is not here,

The Palace of St Michael and St George, by Joseph Schrantz.

having left 4 days ago only; but, as he is gone to Kefaloniá, I am going off next Saturday in the Ionian steamer to catch him, & shall then have the opportunity of seeing Zantë etc. in his company — a great advantage as he is Rector of the college* here & has his office all over the Ionian islands. So you see I fall on my legs again, don't I? I ought really to be most thankful for the number of friends I find. No sooner am I here than the Lord High Commissioner asks me to dinner, so there I dined today — & here come 2 more invitations! Gracious! I had need have as many heads as a hydra to eat all.

Being now most comfortably settled (my room looks like the one at Knowsley* or anywhere) I must tell you a little of the place . . . Corfu, the island, is — as you may see by the map — very long & narrow & close to the coast of Albania. The city was Venetian until 1780, but it has little to recommend it — narrow streets & poky houses. But nearest the sea, there is the most beautiful esplanade in the world (on the corner of which I now look). On the farther side is the magnificent Palace* of the Viceroy (now Lord Seaton) & beyond is the double-crowned Citadel — very picturesque . . . This afternoon I have been wandering all about & nothing can be more lovely than the views; I never saw more enchanting. The extreme gardeny verdure, the fine olives, cypresses, almonds, & oranges, make the landscape so rich, & the Albanian mountains are wonderfully fine. All the villages seem clean & white, with here & there

The Esplanade, by Joseph Schrantz.

a palm tree overtopping them. The women wear duck, black or blue, with a red handkerchief about the head; the men, the lower orders that is, mostly red caps, & duck full Turkish trousers. Here & there you see an Albanian all red & white, with a full white petticoat like a doll's, & a sheepskin over his shoulder. Then you meet some of the priests who wear flowing black robes & beards. Mixed with them are the English soldiers & naval officers, & the upper class of Corfiotes who dress as we do; so that the mixture is very picturesque. . . . Greek is the national tongue; but they speak just as much Italian — for the Venetians ruled them for so long a time. Many of the tradesmen speak English.

It is astonishing how little accomodation for strangers there is here; the only hotel is quite full, & poor Lady Duncan is in a wretched lodging. As for me I should have been very badly off, had it not been for my kind host. What with sea sickness & no sleep for 4 days I am so sleepy I don't know what to do, & I wish I were going to bed instead of dining out; for all that I must now go & dress. I wish you could see the sunset & sea; it reminds me of the old days of Amalfi or Sorrento. [A.L.]

I wish I could give you any idea of the beauty of this island — it really is a Paradise. I have not drawn very much because I have been looking at it so often, & taking fresh walks. The chief charm is the great variety of the scenery, & the extreme greenness of

14 MAY

Corfu from Aghii Deka, 18 May 1848.

every place. Such magnificent groves of olives I never saw — they are gigantic. The people are a most quiet harmless race — & exceedingly civil. The Albanian shepherds in their beautiful dress are very striking. We are expecting the Malta steamer today, & with it news from England. The Ancona post-line of communication being stopped makes us all behindhand. I don't quite like the climate here; it is very variable. In the middle of a hot day the wind changes & blows from the snow mountains of Albania — you are glad of cloaks & coats. I am still wearing cloth all over, whereas last year at this time I was melting in Sicily in linen. . . . Today I have bought a Greek grammar & must begin to speak. [A.L.]

3 JUNE
ATHENS

Since I wrote on the 22nd of May I had resolved to make a little tour to the south end of Corfu, & did so from the 26th to the 29th, when I meant to return & wait for the next Malta steamer which should bring Lord Eastern to make some tour — or perhaps Wilmot-Horton would then have been able to go somewhere, or, if not, I should then have decided to go alone for a little while, as I already know enough Greek to ask for all I want. But the 29th was a very hot day, & though I had fixed on going to a little village, Aghios Matthaíos, to sleep, yet I was lazy, & at the top of the

Corfu from Vido, showing Fort Neuf, 23 May 1848.

hill I debated for 5 minutes whether I should or not. At last my indolence prevailed, & I determined to go back to Gastoúri for the night & return to Corfu on the 30th as I had first intended. But before I got to the corner of the Gastoúri road I sate down to sketch, & lo! who should come by with a great train but all Lord Seaton's people — & Sir Stratford & Lady Canning to my infinite surprise. They were on their way from England straight to Constantinople & were to remain a week at Athens besides. Nothing would serve kind Lady Canning but my coming with the embassy; so Lady Seaton whirled me off to dinner, the next day I packed up, & on the 30th I was actually bag & baggage in the private steamer conveying His Excellency to the Grand Sultan! Did you ever hear such a funny affair, so evidently without my own will almost? Of course everybody congratulated me very much. Just think: I am always with this most delightful family — or the secretary Lord Augustus Loftus; I am at no expense, see the fiinest scenery in the agreeablest way, & shall have advantages at Constantinople no one but the Ambassador's friends or family could ever hope for. You know Sir Stratford Canning is considered as one of the very first living diplomatists & has been for ages in Turkey managing Eastern affairs; he is besides a most cultivated & amiable person, & thus this journey is in all respects very desirable ... Lady Canning is goodness itself & so are the 3 daughters. Well, on Wednesday the 31st I said good-bye to Corfu for the present, & was sorry to do so. The extreme kindness I have received there, not only from Bowen with whom I stayed but from all the officers & the Lord High Commissioner's family, will always make me look back to the time I passed there with pleasure. Besides, it is really a Paradise ...

[A.L.]

DECEMBER 1855 – AUGUST 1856

4 DECEMBER
THE CLUB HOTEL

I am once more in Corfu. We left Trieste on the afternoon of Friday the 30th, in the Austrian Lloyd steamer, the *Europa*, the boat being pretty full so that F. Lushington* & I were glad to have taken the precaution of procuring a cabin to ourselves. Was there ever such luck as mine in sailing! The sea was perfectly smooth so that one ate & drank & read & wrote & slept just as if in a house. Next day, 1st December, was also beautiful all through, but the voyage is not so interesting as I thought, for I fancied we should go close to the Dalmation shore, whereas we steamed away quite in the middle of the Adriatic sea, seeing nothing at all but water, except here & there a leetle bit of island or mountain. On the 2nd of December, the weather changed & became cloudy with rising wind, but the sea was never rough enough to keep me from eating & walking, though it grew much more so in the night, & there was too much pitching about to sleep. By six o'clock yesterday morning, the 3rd, we were all safe in Corfu harbour, some hours later than we should have been had the wind not been against us.

As usual, every inn was full, & as Mr Bowen could not take me in as well as Lushington, I had some difficulty in getting a bed which at last I did here. Nearly all day yesterday it poured torrents of rain, but in the afternoon it cleared & all the beauty of the place seemed to return at once. I am very busily inquiring about rooms to live in, & after breakfast am going about with a house agent to see what turns up. It is not easy to find any rooms here at all, still less so when the light & situation & aspect are all so important. I should have loved an end house of the Condi Terrace, a new lot of buildings which look north & west, but they are all taken. The Esplanade (where Lushington has a house) is east & west & will not do for light, though the situation is good. I rather hope to hit on some place on the Line Wall, where the view is lovely; but if I cannot I must take what I can get. . . . Meanwhile I feel my lungs better already, as it is very nice & warm & the air is so good. . . .

Tuesday afternoon 5 p.m. I have been looking at houses all day long — some too high up — some too low down — some with wrong lights — some too dear — some ill situated. One only seems to suit, but I cannot tell until tomorrow what the owner will ask. I really do hope I shall get these rooms as they look over the north harbour to San Salvador [Pantokrátoras] mountain & there is a room with a real north light window. If I take them I shall have to get a servant of my own, besides occasionally a woman help; I shall have to buy a few things such as sheets, table & linen, etc., to go on with, though Lushington will lend me many. However, we shall see. I have been with Lushington to see his house today — which is very small, & not very nice, though well situated; but I hope he will get a better before long. If I get this Kourkouméli* house, I shall be wonderfully lucky.

All this morning was quite fine, but at noon, clouds came up & presently rain

San Salvador from Fort Neuf, 2 April 1863.

came down, about 3 it thundered & lightened constantly — the rain was literally in torrents; I believe a little child would have been half drowned if caught in it as it seemed to come down almost in one solid mass. But at 5 all was clear once more. We shall see bye & bye how the Corfu winter climate really is; at all events it is warm enough at present. I am invited to dine at the Palace tomorrow at 7....

Wednesday afternoon, 5th December. I have been all day in the country, 6 miles from here, at a place where the landlord of the lodgings I wish to get lives, for I thought it better to apply to him directly at once. The beautiful olive woods of Afra delighted me immensely, but from 1 o'clock till 4 it rained perpetually & in torrents. I looked at the rooms again after this, & I suppose I shall get them, though they want £4 a month for them. Still, they are nearly furnished & have the very light I want & 2 of them are really very nice as to size.... Meanwhile I am now going to dress for dinner, to go to the Palace, & will finish this tomorrow.

Saturday, 8th December. The Palace dinner was rather too stately for my taste; the old-fashioned friendly way of Lord Seaton's kind family seemed changed for etiquette & gaiety, so that I shall not care to endeavour to visit there much, & I suppose I shall not be wanted. On Thursday the 6th, I had to bustle about all day to get the taking of the rooms settled, & after many pro's & cons have done so. Yesterday, the 7th, an agreement was signed, & today I have moved in, bag & baggage — all my first lot of things being safely arrived, & out of the Custom House. . . . I have one larger room which I shall hardly use; then a corner one, very nice & light, overlooking the harbour & across to Mt San Salvador; then a long narrow bedroom, & on the other side of the larger room are 2 which are empty & may be used as I like. At present I have a temporary servant — & I suppose I may keep him. [A.L.]

13 DECEMBER
PALAZZO
KOURKOUMELI

Although there has been a great deal of rain since I came, yet it has never been cold at all, & my cough has quite left me. All those who pass the hot summer here feel the want of fires, & have them; but I should not like one at present at all. Nevertheless, today the wind has changed & all the heavy clouds are gone, & the wonderful mountains are as clear as crystal; so I begin to see the possibility of the weather being colder in January, February, March, April, May . . .

Corfu is indeed greatly changed since I was here in 1848. The war* has filled it with militia instead of regulars as garrison, & the officers being all wealthy, more or less, bring out their wives & families, & take houses, so that not a room is to be got but at great expense. I find the lodgings I have taken — for £24 for 6 months — the only ones I could get — very inconvenient in some respects, though there is a good light. But the worst is I am so totally alone . . . The greatest sadness I have is that I shall hardly see anything of my friend. Not that his very high position here would make a difference, but it causes him to be wholly occupied, so that he rides out only for an hour in the afternoon. Besides, the house taken for him would not do, so that he still lives on with Bowen who is now a very great man, & has a splendid palace. In the evenings they go out to various official parties, & would kindly introduce me anywhere, but in the rainy weather one must have a carriage, & that costs a dollar (5s.) each time. Balls there are, 3 times a week, but you know those are not in my way — & besides Lushington & Bowen I do not know a creature, for I do not reckon the court etiquette of the L. H. Commissioner's Palace. Thus, you see, I am wholly alone. And as there is no 2-day post, no newspaper, no chance calling, no daily & hourly invitations, I sit at home all day, almost unable to paint from very dejection.

Nor have I the energy I had in former years, & when I think of the expense I have gone to in sending out all the things here & in being obliged to half furnish these empty rooms, I own I am out of spirits enough sometimes. It is better that you should know this I think than that I should sham & tell you I am happy. I suffered much from loneliness in Egypt, but then I had a never-ending fund of novelty & excitement which kept much distress at bay. Once or twice, finding I can be of no use to Lushington, I have half thought of returning at once, but I think that would be rash & ill-judged. If Ellen Lushington had come out & they had had a home, my days would have gone by in hopes of having someone to speak to in the evening, & some distant resemblance of better hopes might have been looked at, even though I knew they were shadows & not real. But this was not to be; so that you see Corfu, present & future, is, & is likely to be, pain. Should this not diminish I shall perhaps leave it even earlier, if

Kinopiástes, 1 April 1863.

I could get across to Brindisi, & on to Rome for the spring months. . . . Certainly I have made a great mistake in coming to settle for months.

My mode of life is as follows. I have bought a comfortable bed, & with a chest of drawers, glass, etc. etc., have fitted up a half-bare bedroom. I arise at 7 & Panayióti the servant, to whom I am to give £1 a month, gets very good coffee, milk & toast ready. Then I ought to paint & do if I can (have just begun 3 small subjects) till 12, when Signor Stefanizzi the Greek master comes, & stays till 1. I do not make much progress yet with the language of course. After that, when it has been wet, I really hardly know what to do for sheer melancholy sometimes, but generally I have taken long walks — alone always; but that is of less consequence when among the ever beautiful olives of this exquisite island. A great drawback here is the want of good walks near at hand. Only the Esplanade is there, & that is full of exercising troops & endless dogs . . . I return at dusk, & a 2s. 6d. dinner is sent from the Mess rather cold than hot — which I eat up alone — & then generally go to bed as soon afterwards as I can. This is my usual day.

Today is so lovely & bright that I hope to go out to Kinopiástes & draw the view thence from among some immense orange trees, covered with golden fruit. . . . Alas! I see clouds rising in the north — so I fear my orange trees will not be visited today. After painting a little at the 3 subjects I have commenced, my Greek master came, & when he went, I set off for Kinopiástes, 5 miles off, hoping to draw; but the clouds were perverse & soon began to rain a little so that I did nothing & believe it will be best not to think of outdoor work at present any more. The beauty of the villages here is something not to be described, & I certainly should like to do 1 or 2 large paintings of Corfu — for no place in the world is so lovely I think. The whole island is in undulations from the plain where the city is, to the higher hills on the west side; & all the space is covered with one immense grove of olive trees, so that you see over a carpet of wood wherever you look; & the higher you go, the more you see, & always the Citadel & the lake, & then the straits with the great Albanian mountains beyond. However, I have to think of Philae again at present. No one has called today, so I have literally (as usual) spoken to nobody excepting my Greek master. [A.L.]

18 DECEMBER First, you will be glad to hear I am continuing much better in health. Cold as it has been, I seem to have no disposition to cough & all asthma seems to have left me. . . . Saturday the 15th was one of the most bitter of cold days! The north wind blew fearfully, & I was literally obliged to send out for wood, & light & keep alight a good large fire! In the afternoon I walked up to the high ground above Mandoúki; all the Albanian mountains had come out clear in snow, & though there were still storms about every bit of this beautiful island was like purple & blue & gold & crimson velvet as the sun went down. My evening was alone & uncheerful as usual. On Sunday the 17th nothing could exceed the brightness of everything; & I must tell you that in winter we are not well off for churches; one is being repaired & the other so full & crowded that I shall not go at all in the mornings. So I took a book & some cold meat, & set off on a long walk, by Potamós & Gouvio, & then on to Skriperó, & so over the pass of Pantaleóne; on the other side you come quite opposite the Khimariote coast* & I could see all my old friends the villages where I was in 1848. I came back at dusk, having enjoyed my day quietly enough. It is a great comfort in this island that one may walk anywhere in safety. I had hoped to learn the language, but I have given up my Greek master; the grammar work was too hard for me, & worried me too much.

Monday, December 17th. Not nearly so cold; in my walk on the day before, ice, a third of an inch thick, was in all of the puddles *out* of the town; the town of Corfu, lying lower & near the sea, is warmer. (All that long walk of 14 miles was through one immense grove of great olives!) Well — on Monday I dismissed my Greek master & worked a little at F. Lushington's picture & then he & Bowen called — for one minute only; & in the afternoon I went out & up to the village of Análipsis [Ascension] — only a mile from the city — & whence I mean to do my view, if I can make a good large one, for I think it is the grandest of all scenes here. I really think I never saw any one view more beautiful & full of interest. On the way up I saw 2 gentlemen digging in a bank & found they were looking for the trap spiders so common here; these make a

The Citadel from Análipsis, 18 December 1855 and 5 February 1856.

long nest, & shut it up with a door out of which they pounce upon flies & beetles; but if you try to open it they stick their claws into little holes & prevent you. . . .

Today, Tuesday the 18th, has been much warmer again; i.e. I could not bear a coat at all, but then the wind has changed to south & rain is coming. In one respect, I gain by the change. The sea does not beat as it does when the north wind blows, so the night is quiet. All this morning boats have been bringing over loads of peasants from Khimara, to cultivate & gather the olives here, as this island is so thinly peopled that they are obliged to send for help in agriculture. I painted this morning until 1, then went to get some money, & to make some calls; for, at what cost it may, I do not think it will be good for me to be so completely alone. I met one lady (Mrs Sutherland) & sketched with her; & then I heard that Bowen was to be married — a matter that makes an immense sensation here, as he is to wed a beautiful Greek lady, the only daughter of the president of the Senate. So I went to congratulate him; then, at 4 or 5, I went to the weekly reception held at the Palace by Lady Young.* People go in their morning dresses & stay half an hour or so — rather dull work unless you happen to be near someone you know. Lastly, I met with a captain of the militia here, a friend of friends of mine, & he came back with me here & asked me to dine with him tomorrow; so you see . . . I appear to be going on a little more brightly. [A.L.]

25 DECEMBER

Oh! If you had but seen the day here! Perfectly cloudless, warm & sunny, & with every orange & myrtle & olive tree alive with sunshine, & all the bright snow hills on

Pondikonísi and Vlakherné,
off Kanóni,
28 December 1855.

the other side of the water pink & lilac & blue! We have had 3 fine days now but none so lovely as this — the moonlight nights too are beyond everything beautiful. . . . 27th. The Christmas dinner party was very small & pleasant enough in its way, but somehow it did not seem at all like Christmas. I could have wished to dine with Lushington but it was better for him to be with a more cheerful party. Both yesterday & today have been perfectly lovely, the most exquisite summer days — not too hot but quite bright. Today I have been drawing out of doors all day, above the village of Análipsis, whence there is one of the finest views of the town & mountains, over the tops of the beautiful olive trees that cover every place here. Did I tell you that all the trees are now full of frogs? Tree frogs, they are called, about as big as a small walnut & bright pea-green. These queer little brutes make a noise like millions of ducks quacking. . . . Tonight I dine with Bowen & Lushington, & afterwards go to a Major Heathcote's party, where I am to see everybody. One cannot shut oneself up if one tries & perhaps it is as well not.

 Saturday evening. I have been almost constantly out of doors this week, drawing: I go out after breakfast, & put a piece of bread & 2 oranges into my pocket. It is you know necessary for me to get some views before I can copy them for chance purchasers; however, I have done 2 & I mean to try & sell them for £6 each. Every day throughout the week has been the most perfectly beautiful as to climate — no cold, & the sun agreeably warm. Indeed, if it were not for the bare white branches of the fig trees, you would not find out it was winter, for the orange & olive are always in leaf. I wish you could see the loaded orange trees; & the rose trees in bloom. On Thursday, I dined at Bowen's — afterwards I went to Major Heathcote's but I found the rooms too hot. Lushington introduced me to a Colonel & Mrs Ormsby who seemed about the nicest people I have met here. They live in a house on the cliff, out of the town, & have such a pretty garden. Whenever I am drawing early in that part, I am to breakfast with them. Yesterday, I dined at the Club Hotel, but it is noisy & expensive, & today I am going to try a dinner from a Maltese inn near here — I hope it will be good. . . .

My rooms seem more comfortable than at first & the servant is very attentive & regular. As soon as I can make any money perhaps I may grow livelier & indeed I am more so than when I wrote before. Next week I shall ask Lady Young to come & see my drawings; she is like the Queen here, & I cannot ask any more ladies till she has been. They have not asked me at the Palace any more, so I suppose (and I am not sorry) that my vice-regal gaieties are over. Bowen & Lushington, as 2 of the highest dignitaries here, are constantly there. At Major Heathcote's, Countess Valsamáki (Bishop Heber's* widow) remembered me as here in 1848, & came & spoke to me: she has grown so much older I should not have known her at all. . . . Well, the dinner at the Maltese *locanda* cost 1*s*. 6*d*. only & truth obliges me to say it was not *very* nice. The soup was very oily & rich; but then there was a small boiled fish, which was really good. Next, cutlets, possibly of leather — for I could not make anything out of them; then, fried cauliflowers which were excellent; after that two roast thrushes, not bad as at this time of year they feed on the olives & are fat; lastly, a sort of jam tart. Thus you see the whole 1*s*. 6*d* dinner displayed. Besides that, I drank a whole bottle of Zantë wine which cost 8*d*., & having had my cup of coffee I prepared by a good fire to finish this. [A.L.]

I was talking to Bowen last night about the lad Pano, & we all agree it will be better to keep him on than pay more for an unknown, untried hand. So Mr Pano stays at 6 dollars this month. And just now he has brought his account for the week — which is as high as £1 4*s*. but then there are 3 dinners, besides oil, sugar, a slop pail, a jar, & 200 lbs weight of fire-wood. Every morning the breakfast expense is: bread 3*d*., butter ½ *d*., 2 eggs 1*d*. each, & milk 1*d*. Washing, I think I told you, is 1*d*. for each article, which seems funny — to see 2 sheets 2*d*., and 2 handkerchiefs 2*d*., etc. etc. Yesterday, after church at home, I walked to Garoúna — a high hill quite on the west of the island — where there is a beautiful view of the Citadel & city & the channel. Oh dear! how beautiful the olives are — like a great film or veil all over the country. Ah well, I suppose I shall come to know & draw all Corfu, while poor Lushington is here — but I do not, or dare not, think that will be long.

7 JANUARY

Corfu from Garoúna, 1856.

When I returned I found he & Bowen & many others had called & I was to dine at Condi Terrace. At the end house there lives Bowen & Lushington with him, poor dear fellow . . . & I was in an ill humour about a foolish misunderstanding, which I now repent of, as I have too often in life. I find Lord Methuen wants 4 or 5 of my small views, so I hope that if this sort of thing takes that I may really get on. I have done 1 today, so I have 6 ready again now. I am sorry to say that the weather has changed again; all today it has rained hard & is so muggy & hot. About this time the real winter begins in England . . . This room has absolutely a sort of comfort now, the large table being in the centre & a good wood fire blazing; it is laughable to think that 'the furniture' (which causes the rooms to be called 'furnished lodgings' & which makes the rent so high) is a great pier looking-glass, this table, 1 arm chair, & 4 ordinary ditto, & 2 small side tables. But I think I shall hang up some pictures — it is a great thing to be able to make one's daily life comfortable.

The English here, besides those of the Palace, are almost all military or Civil Government employees. Besides, there are 4 regiments, now all militia — Wiltshire, Oxfordshire, Berkshire & Middlesex — each with their colonels & officers, who with their wives & families live in lodgings. Then there are 4 or 5 Artillery officers; resident

The Theatre, Corfu.

military, such as Brigade Major, Quartermaster, etc. etc. The civil employees are Bowen the Secretary, Sir James Reid & Lushington the Judges, with others; & there are 2 families, Walters & Sutherlands, passing the winter here, for there is no room for more. (I forgot the General Commanding-in-Chief, who ranks next to the Lord High Commissioner.)

10th. Things continue to be a little brighter. The weather has again become fine, not clear, but a thick warm grey sort of sky & air — very nice as far as comfort for me goes. I got a bunch of violets today & ate 4 large oranges off the tree of a villa . . . Meanwhile, Mr Walter has paid me 30 guineas for my Philae picture & Mrs Sutherland £5 10s. for hers, so I am already beginning to hope that professionally I may get on. £200 a year would amply cover all expenses, when you know that £300 did not in London. I am now painting a Parnassus, fellow to the Philae, for F. Lushington, & in a week I hope to finish it. I hope also to do 2 or more for Mr Walter. The last 2 or 3 days I have dined at home & really begin to find this place exceedingly comfortable.

On Monday I went to the opera with Lushington, who kindly came in & made me go with him; but I rarely go to theatres now, as the lights annoy me. Tuesday, I worked at the Parnassus picture, & small drawings. Wednesday, I had a sail with Lushington, in his old Malta yacht; this is a great comfort, so far as getting into a good boat, & in 1 hour being at a beautiful new part of the island, so as to have a nice new walk home — for the island is so zigzag that it takes such a time to walk to many points. I did not go to the Palace ball in the evening. I don't care about dancing anyhow. Today I have worked at the Parnassus and, as I said, have had £37 paid me, which settles all my 'furniture bill' here, & leaves a surplus. I declare I am more than half asleep, so I must say good-night.

11th. Today I have paid all my bills here, & still have enough over to go through the month, at the end of which, if I finish my Parnassus, I shall have £30 more. So I really begin to think I see clearer. Someone or other now also generally looks in at midday, & invitations are becoming frequent. Tonight I dine with Bowen & Lushington, on Sunday with the Loughmans to meet the R.C. Bishop of Corfu, & on Monday at Colonel Ormsby's. Meanwhile I am wonderfully well & it is now so warm that I have had no fires for 3 days past. The whole country has suddenly become full of little white lambs — like maggots — & the violets & anemones are beginning to appear. But all unite in saying that March is, like November & December, one of the bad Corfu months.

12th. Another warm day — no fire — & windows open. . . . I went out at 2 today with Lushington in his yacht, & we sailed across to Kanóni point, & got out there, & had a nice walk home. It is certainly very delightful to be able to do this. . . . Meanwhile Bowen has bought a fine house near the Palace. Lushington will have his. The General (at the other end of the Condi Terrace) is said to be going & then I suppose Colonel Walpole, the Quartermaster General who lives in the house Bowen has bought, will pop into his. This is my hope, because the top of that house will be vacant soon, & I might get that; but if the General *don't* go, then the Walpoles will seize on that top storey. As you say, there is wind up there, & I had rather get a good floor on this Line Wall. It would really be a very happy thing to be settled here for winters, & able to come over in summer, & enjoy such improved health as I do now.

[A.L.]

20 JANUARY

It is not very bright now — only about 3 in the afternoon it becomes so, & the sunsets are fine. Sometimes it is cloudy all day long, & sometimes a shower or 2 falls. I wait always expecting at least a month of dreadful weather before the summer comes, for I know March always brings storms everywhere. The reason that no other houses are built here — or at least, one reason — is that the town, a fortified walled place, is already full, brimful of houses, & you know you cannot build any more over the roofs. Then why not build outside? Because . . . the sea surrounds 3 sides, & it would not be pleasant to live in a house built in the water; & the 4th side slopes from the ramparts so that houses would incommode the battlements & artillery; & lower down are private vegetable gardens & cultivations, & they wouldn't like you to build any houses in their ground. Two doors off this, an old merchant, Paramythiótti, has pulled down his own house, & has built a beautiful one in its place, & the upper story of that I would rather have than any here; but the old pig has gone to law about some ground rights, & now says that he will not finish it at all. To give you some idea of the difficulty attending getting houses, one of the engineer officers has just been ordered to the Crimea, & no less than 6 families are at once bidding & struggling for the rooms he leaves! Bowen has bought a house, & Lushington was to have his (where they now live in Condi Terrace) but lo! the person who inhabits the new house finds out a law which forbids the sale of municipal property without certain conditions, & as this is municipal property, & the conditions have not been fulfilled, it is supposed that the contract must be annulled. So in that case, Bowen will stay where he is, & Lushington *must* move out, as Bowen marries & wants all his rooms. Then Lushington will have the end house, Baker's, when Baker goes, but that is not quite certain, since it seems that the General has a clause in the lease to reserve the house for military residence! Since all this worry occurs in the cases of high official dignitaries, judge what chance I stand of getting better rooms! The only thing is to wait & look out constantly, & seize on anything that turns up at the risk of losing rent here.

Meanwhile, I have sold another little drawing — £5 — which pays for rent up to April; & I hear of others about to be ordered; & Lushington's picture of Parnassus (£25) is nearly done; & so is Mrs Clive's (£25), so that in the 2 months, dating from 8th December, when I took these rooms, to 8th February, I shall have cleared £80; of course, that will not always go on, for I shall require time for painting from nature; but if I can make £250, or even £200 here, with health, I shall certainly be a gainer.

This last week I have been pretty regularly working indoors. Monday was bright & cold, but too chilly to sit & draw; in the afternoon I dined at Colonel & Mrs Ormsby's, some of the nicest people here; they live in a villa on the cliff, & are the only people who live out of the town — because there are, as I said before, *no houses* to be got. Tuesday — a pleasant gray day — I passed in looking out for places to draw in among the olives, wandering about, & now & then sketching. Dined at home — having now instructed the cook-shop to send 4 things only, so that they are good: soup, boiled beef, brains, & fish. Wednesday, painted at home all day. Dined with Frank & Bowen, & went to Lord Methuen's ball. Thursday, painted quietly at home, went out at 4 & by degrees met with others, Frank, Lord Methuen, Captain Butler & Mr Walter — had a little walk. Dined at the Palace, rather a pleasant party — Doctor & Mrs Sutherland, Captain & Mrs Prower, Mrs Barrington, etc. Friday, worked all day at home, calling at Colonel Ormsby's for a walk before dinner at home. Saturday, wrote letters, & at 1 sailed with Frank in the *Midge* over to Barbáti, & then had a lovely walk back. This was a part of the island I had never yet seen, & really I think it most exquisite. We got home by moonlight, & it was too late to get dinner for me, so I went up to Condi Terrace & ate half Frank's. Today I dine there again, to meet the 2 Greek judges; so you see, life is becoming much more cheerful & agreeable in Corfu than it was at first....

The last 6 days, barring Tuesday which was wet in the afternoon, have been always lovely — i.e. warm & pleasant. Yesterday & today quite cloudless & brilliant. But as the days grow longer I begin to feel the inconvenience of these rooms, as the sun comes in earlier. Some others *must* be got by April. But how & where, I can't think. The last steamer has brought a fresh batch of officers & their families, & prices, even of the rooms already let, are raised, if taken by the month. Meanwhile, F. Lushington's & Mrs Clive's pictures being wet, I have begun to work on Sir John Simeon's, & have been out very little, only a walk in the late afternoon. I have begun my Greek lessons again, my master coming from 7 to 8, when I breakfast....

The Citadel, with Maitland's Rotunda in the foreground (undated).

Saturday 26th. After the last lovely days, the weather has suddenly changed. Last night at 10 it began to cloud & the south wind to blow up, & today is a dim dreary *pouring* one. We had a very nice party at Mr Walter's — my little picture of Philae being hung up, & looking very well. I hope he will have 1 or 2 more views of Corfu, & they talk of returning next winter. They, by good luck, got a floor in a capital house on the Esplanade — 10 rooms — & only £30 a year! Meanwhile I have set my Greek master to inquire in every direction, & must go on hoping. Today, as there is no sun, I can paint well enough, but the dark, dull, sunless days are few here. It will be good fun when I can understand Greek well, as I can then get many things more as the natives do, than after the extravagant English modes....

Today, many boats have come over from Albania, full of cattle, horses, pigs, & sheep. Every one is bundled into the sea & they swim ashore. Just now all the harbour is full of black pigs, swimming away like a shoal of porpoises!... On Monday, there was a regular burst of people into my rooms & they ran away with £28 of little drawings! So, allowing for frames, I have cleared £23 by the morning's work, & several of the people who came wished for other views, so that it really does seem as if one were going to get a comfortable living after all. It is now 9.30, & I am going over to the Citadel to Lord Methuen's ball — for an hour...

February 1st.... I sold another small drawing yesterday, so that there seems no lack of work. The weather has been very stormy — today bright, very cold, &

The Citadel, 27 December 1855 – 6 February 1856, 11 a.m.

extremely windy. My object in changing rooms, if I can, is twofold; I took these when the sun did not shine, so was not aware that the reflection from a yellow house on one side, & the sails of the ships below, would make the light perfectly useless. When the sky is cloudy it does very well, but after March, there will be no more clouds. I shall try to get the refusal of the floor the Walters live in. It has many drawbacks, & is on the noisy Esplanade; but it has 2 good large rooms, one looking north-east, which I could well paint in. I fear, however, that some civil or military employee will be beforehand with me. We shall see. [A.L.]

10 FEBRUARY

The weather nowadays is, day after day, something you can hardly imagine. There is never any cloud & no variety in the sky but towards the morning & evening when rose colour & crimson are the fashion. It is neither too hot nor too cold — warm in the sun & pleasant in the shade, & with a nice breeze. The turf is becoming more & more covered with flowers: lilac & pink anemones, white hyacinths, crimson cyclamens, & other flowers are coming out in a universal crop — & really I do hope some day to be able to give a good representation of this beautiful country. It is not easy, however, to do all at once, for I must of course attend to supplying drawings for those who want them. This week has been as usual very busy; I finished & gave Bowen & Mlle Roma a drawing for their wedding present, which was liked very much. Some days I have been out, sketching the peasants who are still picking the olives, & form a very pretty feature in the Corfu winter landscape. (They often come to me, & say, 'Don't draw me so! I am quite ugly in this working dress; draw me on a Sunday or fête day, when I am in my best clothes.')

On Wednesday 6th a very curious thing happened to me . . . It is determined to establish a School of Art in the university here — & the offer of director has been officially made to me with a salary of £100, & a house worth as much, & — I have refused it. You stare! & can hardly believe I should refuse £200 a year, but so it is. The place involved duties, to be regularly performed, to which I do not feel myself equal: the arrangement & overseeing of schools of Art, lectures in Italian, & attendance to tuition (with assistance) 4 times a week for 8 months, etc. etc. I think you know me well enough to be aware that I could not conscientiously undertake such a position, however advantageous in some respects. Again, my progress as a painter would be wholly knocked up; & supposing my health required change in the summer months, I could not lightly throw up a place once held. Then, there are the *relazioni* with the Government of which I should be a part — & thenceforth no longer an independent man. So, after thinking the matter over, I wrote a letter to Bowen — to be shown to the Lord High Commissioner — declining the offer altogether. The worst is, I can get no advice from anyone about this; for Lushington, in his post as Judge, never gives the least opinion on matters connected with the internal government; nor was I allowed to impart the matter to anybody, even if I had desired to do so. So the whole result of the affair is that I have literally lived to 43 to refuse a 'Government place' — if there is any virtue or fun in doing so.

There is the Trieste steamer bubbling into the harbour just opposite my window! I wonder if she has any letters for me. Every little sail & mast & rope is reflected in the water today, it is so clear & lovely. All the talk now is of peace, & then that the militia regiments will go home. Neither the officers nor their wives, nor we, like this idea. It is very unusual in a garrison to have such a collection of nice families as there are now here, & I hope they won't go away yet. . . . I have not been out sailing or walking all the week, but only pottering with a sketch book, & sitting on the top of the Análipsis hill. For at the end of May there is a great *festa* there, & all the peasants come from all the parts of the country, in beautiful costumes; & I want to be able to prepare in time for a large painting of this scene, which I believe is one of the most remarkable in Greece, both for beauty of scene, & variety of dress.

Meanwhile, all the Court (as I call it) came to my rooms in a body on Thursday, & Lady Young bought one small drawing, & her brother-in-law ordered a large £10 one; & the week's expenses were only 15*s.*; so that one has now got £70 ahead — not reckoning debts in England, which I shall pay by sending drawings there for sale. To my dismay however, as I am becoming known as a resident artist, the Court has taken a whim of coming to see me sketch, which disturbs & annoys me. That is to say, Lady Young & her suite, galloping furiously on 12 or 16 horses, come rushing through my quiet olive groves, & quite destroy the repose of the landscape. However, they are soon off again, for Her Ladyship (our gracious sovereign) seldom remains long in one place. (Do not quote what I write in this way, to any people at your house, for there is no knowing how things come round, & this is *such* a place for gossip!) One evening I drank tea quietly at the Cortazzis' — very nice people, & now I think I have told you my week pretty well. . . .

Beyond the gardens I told you of — & they are all private property — the olive plantations begin, & though old trees are cut (or blown down) & used for fire wood, others are always planted; & as the owners of estates live in the town, they don't give up their trees — by the sale of whose olives they live. I go on with my Greek pretty regularly now; & hope to make good progress bye & bye; but it is very difficult. Latterly I have been dining a good deal at home & now I have really got to have excellent dinners — so far as they go: first-rate macaroni, fish, & sometimes roast lamb & salad. Sometimes I go out afterwards to Mrs Cortazzi's, or Mrs Loughman's, & pass an hour or 2, but as I rise at 6, I generally go to bed early. [A.L.]

It has occurred to me that you may think that some of the dark-sided views which I set forth to you of Corfu life may arise from tempers or discomforts of my own, & that I am not able to see Frank's position justly by reason of some selfish crookedness twisting my perceptions. But this is not so, I can assure you; & though I know I used many phrases of dislike about this place, yet you know my exaggerated way of writing & talking & can weigh what I mean; & regarding myself, I have so little real care about the minor uncomfortables (tho' I growl enough about them in my way) that I could look happily to staying here all my life, were other things more turning out with a chance of comfort & pleasure. The trees, & the sunshine & the rocks & water, & the hope of progress in art, & study of Greek etc., all fill up my time well, & only leave me with room to growl, so far as Frank is concerned, about creaking tables, breaking chairs, low & badly-lit rooms, dirty dinners, etc. etc., all of which are easily forgotten. . . .

15 FEBRUARY

And now let me give you a day of Corfu life — & by degrees if you like, I can set the island before you. 6.15 rise, & before 7 a.m. in my room; this week the Greek master don't come but I write out a lot of horrid nouns & adjectives till 8. Thereon comes Pano the boy, & brings 2 eggs, 5 pieces of toast, sugar, coffee, milk, a pat of butter — out & out the most perfect part of my day's treatment. Then, after breakfast, I work usually till 1 or 2. But today I went out at 12 & returned, & I meant, ere I said so, to have described a lot of people I met — but that involves a key to general Corfu society, which I could give easily only it is too late tonight. At 3 then I walked out with my sketch book — dinner ordered at 7 ('dinner ordered' means an 18 penny collection of irregular food, which one eats or not as may be). I walked out of the gates along the suburb road — what clusters of turkeys go fidgetting & gobbling about among the ditches by the roadsides: how they fight! But they are very picturesque & one day I will do a foreground of them. Then I go slowly by the road to Kastrádes* — it is a gray, overcast & warm afternoon. . . .

But today I did not go on to Kanóni. I left the carriage road & went down towards the lake, by a district of gardens & cottages, with here & there a white chapel & cypresses shining through the filmy olives. (Said a blind beggar by the road, 'O my lord! for the sake of the All Holy, give me something to relieve my misery!' So I gave him a halfpenny, & he said, 'Humph! — that's less than (or as bad as) nothing at all'!

59

Pondikonísi and Vlakherné (undated).

Then I walked on till I came to the Kanóni cliffs, where you see the little island called Ulysses' ship — & very charming it is: I made 2 drawings there today. There are 2 islands — I don't know which is the ship. You see hills of Benítses above them & I hardly fancy a prettier picture than the 2 make together. The nearer is a mere church & walls — the further a larger rock island: I have never been there yet but Frank & I will go some day.

Well, I finished my 2 drawings, & yet it was only 5.10; so, said I, I'll go round (if I can) by the rocks; whereby I slowly began to scramble all along the shadowed shore. Queer it is & no one knows why, that the sea recedes here for a week or so, *sans* rhyme or reason, & at other times you can't get around those rocks at all. So on I went & as it's full moon I laid myself out for the whole hog — to get to Corfu. Halfway I saw a fisherman, naked legged, slopping for queer fish. 'Many fish?' said I. 'None,' quo' he. Then another corner to round, & I wished I had nails in my shoes. But one got by it. There was another human-being poking about in the shallows. 'Lear!' he said with a shout, & it was Franky. Now that I call a mesmeric chance. He had read from dawn till dusk, from 9 to 5, & then had walked up to Análipsis hoping to find me, but not doing so had come down to the sea edge, & was full of molluscous sea-slugs, shrimps etc. . . .

And so we wandered on by the rox. Now & then Frank took my big book & I howled to him to give it back, for a chief justice ought not to carry dirty artists' books.

And so we came to the old Venetian landing place, where the great fig trees overhang the rocks, & so by the endless speaking olives. (I say speaking because every olive has more individual character than any other tree I have ever seen. One says, 'Look at my wide arms — how I stretch them about! none bear so much fruit as I do.' Another can say very little, he is so very very old; a third droops & looks ever at the ground; & so it is with all, no tree is so varied.) [E.T.]

19 FEBRUARY

The view from the Análipsis hill is certainly a wonderful thing, & when, on the fête day, all the ground is covered with gaiety & costume, nothing can exceed its beauty. Do you know there has been literally no winter here; they say it is 27 years since there was so little cold, & still some think we shall have a touch of rigour in March: in fact, I have scarcely any asthma, & no symptom of bronchitis at all. . . . The Balls are all over now & gaiety generally, dinners excepted, though I am going to soon back out of all, by dining early. The not being able to get any properly lighted painting room annoys me horribly, & I confess still to being at times very low-spirited & depressed, but not so much as before . . . The sort of lonely feeling of having no one who can sympathize professionally with one's goings-on is very odious at times. Lushington would more or less, but his work is tremendously heavy, & when he gets any leisure he rides or yachts, or shoots, all out of the way sports for me, except the former: I *did* ride all last Saturday for a wonder, & wish I had tin to keep a horse. . . . The Lord High Commissioner & Lady Young are very good-natured, but I don't take to Court life, & not playing cards am doubtless a bore, or rather useless. But I suppose they are good people. [C.F.]

22 FEBRUARY

I have suffered much during the last winters in London, & was so unable to work as I wished, that I resolved to try what climate & scenes I was desirous of revisiting would do for me; & accordingly I have come hither, intending to make Corfu my headquarters for some time — visiting as opportunity may offer many parts of Greece & Albania which I did not see in 1848–9. Already I have nearly lost my asthma, & bronchitis — the old enemy — has ceased to torment me, so that I hope by degrees to paint some of these places. Of Yannina for instance I greatly wish to make a large & careful picture, but my first effort will be to represent this island & town, with the opposite coast, from the little hill of Análipsis during the great *festa* in May. This picture I hope to send to England for the Exhibition of 1857, but of course I shall have nothing Greek there this year. . . .

I really think no place on Earth can be lovelier than this. The olives in their half wild & uncared for semi-culture are so perfectly beautiful, & the views of every part of the Albanian coast so exquisitely majestic. But there has not been for many years so very mild a winter as this, & indeed only one single bright day could be called cold, all the rest of the 3 months I have been here having been like autumn weather in Devonshire – often wet & cloudy but mild. On the high mountains by Santa Quaranta there has hardly ever been snow, & only the furthest range is thoroughly white. I long to land there once more, & draw the great rock of Filátes, & to see Butrínto.

The Bay of Garítsa, 26 February 1856, 5 p.m.

Corfu is much as it was when I was here in 1848 & '49 — or rather if possible more inconvenient & disagreeable as a town. Nothing new by way of hotel, no new houses except one terrace near the University, filled at once by resident officials from end to end. The garrison here now being all militia, & the officers well-off for money, every available corner of the crowded little town is taken for their wives & families, & so far as balls & dinners make happiness a London season could not exceed the winter gaieties. But the drainage, & lighting, & all the essentials of life-comfort are as formerly — i.e. abominable. And out of the town cultivation is exactly where it was, or worse, except only the estates of Kourkouméli & Capodístria. Everywhere else you may walk ankle-deep even now in olives, spoiled on the wet earth, while every now & then 100 or 200 Khimariotes come over to help the tardy natives. But as a set-off to all this one may ride & walk for ever among fern & anemones undisturbed by fences, & with the eye unannoyed by lopped trees....

The greatest drawback to me here is the want of sympathy as to the antiquities or the topography of Greece, always excepting my friend Lushington ... but he is so busy ... that he can command but little leisure; & Bowen (who wrote much of Murray's Handbook, & an account of Mt Athos in the Edinburgh Review last year), but he is now principal Secretary of State & as such has his time filled up.... [W.L.]

After church last Sunday, Frank & I walked to Kalafatiónes — a village some miles   5 MARCH
off — & by chance we arrived there to see the dance with which all country weddings
conclude; it is a very pretty sight. On a sort of rising ground, where the churches are
usually built, this ceremony takes place: a long string of couples hand in hand, & close
together, moving in a circle to music, & proceeded by the *choregós* — a
man who capers & dances before them, backwards. The first couple
are the bride & her mother, & all the jewels & finery they possess.
The 2 we saw were literally covered with plates of gold, & coins
threaded like necklaces about their heads & necks. Each of these dancers holds a
handkerchief in one hand, which the next in order holds also; they advance 3 steps, &
go back 2, & so by degrees get round the circle. The bride & her mother keep their
eyes fixed on the ground. There were perhaps 40 couples ... [A.L.]

View of Corfu, from the south-west, 11 March (1856?).

At last, I have decided on taking some other rooms, which in many respects are   3 APRIL
preferable to these, though not as to situation, that is to say, they are badly off for
entrance, & there is more street work to get through before you reach them. On the
other hand, they are much larger & loftier, & there are 3 on one floor with a servant's
room, & little spare room above, for £3 a month, whereas these cost £4 a month, &

Corfu from the island of Vido, 1856.

there is only one room for study & sitting room, greatly to my inconvenience. As yet I have not taken the new set, for I said I would on the conditions of the upper floor being new ceiled & a water closet built; but the landlord is doing that at present. The light is not good, but far better than here, & the view nearly the same, that is the north front looks over the harbour to San Salvador & the island of Vido, with my particular Santa Quaranta mountain beyond, while the west looks at Fort Neuf, just as my rooms here do. As yet I have got no servant (for Pano can't leave the people here, nor can he cook nor speak Albanian), nor have I got funiture, so I shall be here through May I dare say. . . .

 Meanwhile I have sent to England for some large canvasses for a big picture for the 1857 Academy Exhibition, & while all this goes on I am at work on different drawings out of doors, as my painting at the orange garden, which is not a picture but a study, for the colours of the oranges & lemons & dark leaves are not to be imitated at all if one does not try from nature. This garden (at Virós) is about 4 miles off & I walk there about 12 or 1, & sit till 5. . . .

 You really cannot have the least idea how wonderfully the whole place is now covered with flowers! There is hardly any green left since an immense crop of marigolds, geraniums, orchises, irises, & caronilla have come out. The little hills are positively an immense crop of geraniums all gold colour, & in the olive woods the large white heath looks like snow, & the pale lilac asphodels in such profusion as to seem like a sort of pale veil over all the ground. The hedges are *absolutely* pink, & in fact the whole thing is almost absurd from its very oddity. [A.L]

At last I have taken the other rooms, for 6 months, & now I have to get them cleaned, & partly furnished as soon as possible. The expense will be very considerable, but it only comes once, & then I shall know my expenditure with certainty. When people leave Corfu, they sell all their goods again; & tomorrow I go to Mr Baker's house, & order Taylor (who is the universal man of business here) to buy such things for me if they go at reasonable prices: a table, 8 or 10 chairs, chest of drawers, press, etc. etc. . . .

6 APRIL

I have also found a good servant — at least he seems so, & as he is a brother to Lushington's man, that is in his favour. George speaks Albanian as well as Italian & Greek (being by birth a Souliote) & he can cook; he was 7 years with General Congers

George Kokális
(said to be by Lear).

& has an excellent character.... Well, I have just been to the new rooms with George, who seems an intelligent & good sort of fellow.... Drawbacks of course there are, but I find that the situation is far better than I thought, except that it is very noisy, being in one of the principal streets — though the hum is far below me. Out of the bedroom & study windows you look over the Police Office & 2 other streets of low houses, to the back of this where I live now, & straight over *it* to the harbour & beautiful Santa Quaranta mountain. As far as I can see these rooms will suit me very tolerably, & I shall begin on oils at once....

Meanwhile, there has been once more a rainy day, but now the summer has really set in, & it is quite warm. But lo! all the hedges & trees have said to each other, 'Bless us! here is April the 10th, there is no time to lose', & out they have all come in full leaf most wonderfully! As for flowers, things have now reached their utmost, & I suppose there is now no more possible room for any more, for all the fields have ceased to be green & are sheets of pink & lilac & yellow & blue. I never beheld anything so amazing! Yesterday's dispatch made Bowen a knight, so he is Sir George, & his Lady (on the 28th) will be Lady Bowen. [A.L.]

18 APRIL   You will be glad to hear I am settled in my new lodgings, but how comfortable they are after those I have left I cannot tell you! On Monday & Tuesday I moved in gradually, all the things being taken on men's heads here. Wednesday & Thursday I was arranging, & today I have drawn all day long at home, breakfast, dinner, & supper (I hope) all without going out of the house. My study is really delightful; the light is quite good, & I can make it less or more by some shutters I have put up for half the windows. A large double table for water-colour drawing, a large one for my oils, 12 chairs, easels, & frames etc., are all its furniture. If I want change, I open the wooden blinds & look at the little bit of harbour & Santa Quaranta mountain over the tops of the houses on the Line Wall, one of which is my former dwelling. Or I can look out of the window & see the people below; or I open the blinds of the west window, & watch the very amusing groups of every sort of dress coming up from Fort Neuf. My bedroom is even better (& all are so lofty & airy!). There I have my chest of drawers & bed, & wash-stand, besides 2 old wardrobes which I bought at Mr Baker's sale for £2 each. Then my dining room has one very good table (cost £3 10*s*.) bought at Walter's sale, 9 chairs, a black horse-hair sofa, a capital book case (I gave £6 10*s*. for it) & 2 small side tables; I have hung 14 of the old Oxford Terrace* drawings round the white walls so that the room really looks very decent; besides that, the 4 windows have cambric blinds, for there is nothing to look at outside. Below the rooms ... I have put up a door, so that my 2 floors are quite shut in & private. The kitchen is not yet in complete order, but it has been pretty well used today, & with success.

At 7 I had my usual coffee & toast; & at 1 — the first dinner here cooked by George, who I rejoice to say can cook very decently indeed. There was a pilaff of rice & mutton — the very best dish in the world; & a dish of Jerusalem artichokes, an omelette, & pancakes, oranges & biscuits, & Kefalónia wine. We shall see how the expense of this turns out, but it is really a great thing to get one's meals hot & comfortable. I have ordered an omelette & a salad for supper. Besides the cookery, George seems a very good valet & servant in every way, & it is pleasant that he is a brother of Frank's man Spiro. So you see, I am quite in a good humour today....

Really, the flowers are now quite absurd; every day brings out a new set, so that

The procession of St Spirídon c. 1821, by G. Cartwright.

there are really too many. The last 2 days have brought out millions of trumpet lilies stuck as thick as can be all over the fields (they look like so many white paper scrolls!). And rose-coloured cistuses, & white convolvuluses, & pink orchises besides all the peach & almond & may trees, & the oranges have all burst out at once...

On Sunday is the great procession of the body of the Greek saint, St Spirídon,* who is carried all about the town, with a world of costumes after him. On Monday I hope to go out with Frank for several days' holiday (it is the Greek Easter, & Courts of Law shut up). We shall go in the yacht, but only along the coast all round Corfu, touching wherever we like, & I shall make drawings while Frank reads & writes. This will be very nice if we have fine weather, & now it seems all but settled. The last 3 or 4 days have been very warm, & summer seems to have come — like the different flowers — all at once. I am working very hard to get Mrs Prower's drawing of Aghii Deka done, but now, having money beforehand, I must begin to study a good deal for my paintings. . . . I shall be very glad to be out of the way all the next week, for the Greek Easter is very noisy, & they beat drums & fire guns till one is sick, besides the odious custom of killing a sheep before every house, in the middle of the street! Everybody, rich or poor, brings a lamb on Easter Sunday, just as at Christmas everybody eats beef or pudding with us. Here comes the supper, so I will say good-night. [A.L.]

27 APRIL
PALAIOKASTRITSA

In the yacht (the *Midge*) off Palaiokastrítsa. . . . Well, the 20th was Sunday, & Palm Sunday of the Greeks. Having seen so many fine Roman fêtes I went to see this Greek one. The variety & prettiness of the peasantry costumes greatly pleased me, but on the whole the affair is so mixed — half Greek, half common European fashion — that it is hardly very characteristic. Only the long double line of clergy, whose dresses are certainly most magnificent, & immediately before St Spirídon's body (he is carried in a glass case) walks the Archbishop, with a magnificent tiara of gold & jewels. The Greek priests, you know, wear long beards, so are finer to see than the shaven Romans. In this procession they use enormous candles, perhaps 2 feet round in size, & 12 or 14 feet long, & the effect of all this bright colour against the blue hills I thought was very nice, though the best view of all is from my own windows, as the procession came up the Strada Mercanti. I dined at the Palace that evening but did not find the party over agreeable.

Next day — 21st — it was cloudy, but having packed up, F. Lushington & I got to his boat about 1, & we were off by 2. The wind was a quiet south breeze, so it served to take us to Serpa . . . a harbour at the north east corner of the island, close to Albania. Here we arrived about 7, but it rained hard all the way there, so we only wrote & dined, & wrote, & went to bed. The *Midge* is said to be a comfortable boat, but I do say that all boats are hateful. What with screwy & bumby & squashy & other fidgety noises I got no sleep at all. 22nd. Fine again; & after a latish breakfast we set out to go to the top of San Salvador. The first part of the way was truly lovely from the wild flowers, so fresh after the rain, but the ascent of the mountain, the highest in Corfu, was tiresome, & did not repay the trouble, though the view is very extensive, & towards Albania beautiful. We got down to another harbour . . . called Kassiópi, the scenery about which is delightful. Wednesday 23rd. After bathing & breakfast, we set off to Fano [Othóni], one of the larger islands close to Corfu. Oh dear me! how tiresome I thought the voyage, all on one side, with no interest, & yet just so much motion that one could do nothing but lie still! How people can like yachts I do not know. We passed Merléra [Eríkousa] about 3 or 4 o'clock, & got to Fano about 7 or 7.30. Here there is no regular harbour, only a roadstead, so I ordered myself on shore, & had a mattress sent to some rooms, where I slept somewhat more than if I had stayed in a rolling boat all night.

Thursday 24th. Frank came on shore early, & we employed the morning in seeing all there was to be seen in the poor little island: rocky, but with little gullies full of olive trees, & with cottages neat & nicely kept by a hard working set of civil people. At noon

Palaiokastrítsa, 15, 16 and 18 April 1862.

we left, hoping to get to Palaiokastrítsa before night, but before we had passed Diáplo it became a dead calm, & until 9 at night there we stood roll – roll – pitch – pitch – creaking, flapping, & bumping, till I could have thrown myself overboard from sheer disgust. We only got to a little port, Kravía, very late. However, the day was lovely. Friday 25th. A nice breeze brought us here, Palaiokastrítsa, in 2 hours, & we went to the quiet little bay where I am now writing ... Such a pretty little place! It is surrounded by great rocks, on one of which is a convent, & on another an old castle; & if this place were anywhere else it would be a watering place. The beauty & quiet of the place is delightful. We walked about till 7, & then returned to dine. Saturday 26th we employed in going up to the old castle, a beautiful excursion half way, the rest barren. By 6.30 we had come down again to dinner. Frank sent out for letters & a carriage — to return tonight to Corfu. . . .

    Meanwhile I have come to the conclusion yachting does not suit me at all: all the week has gone without my having done one single thing of any sort, & the nuisance of knocking one's head, & being in a cramped cabin is not repaid by any society in the world. I really believe the liking for yachts is merely a fashion, just as many women will bear the utmost pain in lacing rather than not appear in the mode. Nobody will ever persuade me that this boat life can be pleasing to any one. At all events I think it is the last as well as the first yacht trip I shall have to write about, were my life to last 100 years.

It is getting very hot now . . . Oh! I never told you about the fireflies: they are here by millions now from 8 to 10 every night, & are certainly better animals than the frogs. The whole land is like a fairy scene lit up with myriads of tiny lamps. At present the weather is mild, but very rainy again, that is, morning showers for an hour or 2: these do a great deal of good, & the fig trees & others are already out in full leaf. As for the flowers, they are more & more & more, & every place is like Covent Garden Market. Only think of streets of crimson gladioli, hills white & pink with large rose cistus, or yellow with bright asphodels & tulips. Except the fern & myrtle the flowers have swallowed up all the leaves. Some beautiful birds are come too. Hoopoes, & yellow orioles are quite common; blue rollers & turtledoves & quails . . . [A.L.]

11 MAY   The weather has scandalised me very much: very cloudy, no mountains visible; muggy, & often rainy, with several thunder storms; today, however, all is quite bright

again. . . . George has really proved himself a good cook, & we have managed as well as if we had been in Oxford Terrace. I have not, however, done much work, as you may imagine. Bye the bye, the General has given me commissions to paint 2 pictures — about £30 each — so you see I still get something to do. I believe staying here for the present will be quite the right thing for me. . . .

Wednesday I went to the woods above Gouvia . . . nothing can be lovelier than those olive woods, when once the odious 3 miles of high road, the bane of Corfu, are accomplished. The olives in the northern centre of the island are not so fine, but younger, & if you go up any of the hills you see all the landscape through the foliage just as if you looked through a thin veil. It is this effect I mean to try to get in one of my larger pictures. Then, as I sat drawing, the whole place is quite still, except that a hoopoe or a turtledove or an old raven, or a very large lizard, bright green & in a dreadful fuss, breaks the silence. The flowers are beginning to die. The anemones & asphodels are gone; the cistus is going; only the orchises are as plentiful as ever. But all the woods now are suddenly covered with a carpet of bright green fern all over — though how long that will last I do not know. [A.L.]

11 MAY

Do you know I am half in love? There are two *awful* sisters here (I call the house Castle Dangerous), English, but brought up here — & so simple & good! — & so full of poetry & good taste, & grace, & all the nettings whereby men are netted. I begin to feel I must either run for it, or rush into extremes — & as neither they nor I have money, am not I a fool for thinking about it? Yet sometimes at 43 I cannot help believing that half & half life will get too wearisome to bear ere long. The older is my alarm, but the younger is the prettier . . . [H.H.]

24 MAY

It is now *really* getting hot & think what a comfort it is that I can sit in the large room with my 2 windows wide open & yet with no sun at all. . . . 20th & 21st — mornings of both days passed in working at drawing, & in setting my spare room in order to work at a photographic machine I have just purchased. I have often wished to possess one, & just now a really good one was for sale, at just half its original price. So I have bought it, & hope before long to be able to send you & others some real views of Corfu. If I can come to use this mode of working it will be of great service to me in copying plants, & in many things which distance, limited time, heat, etc., would prevent my getting. We shall see. On the 22nd, I went out very early to Signor Kourkouméli — my former landlord — & I only returned last night . . . The run into the country has done me a good deal of good; just about Kourkouméli's house the country is too cultivated to be very picturesque, but half a mile off there are very wild scenes, of olive grounds — great spreading trees, with the hills of Aghios Yiórgios peeping between. Early yesterday morning I had a very nice ride; the ground was quite dazzling: *covered* with rose-coloured cistus, & pink everlasting peas besides innumerable large white convolvuluses. The Kourkoumélis were very agreeable & good-natured, & reminded me of days passed with the Buonapartes & others in Italy.

Demétrius Kourkouméli.

They rose at 6: breakfast (very light one) at 8, & then a long huge dinner at 3 — an infinitely more rational mode of spending the day than that of the English here, who persist in coming in at the only tolerable hours of the day in summer — viz. 5 to 7 — to dress for late dinners. As for me, I dine today at 1, & give up late dinners altogether after the next week. . . .

Did I ever tell you that the dirty little urchin boys in the streets here have a queer habit of going before all the military bands when they play through the streets, turning over head & heels in the most funny manner? Sometimes they spin over 5 or 6 or more times without stopping, then run or skip on, to the time of the tune, a few paces, & then set to, to turn over again. Generally they twirl sideways, & so look just like so many wheels spinning before the band, just like this — Queer little brutes! Today is the Queen's birthday — & such a noise of canon & guns & bands of music! I am glad to be well out of it. And tonight there is a grand ball, to which I shall just go for half an hour or so. Now I shall leave off again. $Τὸ\ γεῦμα\ εἶναι\ ἕτοιμο$ — which means, the dinner is ready. . . .

24th, 9 p.m. I have been walking to the One Gun Battery [Kanóni] by the lower road & orange gardens, returning by the cliffs & olives. How beautiful is that village of Análipsis, with its scattered sheep & lambs, & the little cottages, with kids & calves round the door. At 8.30 I got to the Esplanade, when behold! it is all thickly covered with tents! The 46th regiment has arrived, & there is nowhere to put them till the forts are empty — the Berkshire & Oxfordshire go all away on Monday or Tuesday. I have come home too lazy to dress for the ball, so I don't go. The night is very sultry, but I am glad to have these large rooms; & though they are right in the middle of the city, they are quieter than any house on the Line Wall at night, because all the populace walk up & down there & sing more than enough. Dear me! it is a sad bore to find all the people one was beginning to know, & many to like, hustled away at once as if by a hurricane! 26th. The Trieste boat not in yet. The bustle of Corfu is something unheard of — poor little quiet stupid old fish pond: 2,000 men rushing in, 2,000 more rushing out, & all the fuss of embarking, etc. etc. In a week we shall be all stagnation again. . . .

The chestnuts now are all in full leaf, &, dear me! such a lot of new flowers; for my part I don't see where the flowers are to stop, they are so endless. The island is now in full beauty, as the pomegranate, orange, quince & almond are in bloom, & the magnificent fig trees all in leaf, while the corn, Indian corn, & mellons, are growing fast. We walked back by the lake, as the marsh is now dry as a bone; & then we dined at Frank's new house, to try his servant's cooking. Being brother to my man, we suppose their talents might be similar, but were not prepared for all & everything being exactly the same: red mullet, pilaff, cutlets & pease, bread & butter — a twin dinner to mine. . . . Frank's house has burst out all over black beetles, but I have given him a σχαντζόχειρος — viz., a hedgehog — to devour them. And everybody's house possesses a large supply of the domestic Julus* which is not pretty — being in appearance between a long caterpillar & an earthworm, only polished up with Warren's blacking. He sticks upon the walls confidingly, & don't bite, or do anything disagreeable, only when you touch him he comes down — snap — & breaks into little bits like an old tobacco pipe. On the whole, 4 or 5 Juluses on a wall may be looked on as rather ornamental than not. [A.L.]

On the 4th Frank & I went up to see the preparations for the great Análipsis fête, but alack! alack! it was just like Greenwich fair! A crowd & bustle — soldiers, sailors, no costumes, innumerable booths & places for roasting lamb, & altogether a total spoiling of my quiet olives. On the 5th, the day of the fête, as I had given up all idea of making use of the *festa*, I had no excuse for declining a party at the Cortazzis, who have a villa on the hill, & who give an annual sort of little fête or dinner, from which their guests go to the top of the village.

4 JUNE

So at 2 Frank & I went round in his boat, & met the party — Shakespears, Ormsbys, Finucanes, & 5 or 6 more — & a very pleasant afternoon it was. At 6 or 7 we all went to the fête, but I found it an immense bore — like Greenwich without the fun — & the dust & the crowd & the noise were so extreme I was truly glad to get back. Moreover, the dancing & costumes are not in sight (as I thought they were) from the place of my view.... so I could not have made any use of them, & now I shall make my foreground of shepherds & sheep, & a few figures, as there always are in the winter. I have decided also that the winter aspect is the best, on account of the snow on the hills, which, on the 5th of June, is nearly gone — even Pindus is beginning to be patchy. By degrees our party broke up, except Frank & I who had a quiet end of the evening — tea & music with Mr & Mrs Cortazzi & their daughters. They are nice natural simple girls, but never having been out of Corfu it is the world to them, & I think they did not like our not being enraptured with the miserable Cockney Fair, though we admired it as much as we could to please them. [A.L.]

19 JUNE
HOROEPISKOPI

I think it highly probable that you will not be able (all at once at least) to pronounce the address of the place from which I write this; so you had better call it Hokus Pokus at once, as all the English do here. Hokus Pokus, then, is a village 14 miles from Corfu, & as I wanted to see this north side of the Pantaleóne pass, I got leave from Count Voulgari, who has a country house here, to make it my headquarters. The village is on a double rocky hill in the midst of a valley entirely full of splendid oranges &

Horoepískopi, 12–14–18 June 1856.

cypresses, just as if it were in a basin; on the other side of the basin are several other villages, & to the north all the hills slope away to the sea, beyond which my old friends the Khimariote mountains are seen. This Hokus Pokus is the centre of the villages in the north of the island, so I meant to make excursions & stay a longer or shorter time as I found it desirable. But, although the scenery is exquisitely beautiful, yet it has too little variety to engage me much, nor are the lines of the hills so fine as on the south or city side, so that I shall go away back again at the end of next week.

I brought out a good lot of things, books, drawing materials, clothes, etc., besides George & the canteen or box of plates & dishes etc., & a bed; for these Greek country houses are empty, except for a few chairs & tables. (N.B. There are *some* fleas also.) This house quite overtops the village, & out of my bedroom window one sees a wonderfully lovely valley, not unlike that I stayed in at Lydford in Dartmoor — only there is no river; an undulation of olives — at this season as green as elms — all the way up to San Salvador. I seem to have done very little while here — the places are so far apart, & it has taken so much time to find out what was worth drawing or not. Pagus seems pretty, but there is a monastery at Nimfes which is really placed most picturesquely: immense cypresses stand up like columns against the evening sky, & the great rocks & far, still landscape & lilac channel are very noteworthy. I go there on Monday from here . . .

Horoepískopi, 13–18 June 1856.

Horoepískopi,
14 June 1856.

    In the meantime I delight in the heat, & would it were never less! It *is* so nice never to cough or use one's handkerchief, but to be able from waking to look out at the clear, pale cloudless heaven, never altered at all day or night. I have not felt so well for many a long day indeed. I rise very early, having brought out a comfortable bed, & after coffee go out from 5 or 6 to 8 or so, when I return & open out or arrange my drawings, write Greek, parts of letters, & see to George's writing lesson, till 12, when I dine — mostly on fowls nowadays, boiled, roast, curried, in soup, or pilaff. Vegetables make the rest of the dinner, biscuits, mulberries, coffee & a cigar finish it, not to speak of a whole bottle of country wine. Then I read, & then sleep, till it is time either to

Horoepískopi, 14 June 1856.

work, or to explore some new part of the land. (The last 3 afternoons I have sate below the village, tempted by a wondrous group of immense olives shading a slope of fern; here a whole family of the village cook & sleep out of doors watching their corn planted close by; a most beautiful scene, but poor owls, they have spoilt it all by moving quite away, not liking to be drawn; they cannot naturally understand why a queer looking stranger should come & stare at them day after day & write them down as they express it; so they have all gone & my 3 days drawing is spoiled.) At sunset I retire, have an omelette & salad for supper, & another bottle of wine; read & write a little; & then go to bed — a mode of life more adapted to this climate than the rising at 8, & late heavy dinner at 7 (the only best out of door hour), including hours of intermediate lassitude. . . .

What nonsense I talked about the flowers being over — the whole place is all over acanthus flowers & clematis beyond credible, not to speak of dog-roses & all kinds of wonderful grapes. . . .

June 20th. My expedition yesterday was charming, but so distant are the places here I grudge the time one has to give to them, since sketching is out of the question,

77

as the subjects are very elaborate & require hours to do any good with. The whole 2 hours walk to Sokráki was under wide olives, by the side of a stream where blue dragon-flies, green frogs, & lizards, & yellow butterflies abounded. The village itself stands high at the end of the valley, & just above it is a rock, from which you see, looking south, all the old Corfu world ... I am staying on the north side, divided by the Salvador mountains from the city part. I should have liked to draw a map of that view, but it would have taken 3 hours at least; yet it was so clear that I could see (with my glass) every house in Corfu, & also those in Gastoúri, 20 miles off. ...

On the evening of the 9th I dined at the Palace, where was Smith O'Brian* — odd people one falls in with here & there. The party was very pleasant — now the great dancing fuss is over things are much more enjoyable; & I don't say that Bowen's being away hasn't something to do with it. If being a guest as well as an artist in this very little fish-pond of a place would elate a man, there is enough of that for me, for the big room at the Palace is all over 'Lear', Lady Young having 3 drawings of her own, & borrows everybody else's to copy — & indeed she copies them very nicely. The 10th — the day before I left town — was mostly bustle & packing up my lodgings: dining quietly at Frank's late. Did I tell you I had got a large hedgehog for him, to eat beetles? &, though all unexpectedly, Mrs Hedgehog has produced *four* small hedgehogs, for all the world like little hairbrushes? Now, I maintain I only present one beast, & that these 4 are consequently mine, & very possibly the judge & I should have gone to law about the case, only the 4 little brutes have considerately died, one & all. ...

You have often heard me say that from 1848 a long season of war was only *beginning*. In no time of history was all Europe so unsettled as now. ... [A.L.]

29 JUNE   There are *no* pheemail servinx in these houses. The floor below me is inhabited by some old Paxos merchant & his wife, but I declare I never see them; how should I, even if I met them on the stairs (which I never did), the stairs being so dark? Menservants do everything; my man makes my coffee & toasts my bread; then 'does' my rooms, all of which are capitally clean; then buys, brings, & cooks my dinner; takes out notes & runs on errands; & so on — all through the day. And during the 3 weeks I was away I never had to ask for anything twice, nor to complain in any way, cleanliness, punctuality, & general good service making him a most valuable attendant. His brother, Giovanni, is becoming as much so to Frank though we really *do* expect Spiro home tomorrow — but Frank wants 2 servants in his position, & will keep both most probably. Certainly for £2 12*s*. a month (provisions not included) such servants are cheap. Moreover, as they could not starch or iron linen in the mountains, I found George did all that department himself.

Lizards don't make any noise, only for hustle, bustle in the hedges & grass. There are very few venomous snakes in Corfu, & only near water; I saw one the other day in the ditch, with 6 fat frogs croaking & squeaking at him as fast & loud as they could, whether in compliment or abuse I could not learn. If I go out in the yacht again, it will be for a half hour's sail to the other side: no more long trips for me.... Of what you call the 'Zantë Currant Tree', there is scarce any here ... it is merely a low-growing small sort of *vine*, producing large bunches of very little grapes, which are dried. But for 4 years the 'currant crop' has failed, & this year also the vines are ill. Like the 'potato disease', no cure is found for this malady, which comes all over the plant like mould, & the grapes stop growing when they are as big as ◯ that. Wine is almost ceasing to be made here, & from one farthing a bottle, is now at 9*d*., so that the poor get none at all....

To return to my country excursion, which, so far as it relates to the north of the island, is now finished, for there is no one place I should greatly care to return to, although all are beautiful. I stayed at 'Hokus Pokus' till the 21st when I made a move to Nimfes, leaving some of the things at Count Voulgari's house to return for them afterwards. Nimfes (pronounced Neem-fess) is a larger place than Hokus Pokus, but more remote, & more dirty, though more picturesque. There is a quiet valley below it, almost as good as Italy, & from the high parts of the ground you look over innumerable distant olives to the western sea, where Fano & the little isles lie very prettily at sunset. I stayed at Nimfes & was glad to go, because I could only get lodged in a most filthy little house, where the fleas were something serious I can tell you! There were 64 fowls in the little dark hole of a kitchen, & how George turned out clean dinners daily was a marvel.

The monastery at Nimfes, 23 June 1856.

Askiteriá at Nimfes,
22 June 1856
6 a.m.

However, I was little indoors, having been mostly at the Askiteriá, a convent close by, where there is a fine terrace & cypresses; & one day I went to a fête which was really worth seeing: there were 7 sets of dancers. One dance alone contained 84 women, who danced that slow circular dance, 6 of them in a row, linked on with coloured shawls to the next row. The first 6 were chosen for beauty, size, splendour of dress, or knowledge of the dance, so that sometimes a fat old lady, bending with scarlet & gold, led the procession, & all danced 3 steps on, & 2 back as gravely as if it were a funeral. This was a much better fête than the city Análipsis fête, as everybody was in costume, & there were no crowds to prevent the 6 *choregoi* jumping as far or as high as they pleased. I can't think why they don't break their necks, or dissolve in a

A village fête in Corfu.

heap, for the dance often lasts 3 hours without stopping! I observed the women of one village, Agrafí (for the villagers of one place make up a single dance to themselves), quite loaded with finery, at least the advance row: purple silk-striped full skirts; orange-striped aprons; crimson velvet vests worked with gold; rose-coloured silk under vests; heaps of chains & gold ornaments, & rings on all fingers: shoes all buckled, a headdress of white silk . . .

From Nimfes I sent George with my things to Spargus [Pagus] on the 24th, to a house of Cavaliere Damaskinós, & I passed the day in walking round the coast to various villages, all, as I have said, in beautiful scenery, but none possessing very good

24 June 1856 (Spargus?).

Kastro St Angelo from above Makrádes, 26 June 1856.

or very pretty qualities for landscape compared with what I see on this side of the hills. The house, however, at Spargus was a perfect bit of comfort — so perfectly clean! — with a larder, kitchen, etc., which might do justice to an English housekeeper. If you look at my 'Albania' you will find I stayed at Yannina with our vice-consul, the brother of this Mr Damaskinós, in 1849; & on the score of old acquaintance, I was not allowed to purchase anything at Spargus — but was dined at my host's expense, though always on those everlasting chickens: though indeed there is no other food in those villages! For 2 days I explored the coasts, which are rocky & fine ... I am now going, if I can find any sort of lodging, to the village of Análipsis, to make studies for Lady Reid's & other pictures, for it is now far too hot to walk there, at however early an hour....

Last night the mountains at sunset were of the purest vermilion rose I ever saw, & all the sea, like glass or oil, was amber colour, reflecting the sky. My servant has perhaps a fault in a tendency to collect pets: my having given Lushington the hedgehog has made him imagine a zoological collection to be a part of my will, so at Hokus Pokus, I found one day 3 tortoises, another day a young fox, a jay, a nightingale, & various other animals, all of which I had to deny myself the pleasure of accepting . . . Only the tortoise has come here — & I can't well turn that off, as he gives no trouble: only I would certainly not allow him to have the run of the passage, as one will tumble over him continually. Oranges are still excellent here — what a comfort they are! — & figs are now beginning: with cherries, & mulberries (the white are best, although are horrid like fat caterpillars!). Red mullet every day now one has got back to the sea. So far from the country being dried up (though all about the city where there is no shade it is brown enough certainly), the fern is most magnificent now, & such a green! — I never saw lovelier park-like places than there were in my tour, & I mean to make the fern a great point of my second big picture.

June 30th. This morning I went up to the village of Análipsis early with George, & I have absolutely got the only decent place there! For the sum of £1 5s. the whole family turn out of their rooms, which are mine for 6 weeks! They are small, but very airy & overlook all the most beautiful part of the islands, & besides that, the house is quite close to all the spots I most want to work at. I am in great spirits at this bit of luck . . . In one minute I am within all those fine olive walks you have heard so much of. I have some idea of devoting a good bit of time to illustrating this little promontory, for it is full of interest, as the old city of Análipsis [Corcyra] was built on it, & ancient coins & marbles are still found. [A.L.]

All the week has gone, & very little written, nor indeed, much to write about; however, to tell the truth, the life at my village villa is not very agreeable after all. That is, the early morning, & the late evenings out of doors are pleasant, but the indoor life is not. On first coming here I sent my 2 carts (small carts) of furniture — i.e. bed, wash-stand, tables, chairs, etc. etc., & the rooms looked very comfortable after a fashion, & so they were. But soon after I came (on the 3rd) the high north wind, so prevalent at this season, set in, & I could not work out of doors at all; & as the heat was great, & the flies abundant, & my room very small, it was pretty well a dissolving view of things in general, I can tell you. However, I did work, both at Lushington's last picture, & at Sir Simeon's (both Philae) — & L.'s I have finished, & on the 14th send it home to him. It is a sunset, & is thought by far the best little picture I have done yet. Strange that what to me is always painful & disagreeable work — painting — should in a couple of months create a work which not only gives pleasure to its possessor at present but may continue to do so to hundreds of others for a century or more — a very unfair division of happiness I think.

My man gets me a very fair dinner at noon, & at 8 I have tea, & then go to bed very early to rise betimes next day. One evening I went to the Cortazzis', who have now come to their villa just below, & another to Colonel Ormsby's close by, but in each case I had to sacrifice my evening's work, & also that of the following morning by over-sleeping, going to bed at 11; so I find I can't visit at all, & consequently am more alone than I like to be. So 10 or 15 days more will be as much as I can bear here, I think; though it may depend on the studies I have to make. . . . I do not mind a lonely

20 JULY
ANALIPSIS

83

Corfu from Análipsis, 1856.

life if I can get exercise, but here, at this season, there is only the opportunity of walking a few paces morning & evening, because the subjects I am painting are close by. Nobody of the English in Corfu seems to care a jot about these beautiful scenes: one & all drive vulgarly to given spots, & rarely twice to the same except the high road, Esplanade, or Kanóni . . .

 The hay was cut here last May . . . the corn has been cut a month past. All that was so beautifully green up till June is now all pale yellow & parched dry, even under the olives, near the city, where the trees give but little shade; I have not been at Virós lately to see if the fern is green yet. All about here the ground won't leave off bursting out into flowers as far as it can, & a vast crop of yellow thistles has just come out, which certainly don't give a cooler effect to the landscape; but the yellow ground contrasted with the blue & purple hills & sea is very beautiful & I do not know what season to paint in my large picture — green or yellow. I forgot to say, the wind only lasted a week, & it is now always calm & clear, though there is always too much wind for my taste from 5 till sunset. This wind, though, is what makes the island so healthy, & I never could understand why there were no fevers when there are marshes of such extent . . .

Corfu from Análipsis (undated).

You ask about the costumes at the Análipsis fête — there were lots of costumes, but such crowds of people you could see nothing; perhaps above 1,000 soldiers — & 3 or 4,000 of the Corfu gentry in hats & coats; so costume was scarcely visible.

The church is not so crowded now in the morning, & therefore safer from colds; I fear we shall lose Mr Clark, whose wife is ill & must go to England, & he will not return I think, if he can help it. . . . On Thursday I went into town to see S. Saunders the Prevesa consul, & coming away from the inn, old Mrs Castro said, 'There is a gentleman, Sir, & enquiring after you; he is at lodging so & so'; & when I found him out, lo! it was James Uwins* with a great gray beard, come from Athens. We had a walk together that afternoon, & he drank tea with me here, & last night he called when I was out; this is all I have seen of him, but I hope he will not go yet. It seems but the other day — though really 19 years ago exactly — that I walked from Rome to Naples with him. He says, having just come from Sicily & Greece, that Corfu is the most beautiful place he ever saw yet. . . .

Did I tell you of the bright blue thistles? Out of spite because she has got so few flowers, Mrs Nature has turned one sort of thistle brilliant blue — leaves, stalks, & all — & they look like bright blue flowers at a distance. These rooms are wonderfully clean. I have only really seen 2 fleas; it is quite melancholy. It is an old widow's house, & she keeps a nephew & niece, & 2 small grandchildren who never cry or make a noise all day — Fotiní, & Christina. I cut them out 2 paper birds the other day — & the whole village has been to see these 2 *«πουλιά τοῦ Μαρτίου»* ['birds of March']. The view of the lake, westward, when the sun sets, is very grand. But I hear George bringing up my everlasting omelette . . .

As I am writing, the villagers one by one have gone to bed, & the priest, who lives next door, also; & now one only hears the pretty brown owls whistling in their sad one note. Some friends here have got 2 young owls, tied to a post, & every evening the paternal & maternal owls bring them mice & worms in the prettiest way possible. 'I am sure nobody ever gave *me* mice & worms' (as poor Mrs Warner* would have said). The headdress of the priests here is very picturesque; the married ones wear a squashed hat . . . but the unmarried clergy, of whom alone they make bishops, wear a beautiful globular platter-like, pipkin-form, abstract lunivolvular sort of tile . . . All wear beards & long robes, & they are about the most picturesque of all the people here. As soon as I go to town, I mean to have a Greek master again twice a day for I am just beginning to be able to speak more quickly, & if I can once overcome my indolence so as to conquer grammar, a language has lost all difficulty with me on account of the quick character of my ear. I have also learnt to write it pretty nicely . . .
[A.L.]

Once upon a time a bird was ill, and a cat, bending down to it, said, 'How are you and what do you want? I will give you everything, only get well.' And the bird replied, 'If you go away I shan't die.'

Yesterday I was at the Cortazzi villa when Mrs Cortazzi brought in a large packet of Zantë grapes — or currants, as they are commonly called; & as I thought them very nice to eat, my amiable neighbours gave me a good basketful to take home. . . . The villa, close by here, is a great gain to me, as I often go in to tea, though I am beginning to call the house 'Castle Dangerous' because of the 2 young ladies, & of the difficulty of getting away when one has gone there. If I were not such an ancient owl, I believe I should fall a victim to the eldest, but I am resolved to run if I find myself growing silly. I shall be a week longer here, if not 2, & then go back to my lodgings, or to Aghii Deka on the hill for a week or so. The weather is hot, but never too hot for me — & today it is very nice, as there was a thunderstorm & heavy rain yesterday early. My! how it *did* thunder & lighten! [A.L.]

29 JULY
ANALIPSIS

When I came to town I went and stayed a day or 2 with Frank till my rooms could be cleared properly. And, as my big canvasses had not come, I made up my mind to see a little bit more of the world before working hard again. Frank & Colonel & Mrs Ormsby were to go on the 7th to Delvino, so I agreed to join them, as I had never seen that part of Albania; & then, I planned to go to Yannina, & if possible on to the long desired Mount Athos, so as to return to Corfu as early as possible in September. Now you are to be clear that in these days things are not as they were in 1848: we now have consuls at many places, & although I take a bed & cooking things, yet I shall want them but little. Our yacht trip over to Santa Quaranta was delightful, & for once I am beginning to like yachts — at least, the *Midge*.

13 AUGUST
FILIATES
(OPPOSITE CORFU)

On the 8th the Ormsbys, Frank & I, went early to Delvino, which is immensely picturesque; it seemed odd enough to come all at once again into the use of divans & round tables & cross legs! But the wonderful picturesqueness of Albania is as new & beautiful as ever; & after the eternal, though lovely olives of Corfu, I must say we, Frank & I, found it very refreshing. On the 9th we returned to the coast, & there Colonel & Mrs Ormsby left us, & we 2 ran down in the *Midge* to Skala Sagiáda where early on the 10th we landed, taking also my man George & my luggage. We were soon at this place, & well lodged in the house of Jaffier Pasha — & how I wish you could see it! It is one of those strange all roof & lattice Turk houses, enclosed in a court with walls & towers; the walls are black with jackdaws, & the towers white with storks who clatter as of old.

I am sorry to tell you that in the afternoon I had a baddish fall, down a flight of stone stairs; the matter might have been serious, but happily I broke no bones — though I did not feel able to move for travelling until after a good rest. So I have stayed here through the 11th, 12th & 13th, & tomorrow I shall go as far as Keramítsa on my way to Yannina, but if I find the least chance of my being unwell shall return to Corfu at once, which I can see from the hills close by. My going on to Athos depends on that. [A.L.]

OCTOBER 1856 – MAY 1857

8 OCTOBER
QUARANTINE ISLAND
CORFU

I came back all right yesterday morning, exactly 2 months to a day from my starting on August 7th, but as there has been a report of cholera at Constantinople, these idiot Corfiotes have put on a quarantine of 8 days — as if any quarantine ever kept out cholera at all! So instead of going at once to my room, I have to stay here 3 days (the other 5 being counted in the voyage), an expense & annoyance not over agreeable. However, this quarantine house is very good, & I have a very large good room to myself... Frank came yesterday in his boat (having previously sent off a basket of wine, fish, fruit, meat, & vegetables) & brought me some books; & thus... having my drawings to pen out besides, I am not likely to be very doleful, particularly as I am in such good health...

There are all kinds of books at Corfu, but I have no time for reading them: Frank has all the best new ones, for he can read & understand in 10 minutes what it takes my brain as many days to go through. My Greek will occupy every leisure moment, besides penning out the valuable Mt Athos collection of drawings. [A.L.]

PRITVATE and ΚΟΜΦΙDΕΝΤΙΑL

9 OCTOBER

Had I been ever to the north of the island when I wrote last? There is not much to say of it: in point of scenery it is far below all the centre in interest. But any particular reason for all account of it — should I write on Corfu — is the improper name of one of the towns — 'smack-your-arse' — Σμακιεράς. What could a decent man do with such nomenclature? So I came back to Corfu — pleased only that the north of the island had been 'done' & was not to do. I then took a lodging in a village close to the town. I trust to paint a magnificent large view of Corfu straits, & Albanian hills. This I trust to sell for £500 as it will be my best, & is 9 feet long. If I can't sell it I shall instantly begin a picture 10 feet long: & if that don't sell, one 12 feet long. Nothing like persisting in virtue. O dear! I wish I was up there, in the village I mean, now, on this beautiful bright day! However I got unwell, & Bluedevilled, & I made up my mind that I could work no more till something called out my boddly & mentle N.R.G.s.

So I said, I'll go to Mt Athos (I should have gone to Montenegro with A. Seymour had I not missed the steamer). And off I set on August 7th taking my servant, canteen, bed & lots of paper & quinine pills. F. Lushington saw me as far as Filiátes, but then I fell down a high flight of 19 stone stairs & damaged my back sadly. I thought I was lame for life, but after 4 days on a mattress, I got on pillows & a horse, & went over to Yannina & to Pindus, & (in great pain) to Larissa, & finally to Saloníki. There getting better I went slick into τὸ Ἅγιον Ὄρος or the Holy Mountain, altogether the most surprising thing I have seen in my travels, perhaps, barring Egypt. It is a peninsular mountain about 2,000 ft high & 50 miles long ending in a vast crag, near 7,000 ft high, this being Athos. All but this bare crag is one mass of vast forest, beech, chestnut, oak, & ilex, & all round the cliffs & crags by the sea are 20 great & ancient monistirries, not to speak of 6 or 700 little 'uns above & below & around. These convents are inhabited by, altogether perhaps, 6 or 7,000 monx, & as you may have heard, no female creature exists in all the peninsula: there are nothing but mules, tomcats, & cocks allowed. This is literally true.

Well, I had a great deal of suffering in this Athos, for my good man George caught the fever, & nearly died, & when he grew better I caught it, but not so badly. However, I persisted & persisted & finally I got drawings of every one of the 20 big monasteries, so that such a valuable collection is hardly to be found. Add to this, constant walking — 8 or 10 hours a day — made me very strong, & the necessity I was under of acting decidedly in some cases, called out a lot of energy I had forgotten ever to have possessed. The worst was the food & the filth, which were uneasy to bear. But however wondrous & picturesque the exterior & interior of the monasteries, & however abundantly & exquisitely glorious & stupendous the scenery of the mountain, I would not go again to the Ἅγιον Ὄρος for any money, so gloomy, so shockingly unnatural, so lonely, so lying, so unatonably odious seems to me all the atmosphere of such monkery. That half of our species which it is natural to every man to cherish & love best, ignored, prohibited & abhorred — all life spent in everlasting repetition of monotonous prayers, no sympathy with one's fellow-beans of any nation, class or age. The name of Christ on every garment & at every tongue's end, but his maxims trodden under foot. God's world & will turned upside down, maimed, & caricatured — if this I say be Christianity let Christianity be rooted out as soon as possible. More pleasing in the sight of the Almighty I really believe, & more like what Jesus Christ intended man to become, is an honest Turk with 6 wives, or a Jew working hard to feed his little old clo' babbies, than these muttering, miserable, mutton-hating, man-avoiding, misogynic, morose & merriment-marring, monotoning, many-mule-making, mocking, mournful, minced-fish & marmalade masticating Monx. Poor old pigs! Yet one or two were kind enough in their way, dirty as they were: but it is not them, it is their system I rail at.

So having seen all, & a queer page in my world-nollidge is Athos, I came back to Saloníki, & set sail for the Dardanelles, where being obliged to stay 4 days for a steamer, I spent 3 in seeing Troy. But dear Mother Ida I could not reach, & I do trust to go there in the spring of 1857, for there is a something about the Troad scenery quite unique — if it be not equalled by the Roman Campagna as to grand & simple outlines.

Thence I came by sea to Corfu, getting here on the 7th & being thrust into this place till Saturday the 11th & be damned to the owls for their folly. [C.F.]

Those who know Alfred's poems most thoroughly are the 2 sisters Cortazzi in Corfu, particularly the older — Helena. One evening there was a discussion as to the

9 OCTOBER

comparative superiority of Thackeray or Dickens in drawing female character — other writers were also named — when Miss Cortazzi said, 'Not one of all those you name could imagine or describe such a character as the Isabel of Alfred Tennyson!' She knows every word of *In Memoriam*, & indeed all Alfred's poems, & has translated many into Italian, & set many to music; but in the society of a garrison town you may suppose how few appreciate such talents. And indeed how few of the English ladies — good & amiable as they may be — go one iota beyond the plain housewife everyday thoughts, so that Helena Cortazzi, with her complete knowledge of Italian, French & Greek, her poetry & magnificent music, but withal her simple & retiring quiet, is not thought half as much of as that large Miss A.Z. who can only talk English & dance polkas. . . .

But you have puzzled me horribly, & if you find me dreadfully stupid, excuse me on the grounds of my having had a bad fever — & that I have been sojourning with monks & hermits, whose queer legends did 'all my senses confound', so that I am — to speak Lancashire — 'by common' bewildered just now. Yet here is the paragraph: '*We saw there a Druid's egg.*' May you be forgiven for the frightful confusion of ideas this unhappy sentence has caused me! Ever since I read it I cannot look at a tree without seeing large nests with Druids sitting in them, & when George brought up the breakfast, I beheld three little Druidini chippin' & chirpin' out of the bursting eggshells. . . .

My quarantine life is not heavy, & I sit writing all day long. Outside there is a rocky bit of ground, with a few tombs where wretched people have died in sight of their homes. All is still & sunny & beautiful, & I should enjoy sitting on the rocks & dabbling in the water, if the idiotic quarantine rule did not enjoin a man to follow me everywhere — by which severe surveillance, they must imply that I can fly away as a bird, since by no other mode — unless I swam for many hours — could I reach the city. [E.T.]

13 OCTOBER
CONDI TERRACE

On Saturday morning — the 11th — I was fetched off in a boat, & soon reached my lodgings. But there begins a long story, which has made great changes . . . I found my room all choked with dust, & all the repairs which the landlord had made tumbled & cracked to pieces. It was quite clear, as indeed Frank had told me, that unless Chiessari would expend some £50 or £60 in restoring the whole house, it would not be possible to live there in the winter. In the meantime, I packed a trunk or 2, & sent them up here to Frank's, whence I am now writing, being asked to stay with him for 3 or 4 days; a friend of his — Johnson — is here, & has his lower spare room, so I went up to the top — all these details you will see my reason for writing bye & bye.

The day, Saturday 7th, went in looking at houses: the Palazzo Valsamáki has the best light, on the Line Wall, but the rooms are small, & some are damp; & £7 a month asked. Paramythiótti has now finished his house, but there are many objections, although he asked £26 for the floor still un-let. Other places were impossible — so if

Chiessari would not repair my present rooms, I must either give up staying the winter here, or take one of those I mentioned.

Well — Frank & Johnson & I sat up late after tea — i.e. till about 1 — & then all went to bed, I to sleep directly; but everybody was woken up at 2 o'clock by the worst earthquake Corfu has known for many years. Strange to say, I thought I was in the steamer still, my bed rocking & becoming sick, & I called out to the steward to know when the sea had begun to get so rough. But all in a moment the sound of all the bells of the city going at once & the cries of the people rushing into the churches, which are instantly thrown open, brought me to my senses; & the beams & cornices cracking, I thought it was time to rush down stairs; & there was Johnson, & Giovanni Kokáli. As for Frank, we found him quietly in bed making experiments with a compass as to the exact direction of the earthquake from some water shaken out of a glass by his bed side! I don't think I ever felt anything so shocking in all my life as the movement; but nobody has been hurt in all the city, & no house fallen — though many old ones are cracked.

And here comes more of the story: for early yesterday Spiro came in to say that my Chiessari house was cracked in 3 places, 2 quite unsafe. So down I went, & found it to be so. To make things more confused, George is ill of fever again, at his mother's, so I had to hire a man, who with Giovanni moved out all my books, drawings, & other small things yesterday up to Frank's. Meanwhile I suddenly heard that the first floor — next door to Frank — was to let, & that Sir P. Hunter thought of taking it. So I ran in to see the rooms, & to make this long story short, finally agreed to take them for 6 months — at £6 a month. A great rent, but the rooms are thoroughly good, in a new & strong house; light good; air good; & close to all my friends here.

Condi Terrace
(destroyed in the Second World War).

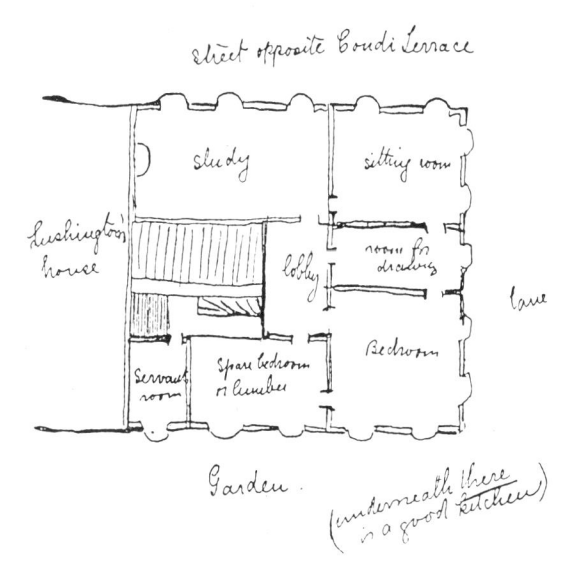

So I am to move in today, & go there as soon as George is able to come. My large canvas will be sent up this afternoon & Taylor will see to moving in all my heavy furniture. There are 6 rooms, a kitchen & a stable; fireplaces in all; lofty; good doors & windows etc. The fault is, that being on the first floor, there is no good view: a peep of the sea at one corner, Mr Scarpass's garden, & the distant hills of Pelekas & Potamós. Over me — second floor — are Major & Mrs Shakespear — very nice people & quiet. So you see me fixed for the winter. [A.L.]

15 OCTOBER In all of what you write concerning Jesus Christ & the Bible I mainly agree with you. . . . My meaning . . . was more to express my own preference for such subjects in the life of Christ as are universal & of daily interest & other than those more occult & dogma-breeding points which do not suit all minds. Nor do I for one cling to the miraculous & supernatural, thinking that I observe from all history the torrents of blood & the cries of torture which have arisen from *disputable* 'idols' of belief. Christ pardoning the woman taken in adultery, Christ blessing the children, & hundreds of ministries of exquisite goodness & wisdom appear to me as being incapable of failing in attracting *all* suffrage. *Nobody* doubts mercy, or affection, being good, but the world will never — as it has never agreed — agree on much that has been written on abstruser subjects, such subjects being (*selon moi*) of far less importance than the facts & rules Christ lived to order & exemplify. [H.H.]

19 OCTOBER The weather has been always lovely, much to my surprise. Rain has threatened to come, but never seems any nearer, except that one day it was cloudy, & one night it rained. Every evening the sunsets are glorious & the Albanian mountains clear as glass. There are always some flowers here — I never saw such a place; the ground is quite purple with cyclamens now in some places, & there are some yellow cistuses; the fern is still green & bright, but the grass is gone. And there are *no* olives this year! It seems the trees in Corfu are habitually ill-conducted. One year, as they did last, they bear so many that half are wasted from want of hands; the next, none at all. [A.L.]

5 NOVEMBER At last the long-delayed rain has come. I made the most of yesterday to draw the mountains before they fled away, but as I walked back from Gastoúri by the beautiful acqueduct path, everything looked leaden & gray, & I thought the end of the fine weather must be very near at hand. So — growl–growl–growl, the thunder began at night & pouring rain, & today I hear the flap–flap–crack–crack of innumerable window shutters whose owners are not fidgety; & upstairs & in Lushington's house I know there must be such a howling that one cannot hear oneself speak, though here, downstairs, it is quiet enough comparatively. Everything is as gray & dull & blotted out as you can desire it in England, & I suppose as the last rain of any consequence was in the beginning of March we shall have a pretty long dose of it. For my own part, now I have got this beautiful large studio, it is rather good for me to be able to work without going out . . .

Bless me, the wind is getting very high! I hope we are not going to have a hurricane. But I must go & eat some bread & 2 apples (alas! the oranges are not so plentiful this year) for it is 1 o'clock; & then I have to give George a writing lesson, for he can't keep the weekly accounts legibly — so that virtue will be its own reward if I can get him to write plain. . . .

Sunday 9th. Gracious: a clergyman with large moustaches & a long black beard — I never saw such a one before — but there he was, & moreover he preached a very good sermon. I don't know his name, but he was one of the Crimean chaplains & on his way to Kefaloniá, & everybody agreed how manly & how like better times he looked, in contrast with the nasty effeminate woman-imitating men who have, since the moral days of Charles II, distorted the human face out of its natural state. I did not approve however of the new military order — church to begin at 10 — it will be such a hustle; but I believe it will be better for clergymen & soldiers. [A.L.]

15 DECEMBER

From the last time I wrote — 25th November — up to December 5th, certainly we had an abomination of Corfu wind! I can't tell you how I hate it, the noise & terrible fuss & nastiness; generally, too, with at least one thunderstorm in the day — such thunder & lightening at night! Well, on the 6th, it burst as it were into a new world: all the clouds went, & the great mountains came out as white as white could be; 2 days were cold, but since those, 7 have been exactly like Paradise as to everything beautiful & calm & quiet & bright. Yesterday clouds rose, & the weather was close & dull. Today it is pouring with rain & blowing a horrible hurricane once more; & so from 10 days to 10 days. November & December, I should fancy, are generally much like this here. January I imagine will be clear & summery; February squashy & warm. As for indoor work, my house is faultless — a good wood fire makes it very comfortable. I go out very little, & indeed, except to Frank next door (he has his cousin Dr Lushington's son with him now), to the Shakespears overhead, & the Cortazzis 3 doors off, & the Palace, I may say I go nowhere. On Christmas day I dine with my neighbours, the Cortazzis just mentioned (the Palace & Colonel & Mrs Gage* having also asked me), & our party will be, as far as I know, Major & Mrs Shakespear, Frank & William Lushington, & Lord Kirkwall;* but I suppose Captain Lawrence & 1 or 2 other stray old residents will be there. I hope too poor Sir James Reid will arrive in time to join something like a social party. . . .

I have now letters from all my old friends I think. I do not know what I should do without letters. Meanwhile I have been working away at setting up for show my Athos drawings & have penned out, coloured, & mounted 40 of them, by dint of hard work. On Saturday last Lady Young & a large party came to see me, & several lots of people have been since. . . . It does not appear to me that I ought to do otherwise than live what is called sociably & comfortably as far as I can, though an artist's life, if he has no capital, must always have its uncertainties & difficulties from month to month. So much, however, of the artist's capacity & strength for going onward depends on his ordinary comforts, that if he were to live wholly alone drinking water & eating barley

'The cat, the clouds, & the Rainbow: — as seen from Mandoúkio, December 19/ '55.' (This sketch may be misdated as it is drawn on the back of a letter from Lushington dated 24 February 1856.)

bread, the money he would save by such diet would be overbalanced by the depression which would soon prevent his getting any money at all. . . .

My Greek master takes great pains with me, & I certainly get on very well. I shall soon be able to write a Greek letter to Charles Church.* One story of *The Arabian Knights* [*sic*] I have quite translated, & in old Greek I am able to read any of the gospels, though the epistles not so easily. Possibly I may take an extra hour for more old Greek, as I long to begin Xenophon. . . . Dear me, I wish I could paint faster & better & had 20 pairs of hands, not to speak of an elephant's trunk to pick up brushes when they fall down. . . . It is also necessary to inform you that my beard is getting quite gray, & all my hair tumbling off; & when I am quite bald, possibly I may take to painting my head in green & blue stripes as an evening devotion; but I have not decided about this yet. [A.L.]

25 DECEMBER TO 11 JANUARY

I will go on with my journal as far as I can, though I am not able to do so very well, because since I wrote last, excepting 4 days I was in Albania, I seem to have been quite bewildered by living in one constant tempest of rain, hail, thunder & lightening, & above all WIND. They say there has been no such continued bad weather in Corfu since 1828. Certainly it was far otherwise last winter. We have had *no* cold — only the 3 first days of December; & although today the wind has changed to the north & it is calm, I cannot flatter myself that we are to have permanent peace of atmosphere. And as my bedroom looks south & west, the noise & hullabaloo keeps me from sleeping, so that I have sometimes been quite unwell. On the 13th, at half past 4 in the morning, there was another earthquake, quite violent enough to wake me, & to be very disagreeable; it was only one bounce, not a 5 minutes of rattle & shaking as on October 11th; & I woke supposing that George had come in to call me, & his light had gone out & he had struck the table. A queer cristling crushing gritty noise soon brought me to know that the doors & windows were what they call here 'settling' themselves. No harm was done anywhere, a little alarm felt; but it ain't pleasant to be shaken about so. Let me see. Christmas day was pouring with rain all day; the Cortazzi party was large, & very full of hospitality & good feeding; but it was not at all like a sociable Christmas after all, since by degrees it had got so many additional guests. . . .

31st. . . . So ends 1856, which has been a very singular year for me. On looking back I find I have painted 11 small oil paintings, & 16 or more large water-colour drawings, besides many smaller ones; a great many oil, pencil, & water-colour studies & sketches; a perfect collection of the monasteries of Athos & partly of Troy as an addition to my topographical collection; besides time spent in travelling, & a large correspondence — 126 letters in all. It is plain therefore I have not been what is called idle, though I am by no means satisfied with my own progress. The paintings & drawings (& the Athos collection will be so perhaps) are a positive addition to the knowledge & pleasure of many families for, possibly, a very long period of time; so that is one consolation — & I can assure you I need no little at times. It isn't very often as I takes to moralising; only at the end of the year one may be pardoned doing so.

January 1st. A finer day. It's a great fuss here, it being the anniversary of the absurd Constitution, & there is a levee, which of course I have nothing to do with. I dined with Frank & we went to the great State Ball afterwards, which, as being Lady Young's birthday fête also, one can't well avoid going to. It is a horrid bore to me for all that.

January 2nd. Pouring rain, high wind, & *very dark*. Worked at large Corfu. Sitting-room chimney — the wind having set in south — took to smoking, & can't be remedied till the weather changes.

3rd. Very wet morning, but people say it will be fine. Went with Frank to Garoúna in a carriage to make a drawing for him — the 4th being his birthday. But it only held up a little. He dined with me afterwards.

4th. Sunday, fine all day. Church, calls, small walk; & dine with C. Lane at Frank's. Tomorrow, Frank, who has a week's holiday, goes with the yacht to Trescoglie in Albania, & is to join Sir P. Hunter & a party to shoot bear at the head of the Butrínto lake.* I, always wishing to draw that lake, resolved to go too, having the yacht in the quiet little harbour all to myself till Saturday next. I think the change would do me good, & I should get these Butrínto sketches at last, after trying off & on.

5th. Finer morning than usual. . . . George got together food & wine for a week &

Butrínto, 7 January 1857.

we packed up all; left Christo, Spiro, & Yanni to look after Lushington's house & mine, & set off — but not at 12 as we had hoped, for Frank had some judicial work, which kept him till 3. The consequence of this delay was that we could not get up the Butrínto river till dusk, when, even if the boat were waiting to take him up the lake, he could not go with his bed, guns, etc. — an hour's journey in the dark; & so he came on with me to Trescoglie, where it was as still & quiet as in a house. The dearest little harbour! Quite shut out from all winds, & looking out on the great mountains above the sheltered wall of rocks, so valuable to boats.

6th. Wet again, but George, the Judge & myself walked across the hills to Butrínto, where I was at all events delighted with the scenery, though I could not draw it as I wished. The lake of Butrínto is a splendid sheet of water, & the lake of Riza is a little one; between the 2 are the great ruins of the ancient Buthrotum & the river of Butrínto runs round them, out of the lake into the sea. No boat was there, & it turned out that none had come; so Frank could not get to the party at the head of the lake, & we walked back in the rain. I bought a lamb for the sailors, from some

Butrínto, looking towards Corfu, dated 1878.

shepherds, for 20*d*. Next day — 7th — Frank took his own boat, rowed up all the rivers, & across the lake, but could meet no one, & had to return. Most lucky it was that I had come & had taken food; so we lived very comfortably in the yacht — the little *Midge* — which has 2 good cabins. . . . The waters were covered with wild duck, & the air full of vultures, & the earth full of dogs. The first we wished we had for dinner, the 2nd we said were nasty ugly brutes; the 3rd we threw stones at & hit their noses. On the 8th the weather was worse than ever, & Luigi (the captain) said it would be worse still. So, as the party had managed so clumsily, Frank did not think it necessary to wait for them, & accordingly off we set, & came puff puff over in no time, & though it was very rough I was not a bit sick.

On the whole this queer Albanian trip did me good deal of good, for it is really most wearying here in wet weather: that everlasting 'one gun' road is pretty in itself, but one always falls in with endless people, & in so limited a society as this, you can't help joining them — a frightful bore to me, who always prefer being alone if not with society I like. I miss William Lushington extremely; Frank is generally so occupied & thoughtful that we go for miles & miles in silence; & military men I know or like at all are either married or busy, or have little in common with me, & Sir James Reid never walks more than a mile or so. O dear! I find Corfu very like a prison I do.

9th. Perhaps the worst day yet; oceans of rain. Storms of wind & thunder all day, & too dark to do anything but paste drawings on to boards. Neither could I have any fires lighted — so I was miserable all day. . . .

10th. All day & all night storm–storm–storm. Work, I could now & then. No fire. Sir James Reid called & took me to the Palace; great dinner. Sat next to a little man, nephew of Dr Powys (of Warrington) & had a good deal of pleasant talk. This was one of the few particularly pleasant parties at the Palace. . . .

Sunday 11th. Usual abomination of wind & torrents. Short walk in a macintosh. Dined at Sir J. Reid's. Letters from Holman Hunt, etc. My Egyptian companion Seddon is just dead, leaving a widow & 1 child, & on the day my poor friend Holman Hunt heard of this (Seddon was his intimate friend & with him in Jerusalem, where now, on his 2nd visit, Seddon has died), his own father died; & his sister, & her infant. Consequently poor dear Hunt's letter is most terribly sad, & I wish I could be with him. And consequently also on all this — the bad weather, my own inability to work, my cold room, & my hearing all this sad & shocking news — I am not particularly lively myself, & wish with all my heart I was out of Corfu. [A.L.]

11 JANUARY 1st some remarks about my Athos tour: I am getting up (by my usual dilatory but sure process of penning out & colour) all my drawings of the monasteries, & have them ready all but 10 or 12, thanks to after-dinner application & stayathomeaciousness. They are a reemarkable lot of work, as I hope one day you will see: mind, if you *do* come while I am here, I have now a better spare bedroom than you'll get anywhere in the town, & you should do just as you liked, barring leaving the windys open all night, because then my landlord's 29 cats would perforate the domestic tranquillity of my establishment . . . I must tell you with a feeling of pride & conflatulation that I have made such progress in Greek as to be able to read the Testament (in *old* as well as modern) quite comfortably; & since I can read the life of Christ in the original, my desire of seeing the actual places he lived in are not to be stoppled any more. I gain more fixed & real ideas from the actual history than from our translation.

2ndly . . . I, alas, am now a long long way off my ideal, & I don't see how it can ever be got at, though I am notwithstanding happy to say that I sometimes DO think I am a little bit nearer the mark than I was. But, hang it, there *must* be an ideal *Mrs* Lear to make up the perfect ideal, & how that is to come about I can't yet tell. Some of your expressions on this head are exactly like my friend Lushington's here, only that yours come out spongetaneous, whereas his have got to be got at by wrenching & imploring, he being, though a diamond as to value, yet hidden in a tortoise's shell, & doing nothing so little as contributing an iota of personal experience for the benefit of others. . . .

3rd. About the blessed Bowen. On the day your letter came, burst out the news that he was, to use his own account, offered the Governor's Secretaryship of Mauritius, such a change being intimated as a mere step to further advancement, & that he should return here as Lord High Commissioner. But it was the popular opinion of Greek & English that a rational Colonial Secretary had determined on sending an unprincipled man to a place he can do less harm in than here, where he is the veriest tool of Greek factionaries. This latter surmise is not, of course, backed by

Sir George Ferguson Bowen, K.C.M.G.

anything but probabilities, but I confess I incline to thinking the same way. Bowen's grossly false conduct here — his barefaced misrepresentation of everyone he chooses to injure, his vanity & 10-fold impudence — could hardly have been tolerated much longer, so although he talks about 'doubting if he shall go', most people believe that he can't help himself. The Greeks, who long ago nicknamed him Κόσκινον — the sieve — believe certain bits of his conduct to mean decadence, though doubtless he will put a paragraph in the papers to prove himself bewept in leaving Corfu. Meanwhile that island is — so far as he is known — in one accord at rejoicing at the removal of one in whom — to use the words of a wise man — it is difficult to determine whether snob, liar, sly knave or fool most predominate in his composing material.

4th . . . O my i! Lady Ormonde! In this queer place very few have ever heard of Maud or Tennyson, & if you hear of such a song spoken of as from 'Maud', so certain are you to hear 'oh! indeed! Colonel Maude of the Buffs! very distinguished officer, but I had not the least idea he was a poet!' . . . Prepare, notwithstanding the ideal, to see me a good deal changed: like Dan Tucker, all de wool comes off my 'ed, & I am older than Babylon in many ways. I wish sometimes I grew hard & old at heart, it would I fancy save a deal of bother: but perhaps it's all for the best. . . . It is George Kokáli's opinion & compliment that the painting I am now doing of Corfu will prevent all other Englishmen coming here, for says he, διότι είναι ώστε τὴν φύσιν, τόσον ἀκριβῶς ὅτι κανένα θέλει νὰ πληρώσει νὰ ἔλθη ἐδῶ — where's the good of people paying for coming so far if they can see the very same thing at home? George is a valuable servant, capital cook, & endlessly obliging & handy, not quite as clean as I should like always, but improving by kindness. I teach the critter to read & write, & he makes long strides! . . .

The Palace folk continue to be very kind to me, & I like them better. Sir John Young is evidently a kind good man, & I fancy more able than he was thought to be. The truth being that it is no easy matter to act suddenly where, as here, language & people are unbeknown & all power is in the hands of an unprincipled secretary. Lady Young lives too much for amusement, but she certainly improves & I believe I should end by liking her very much if I saw more of her. Now . . . I must close this, as the Cyclopses used to say of their one eye. I wish I had written more or betterer, but can't. My 'ed is all gone woolgathering. [C.F.]

12 JANUARY Weather worse if possible. Wrote to Holman Hunt & others all day. Went into Frank's after dinner & penned out till time to come home & go to bed. 13th. Weather abominabler. . . . Dined at home & went to bed in a rage; no sleep till nearly 4 — when the earthquake woke me! 14th. Wind round to the west but as bad as ever. However, fires could be lighted. Worked off & on, got a little walk, & went up to Análipsis, where my landscape is taken from; but it is all too squashy to stand on, & I do not see at all how I am to get sufficient studies, even if it were to clear up now thoroughly, to complete my picture before the spring. But I go on — not liking to give up. No sleep all night. 15th. Did not rise till 12, as one can't get on without sleep. Simple rain all day, & no wind. South wind again — no fire. Gave up going to the Cortazzi party, being so ill at ease, cross, & out of spirits. 16th. Rain, tempest, no fire — ditto–ditto, ditto–crosser & crosser all day. Wouldn't walk with Frank or Sir. J. Reid & begged Colonel Ormsby to leave me alone.

17th. . . . Today is better. No rain. Wind going round to the north. And they mend my chimney, so let us hope it will not smoke any more. Painted the sky of my big Corfu — & George being out, of course the bell rang; I was obliged to send away Mrs & the 2 Miss Cortazzi, as to stop in a sky is to spoil all — a circumstance which all Corfu will be sure to hear of directly, & I never the last of. At 4.30 I got a little walk by the Alíssia road; dined alone — penned out.

Sunday 18th . . . I have had so much cold & headache that I have not been to church, but sit writing by the fire, having told George to get dinner at 6.30; & I don't mean to answer the bell for anyone. Perhaps next week may be a better one than the last 3 generally speaking. But I don't know what to think; & many little matters . . . add to my naturally magnificent capacity for worry just at this moment. If Clowes* goes to Jerusalem, I think I shall go.

In the afternoon, I walked out alone, up to Potamós, & round by the Gouvia marshes. If, after a tempestuous season, you in England are glad to retreat to your fogs & quiet darknesses, think of the difference here, when, after 3 weeks odious weather, such a day as this makes all the earth emerald & the sky sapphire. The mountains were nearly clear, like long ranges of opal, with pearls or cream on their summits, & so calm was the marsh-sea that the great Souli hills were reflected, every peak of white, in the water below the city of Corfu. Certainly, this is a wondrous beauty — after such a batch of ugliness. And it is quite possible that it will last, & that the winter is 'over & gone'. [A.L.]

25 JANUARY

The weather is just the same; it keeps raining raining on, & with such thunder storms! Bye & bye it will certainly begin to get quite an unusual thing to go out at all without thunder & lightening. O dear, I *am* so tired of it — & as all this wet has quite prevented me making fresh studies for my large Análipsis picture (so that it could have been done in time for exhibition), I have at last quite decided on giving it up for the present; accordingly, yesterday it was turned to the wall, & I do not know when I shall take it up again.

January 31st. O dear me, the usual thing — such lightening & thunder as one has hardly heard — & so, despairing of writing any news, I sit down to go on scribbling, which on Sunday last I did not progress with. The oldest people here say they never remember such a dreadful winter as this (though to be sure all old people say such things), & change after change of the moon comes & yet brings no change. Only yesterday was tolerably fine *all* through, & we did begin to think fine weather was coming. I really got a walk along the cliffs, & saw 2 or 3 anemones peeping out. But generally the whole ground below the olives is all soppy & unwalkable. . . .

The black dark weather, & constant noise of wind; the fire smoking in the south tempest; the being obliged to give up my large picture after so much expense & trouble; & the finding it impossible to go on with oils at all without more light — all this made me highly unamiable, & I stayed at home & sulked, till Frank Lushington & Sir James Reid came & pulled me out, whereby I grew better by degrees, & am now at work on water-colour drawings, which I shall go on with until I hear from Clowes, or the weather gets settled. The 20th was a tolerable day; made a drawing of an old man for the foreground of my picture; dined alone.

21st. In the night there was no wind, so I slept all night & till 8 — a vast comfort, for the wind & thunder have put sleep out of the question generally. Rain all day long. 22nd. Wind & rain; chimney smoked less. Sat a bit with the Shakespears upstairs, did not go out. 23rd. Wind & rain — all day long. Today turned my large picture to the wall & had my studio rearranged. 24th. Colouring & mounting Mt Athos drawings. Last night the tempest was frightful, & from 4 to 6 one long thunder peal with incredible hail storms. Dined with Frank.

Sunday 25th. Fine early — church — but storm coming out, & general scamper of alarmed & beflustered congregation. A walk, wrapt up in macintoshes, with Frank, & from 5 to 7 sat with the Shakespears. Major S. is very unwell; the baby highly enjoys her India rubber rattle. Dined with Colonel & Mrs Gage. 26th. Began my Greek early lessons again, which I had given up for a week. Thunder & lightening, hail & rain all day long. Drawings of Athos for Mr Clark of Trinity College going on. . . .

27th. The early morning was clear, but towards noon clouded again, then rain & wind — quite the worst night yet. I burned a lamp all night & got no sleep. 28th. Rose at 10. Rain all day, no wind. Worked at drawings. 29th. Same weather. At 7 dined at the Palace — only Marquis & Marchioness of Drogheda there. 30th. No rain, nor wind but cloudy all day. . . . It is impossible to say how everybody enjoyed the quiet & finish day yesterday: gleams of sun now & then, & the mountains one sheet of snow — & apparently becoming clear. The evening too was clear starlight & moonshine; I dined at Frank's sending in my dinner, because the fire was not lit, & afterwards we went to an evening party at the Palace. 31st. Today all is changed, again no hills — nothing but bleak blank blackness, with such fearful thunder bounces! Yet there are people who say we cannot have fine weather till some much more terrible tempest or hurricane or what not has happened; & the almanack here foretells a frightful earthquake & hurricane on February 5th — a very shameful thing to do, as many of the lower classes are becoming seriously frightened. Let us hope that the next change of the wind may bring some hope . . .

February 1st. Yesterday afternoon, the fire being blown clean out, I took my drawing into Lushington's & worked till 4.30 & we got a walk to the One Gun. At 7 we dined at Sir James Reid's where were Major Daniel, Loughman the banker, & some new officer; the evening pleasant enough, though we had to talk loud as there was a thunderstorm going on always. By midnight it stopped, & I got some sleep till 5.30, when a crash & shakings woke me; merely a most tremendous peal of thunder with a leetle earthquake mixed up with it. It seems these small shakings are very frequent here at times, & are rather popular than otherwise, as there is an idea that they are instead of large shocks; no harm is ever done, to speak of. It has rained, so I couldn't go to church & indeed I did not rise in time. Now it is clear, & I hope it will remain so that we may get a longer walk than of late, or I shall begin to lose the use of my legs. Tomorrow I hope to get letters . . .

We really did get a walk on that afternoon, by the Kombítsi monastery, over the hill by Virós — the only time this winter I have seen those beautiful orange gardens I so constantly visited last year. After returning — half an hour with the Shakespears upstairs & then a quiet dinner & evening with Frank. February 2nd. Cold — cloudy — no rain — no letters. 3rd. Finer. Working all day nowadays at water-coloured drawings . . . I am not going to do any more for £10. It is too much hard labour for little gain; so I advance all future large water-colour sketches to £15 & that is little enough for some I have lately done. 4th. Tolerably fine. The weather seems to be improving at last, slowly. 5th. Once more a day of total pouring rain. Dined alone with Sir James Reid who is extremely kind & friendly. 6th. Cloudy — no rain. [A.L]

7 FEBRUARY   O dear me, I wish I had gone to the Academy when you did, & had been working with you ever since! Coming so late as I did to the light of any kind of truth in painting —

The orange gardens at Virós, 4 February 1863, 4 p.m.

when my habits of life were already but too much formed & my hands & eyes less than ever able to execute what I desired to do — I was never very likely to turn out much of a painter. Moreover, my topographical & varied interests as to different countries, my application split by musical, ornithological, & other tastes, have all combined to bother & retard me — society being by no means the least of the pull-backs. When I say, 'I wish I had gone to the Academy when you did', you may suppose I don't say that out of love for the Academy itself. *Tout au contraire*, I believe that had J. Millais forgone the ambition of place & position, & had he steadily worked with all those who, as he once did, set their faces against conventionalities & still do so, art in England, & who knows where not besides, would have gained life & respectability. As it is, when some half dozen Witheringtons & Richard Cooks are dead, Antony may be condescendingly put on the line when he is 70, & Rosetti & Brown may be allowed to take the place of A. Cooper & Frost — always supposing that Buckner & the man who did the long Florentine procession piktur [Leighton's *Amabne*] are not previously elected. . . .

When you write, put down the names of anybody at Jerusalem or elsewhere who knew you & would be good for me to know. Only, if you write to them, tell them you introduce a most irregular & uncomfortable fool, partly swell, partly painter, who will never do any good, to himself or anybody else; & advise them parenthetically to stop his unpleasant rumblings by instantly emptying a large bucket of hot water on his noddle, & use up his beard for cushion stuffings . . . One of the greatest discomforts here — & one which prevents my shaking off a constant growing moroseness — is the total absence of anyone who can think or feel with me. Lushington's leisure hours are given mostly to shooting or yachting, & we, sad to think, are less together & less happy together (at least I am so) than of old. [H.H.]

8 FEBRUARY Sunday. A magnificently fine day; so, after church, Frank & I set off to the other side of the island, & got there — having started at 12.30 — exactly at 3 — 10 miles. In a little sheltered harbour — not unlike Amalfi — under great rocks, lies the little convent of Myrtiótissa — so called from the myrtle covered cliffs all around. After my great Athos monasteries, this is a wee little one, with 3 monks only; however, it is clean & decent, & they gave us a cup of coffee each, which was not unwelcome. At 4 we set off, returning by a bit of the coast & village of Pelekas, & arriving in town at 6.30 — bright full moonlight — in time for late dinner.

Pelekas, 26 February 1863.

9th. Fine. Interrupted by calls. . . . 10th. Very fine. After 1, went to Análipsis & painted the mountains as a study for my large picture; beyond the shore ridge, the whole line was perfectly white, which I never saw before. 11th. Same brilliant weather — & painting again; today the water is so calm & clear that the snow miles away in Albania is reflected all down to the bay of Corfu. 12th. As yesterday, but symptoms have changed in the sky. 13th. Verily, a thorough rainy day again! [A.L.]

I have, alas! too present a feeling of the want of all kind of sympathy not to find one of your letters most welcome. Perhaps to irritable natures of my temperament, my unsettled early life makes me more susceptible to what devours me here — isolation & loneliness, & sometimes drives me half crazy with vexation. Really, when anyone tells me, as you do, your own inward thoughts & feelings, it flashes across me that after all I *am* a human being, notwithstanding much of the past year & a half has almost made me come to think otherwise. . . . I am so fluffy & hazy, & never know what is right & what isn't. . . . There are hours when I would rather life were abruptly ended, so as not to add weight to weight as my days but too often do. [H.H.]

1857
[DATE UNKNOWN]

At Análipsis, 2 March 1857.

15 MARCH   I am almost sorry I told you so much about the wind & storms, but you know how impressionable an animal I am mentally & bodily as regards weather, so you will not have wondered at my growling. It must be owned however that *everyone* says no such winter has occurred for 20 years. And now, to balance matters, we are all sunshine & anemones & clear skies & asphodels & little green frogs just as usual — nor shall we have any more nastiness, except a cold squall or 2 perhaps. I certainly think this climate a most unequal & trying one to many — persons, for instance, whose lungs were actually much affected; but otherwise I believe it to be most healthy, owing to its extreme purity of air I suppose.

Anyhow, I never remember to have had such continued comfortable health, & in spite of the storms etc., I fancy I shall be here a good bit yet off & on. Indeed, my large picture ties me for the present, for it goes on very slowly, & if sent to England for engraving, the autumn will be the earliest time. There is so much chance of constant improvement here, that I should find great difficulty in giving the place up wholly, for I can run out for foregrounds close by — cliffs, olives, myrtles, etc. etc. — at any time, & as it appears to me more & more that my painter's reputation will be that of a painter of Greek scenery principally, so this place presents on that account many advantages nowhere else to be found, because there is so much of English life that one does not feel an exile as one might at Athens or other semi-eastern places. . . .

So you see I am not always in a growly mood & just now am graciously pleased to be tolerably contented & thankful. In truth, in every other respect than those 2 months of storm, nothing can be more comfortable than these rooms, & my servant is such a good one that I never have a single fault to find. My overhead neighbours *might* be a great annoyance, but the Shakespears are so good & quiet that one hardly hears them except their nice playing on the piano, & as for the baby, it has pretty well left off crying altogether, & plays with anything blue all day long. I fear however that this scene is to change, for poor Major S. has never recovered thoroughly from a fever he had at Varna, & now he has been showing signs of consumptive tendency, which signs have been increasing for some time past. I rather believe they will go to England for some time. Meanwhile, my Greek goes pretty regularly . . .

Regarding my copying my own drawings, it is a thing the effects of doing which would overbalance any good I should gain by making money, because I know my own irritation if I work at anything mechanical, & that my only chance of tolerable ease is constant attempt at progress & improvement. If I constantly copied my own works, I should grow crosser & stupider every day, & finally might turn into something between a spider & a polar bear. I am inclined, when in a decent mood of mind, to think that my best plan will be to stay on here a bit . . . [A.L.]

22 MARCH   My upper neighbours, Major & Mrs Shakespear & the little baby, go in 10 days, a no small loss to me, for they are as good as quiet, & sensible & clever. What is worse, everyone seems to think he is in a rapid decline, & I also fear so. A change of air may save him, & he is ordered off on leave, to return, if well, in October. But I think they

will return no more. Besides this, some odious noisy people will be sure to take their rooms; however, as one leaves off fires now, this won't matter, for I can change my sitting room as I please, & my study is below the upstairs bedrooms, where all is quiet by day.

I have been working a good deal at my large picture — & the foreground progresses pretty well. This next week I have to make careful drawings of asphodels, anemones & daisies, which grow thickly all over the Análipsis hilltop. The doleful part of the business is that the sky is yet unfinished; it is so difficult to do a smooth 9 foot sky at any time that failure is never very wonderful, but here where the paint dries so fast, it is really a half impossibility. . . .

March 24th, 7 a.m. — & such a lovely morning! We have had disagreeable cloudy scirocco warm weather all the week & 1 day of rain; but as it now is, I wish so that I could bore a hole in the wall, & get a room next door for the lovely view. Meanwhile, my large picture has been getting on, though it is so BIG that ever so much work seems to tell very little. There seems an endless lot of work in it, but it is undoubtedly the finest picture I have done, & I ought to get a good large sum for it — seeing that some day when I am gone, it will be valued highly. At present I am doing the rose-coloured anemones in the foreground, & the tall pale asphodels; all the country is full of them just now. . . . O dear! what a place this might be if there were any good people to give it a twist! As it is, a more disorganised fiddle faddle poodly-pumkin place never was. There is only one active man & he is a bad one: I mean active as regards society. For Mr Clark the clergyman is as active as can be, but he does not go into society at all. And surely at the Palace they are active — dancing & rushing about pauselessly & continually. I suspect Lady Young would not be happy in Heaven if she did not get up an immense ball, & land & water picnics, among the angels. It is sadly frivolous work, this life for 'amusement' & that only. But I am moralizing — which is because I have had no breakfast; usually at this time I am reading Greek. . . .

I have made up my mind that, unless any particular event happened to prevent me, I shall come to England in *June*. Today & tomorrow I work hard at anemones. On the 1st I go across, with Edwards (Mr Lister Turker's godson) & George, to Yannina, by Delvino: I can do nothing with that magnificent lake without having seen the mountains with snow on, & so go I must. We shall stop there a week, & make a little excursion or 2, returning here about the 20th. . . . I shall work very hard on returning, & during the remainder of April & the whole of May hope to advance the picture, if not complete it, so far as to send it off very early in June, either shipping myself with it, or coming overland, to be in London before the 20th of June if possible. Lushington goes home in May, but I can't get away as soon as that. . . . So, here's a decision at last. [A.L.]

23 APRIL

Here I am safe & sound, back again. We returned this morning or last night at 2 after midnight — & never was there such a 3 weeks' lucky tour, only with the exception of George's having the fever for 3 days. Weather lovely always — except one storm,

Porto Trescoglie, dated 1862.

which we sat out in a cave. And I bring back — large & small — 98 sketches, so that my illustrations of Epirus go on pretty well. We were off on the 2nd April in Lushington's boat *Midge* — I taking George, the canteen or box of cooking things, my bed, paper for drawing, etc., & Edwards taking his servant, Fillipo (a Maltese). We had a perfectly quiet passage across of only 3 hours & anchored in the little harbour of Trescoglie, enjoying all the afternoon in making drawings — below the tall white heath all in bloom — & comfortable dinner & quiet night.

Early on the 3rd we found some woodcutters' horses by the shore, & as there was no wind to take us on to Santa Quaranta — the proper place for landing to go to Delvino — we hired them, & set off walking . . .

[On the] 21st, we left Delvino for the shore, bemoaning ourselves that the only really hard part of our trip was at hand, namely a passage in a country boat, dirty & slow — for Lushington we knew had gone on his Easter trip down to Ithaka, & we had no friends to fetch us away. But half way to Santa Quaranta (the Scala, or port of Delvino) there we met Sir Paul & Lady Hunter & Miss McKenzie . . . who were to return the following day. Meanwhile, Edwards & I had leave to take possession of the royal yacht (not to speak of some lovely boiled beef (cold) & bottled ale!), so there we housed ourselves quietly, sending back our muleteers who, as if all was to be fortunate in this trip, were a faultless lot, & making ourselves comfortable till yesterday afternoon when, Sir P. & Lady Hunter having returned from Delvino, we all set sail, & creepy, creepy, creepy, tack, tack, tack, got here this morning as I said. I am rather sleepy . . . [A.L.]

Santa Quaranta, 22 April 1857, 11 a.m. 'Penned out the last drawing of all the Albanian tour in 1857, evening of March 6, 1862.'

1 MAY

I am coming to England as fast as I can, having taken a redboom at Hansens, 16 Upper Seymour Street, Squortman Pare, & also a rork-woom or stew-jew at 15 Stratford Place. My big picture is in a mess, & without Holman Hunt's help I can't get on with it, though it is done as to what necessarily must be done here, & requires but 2 months of cropping & thought. Pray heaven I may sell it. I bring to England my drawings of Athos, I hope, for publication. Also sketches of Corfu for separate lithografigging, & sale here. Also 1 or 2 paintings to finish. 'Why are you coming?' say you. Because I can't stay here any longer without seeing friends & having some communion of heart & spirit — with one who should have been this to me, I have none. And I can't bear it. And I want to see my sister. And also another sister who is going to New Zealand, before she goes. And some Canadian cousins. And *you*. And my dear Daddy Holman Hunt, & other people. So I'm off. Whether by steamer to Trieste & by Germany or all by sea to Liverpool — I don't know yet . . .

Bowen goes about saying that Mauritius is very angry that Labouchere* sent them out a *Doctor*, and beg for *him*. Others know better. Moreover, he is supposed to have applied for the Mauritius place, & to have had a refusal. L. could not turn him out, seeing he had already been recommended for knighthood. Meanwhile, while you hold these islands, you cannot govern them while the head man is connected with Greeks. The Greeks call Bowen 'the sieve', & it is notorious that all government measures are got out of him. Little birds say that his conduct about Prince Daniels (his wife's brother-in-law) & some things now going on in the shape of abuse of England in the Greek press, may yet puzzle him. At this minute he is fawning & dinner-giving for popularity. Truth must be very great if ever she prevail against G.F.B. . . .

In my large room they are cleaning out — & selling chairs — & the picture is alone in its glory. O life! life! what is the next to be? [C.F.]

Edward Lear and Chichester Fortescue,
from a daguerreotype taken at Red House, Ardee, September 1857.

DECEMBER 1857 – MARCH 1858

Here I am once more, all right & safe. . . . I left Trieste on Saturday afternoon, the 28th, & set off from the harbour about 3.30. There was very little wind, but a very great swell caused by a storm 2 days previous, & this swell rolled the long named steamer about odiously. But on Sunday 29th, about noon, we got into smoother water, & yesterday — the 30th — we anchored in the harbour at 9.30 a.m., a very good passage on the whole, of only 43 hours. I found George in a boat as soon as we had anchored, & also Spiro — with a note from Lushington saying come & dine today at 6. And when I got up to my rooms, I found everything just as I had left it, so that it really seemed absolutely ridiculous — as if I had not been away a week. Unpacking etc. took up most of the afternoon, & then a call on Lady Reid before dinner time at Lushington's. Today I was up early & found everything going on like clock-work — George bringing in the 2 eggs & 3 slices of toast as if he had done so for a hundred years. The morning has gone in calls at the Palace etc. (for I do these things once & for all, & get them over as soon as I can), & now I am waiting for my 3 boxes from England. . . .

1 DECEMBER

I must tell you that they have had a fortnight's rain here, & now it is absolutely clear & so beautiful that it makes one screech. There is not a single cloud in the sky, & the sea & mountains are as blue & lilac as ever they can be. The olives are finer than I have ever seen them because there is such a crop of olives as has not been known for 40 years. All the trees are literally drooping with millions of fruit so that they look like weeping willows. I went up to the place of my large picture & I dare say you remember the scene well. The old man is still alive though he was not there; most assuredly there is no place in this world more beautiful than Corfu, if so beautiful. . . .

I have been out early this morning, for my old Greek master did not come. So I went as far as Análipsis, & somehow one seemed never to have seen anything beautiful before — the whole scene, in general, & in detail, was so perfectly lovely. After all, one can never hope to give more than the very dimmest shadow of a likeness of nature in the south. The innumerable flowers on the bright green grass, the myriad olives on every branch, the freshness of the dew-clearness of the sky & the water, the splashing of the waves, the sheep skipping about with their lambs, the quiet goats, the fishing boats, the soaring eagle, the pearly mountains & silver snow — all that & much more go to making up the picture, & not a thousandth atom of it can be put on paper. [A.L.]

6 DECEMBER I cannot persuade myself to do anything for more than 10 minutes. Painting, drawing, looking at sketches, reading all kinds of books, German or Greek exercises, sitting still, or walking about, not a possibility of application can I make or discover . . . Just figure to yourself the conditions of a place where you never have any breadth or extent of intellectual society, & yet cannot have any peace or quiet: suppose yourself living in Picadilly, we will say, taking a place with a long surface, from Coventry Street to Knightsbridge say. And suppose that line your constant & only egress & ingress to & from the country, & that by little & little you come to know all & every of the persons in all the houses, & meet them always & everywhere, & were thought a brute & queer if you didn't know everybody more or less. Wouldn't you wish every one of them, except a few, at the bottom of the sea? Then you live in a house, one of the best here it is true, where you hear everything from top to bottom: a piano on each side, above & below, maddens you, & you can neither study nor think, nor even swear properly by reason of the neighbours. I assure you a more rotten, dead, stupid place than this existeth not.

All this you would understand as coming from me, but others would speak differently of the place. Lady Young, for instance, calls it Paradise. No drawbacks annoy her at home, & between horses, & carriages, & yachts, she is away from it as she pleases. The Reids do not dislike Corfu as they would, had they not a nice family, & themselves to care about. The Cortazzis are gone, almost all the military offices are full of new people. My drawing companion Edwards is gone, & I miss him terribly. Frank is just as ever: perfectly calm & although doubtless intends to be kind, is as ever more & more indifferent & passive to all but his own routine of life. I vow I never felt more shockingly alone than the 2 or 3 evenings I have stayed in. Yet all this must be conquered if fighting can do it. Yet at times, I have thought of I hardly know what. The constant walking & noise overhead prevents my application to any sort of work, & it is only from 6 to 8 in the morning that I can attend really to anything. Then ὁ γέρος διδάσκαλός μου ἔρχεται, καὶ ἐργαζόμεθα ὁμοῦ εἰς τὴν παλαιὰν Ἑλληνικήν

Strada Reale, Corfu, c. 1840 (after a drawing 'from nature' by Lieut. H. E. Allen).

$\gamma\lambda\tilde{\omega}\sigma\sigma\alpha\nu$ [my old teacher comes, and we work together at the ancient Greek language]. I am beginning bits of Plutarch & of Lucian dialogues....

At times I seem to turn to stone, wondering what this queer strain of life can mean, & mechanically refusing to go on with it. & then, if I can't sleep, my whole system seems to turn into pins, cayenne-pepper & vinegar, & I suffer hideously. You see, I have no means of carrying off my irritation: others have horses, or boats, in short I have only walking, & that is beginning to be impossible alone. I could not go to church today. I felt I should make faces at everybody, so I read some Greek of St John, wishing for you to read it with — some of Robinson's *Palestine*, some *Jane Eyre*, some Burton's *Mecca*, some *Friends in Council*, some Shakespeare, some *Vingt Ans Après*, some Leake's Topography, some Rabelais, some Tennyson, some Gardiner Wilkinson, some Grote, some Ruskin — & all in half an hour. O! doesn't 'he take it out of me' in a raging worry? Just this moment I think I *must* have a piano: that may do me good. But what the devil can I do? Buy a baboon & a parrot & let them rush about the room? $\Delta\grave{\epsilon}\nu\ \grave{\epsilon}\xi\epsilon\acute{\upsilon}\rho\omega\ \tau\acute{\iota}\pi o\tau\epsilon\varsigma$. [I'm completely at a loss.]

I still hold to going to Palestine if possible.... If I could but get myself comfortable & untwisted by the noise & general discomfort of these houses, I think I could bring myself right yet, but I cannot tell. Sometimes I think I must begin another big picture, as I want something to gnash & grind my teeth on. If Helena Cortazzi had been here, it would have been useless to think of avoiding asking her to marry me, even had I never so little trust in the wisdom of such a step.

That's enough of me, I think, for this once. If you don't write a lot about yourself you are a spider & no Christian. Meanwhile things here are *not* as, by all I was led to suppose, they were represented to you as being. . . . There is one thing here which cannot be grumbled about — at present at least: the weather; it has been simply cloudless glory, for 7 long days & nights. Anything like the splendour of olive grove & orange garden, the blue of sky & ivory of church & chapel, the violet of mountain, rising from peacockwing-hued sea, & tipped with lines of silver snow, can hardly be imagined. I wish to goodness gracious grasshoppers you were here. . . . I believe the cussed people above stairs have goats or ox feet, they make such a deed row. [C.F.]

24 DECEMBER First, I must tell you that since I landed on the morning of November 30th the weather has been precisely the same: 25 days — every one cloudless & bright. It is however pretty cold in the mornings & evenings, but the brilliancy & beauty of the country cannot be imagined. The olive trees are so loaded with fruit that they quite bend like weeping willows, but the Corfiotes say that if rain does not come, the fruit will not ripen well. Meanwhile there have been 3 earthquakes, all small bumpy shakes; & I never felt any one of them, though people ran out of their houses at one of them. I have jotted down from day to day the memoranda of what would interest you, & I find the next note is 'red mullet'. These red fishes are as usual my daily food — & I wish I could send you some; also some Zantë wine which is very good, & only 6*d.* a bottle. . . .

I go often to my old village of Análipsis, from which my large picture was taken. The old man (you recollect him in the foreground?) is still alive, but, as George says, *da giorno in giorno* — only from day to day. The strange feature to me in this place now is the utter absence of wind. Perfect calm has been the order of every hour since I came. I finished a drawing of Zantë, & have sent it off; besides this the 2 paintings for Mrs Empson are all I have completed, & those 2 not quite. I have sold 2 of my 6 remaining copies of Albania, which is better than nothing. By way of fruit one has nuts, oranges, & medlars. [A.L.]

27 DECEMBER My model clergyman, Mr Clark, has been agone & hurt my feelings in a set of sermons on the Sacrament, wherein he has divided his hearers into 4 classes, i.e. those of them who don't 'communicate', those who never think of religion or its duties, those who are wilfully living in known sin, those who are presumptious & will not mix with their fellow Christians, & those who believe themselves too wicked to 'come' — & the whole of these he says break one of Christ's most positive laws! All this I deny, & vow I am in none of these 4 categories: I see no positive injunction [to 'communicate'] except to the living disciples of Christ; I do not regard 'communicants' as necessarily better Christians, because I have known many persons who have strictly conformed to

these outward rules while living a life absolutely contrary to Christian good, & I cannot accept such conformation as a test of Christianity; &, moreover, I believe with the Quakers that a rite, the celebration of which has given rise to such unchristian disputes & horrible enmities, cannot be justly regarded as a binding law. Let those go to it who find it a comfort, as thousands have done, do, & will; but do not stigmatize or upbraid those who do not choose to adopt these formalities for themselves. By all which you see I certainly don't come into the category of those who think nothing of the matter, since I am in a rage on the subject, & have vowed to go to church no more on a Sacrament Sunday, nor will I any more stand up & bear part in the foolish blasphemy, which it makes one's blood cold to hear.

Having burst forth in the above busting, I shall go on calmly.... In my last I used a word, disaffection — which is not correct if applied literally to all the people here. The peasantry — like those in India — have little choice in the matter, & the aristocracy, or one portion of it, I am convinced, have gained much by the last years' progress. It is not to be understood why such open contempt of England was allowed, nor allowed only, but its advocates rewarded.... The uppermostest subject in my feeble mind just now is my Palestine visit. I read immensely on the matter, & am beginning to believe myself a Jew, so exactly do I know the place from Robinson, Dr Stanley, Lynch, Beaumont, Bartlett, & the old writers from the Bordeaux Pilgrim to Maundsell ...

The weather has been utterly wonderful, this, the 28th day since I came, being the first with a single cloud in it! Nor has there been the least wind, or temporal annoyance of any kind, but always a lovely blue & golden sphere about all earth, sky & sea. How different from the 2 preceeding years this! & the olives are one bending mass of fruit. I have however walked but little. I grow weary of the 3 dull miles out & 3 back in order to reach any scenery. And although Frank has walked with me at times, yet it is a weary silent work, & now that he has got a dog, one cannot help feeling how far more agreeable it is to him to walk with that domestic object, to whom he has not the bore of being obliged to speak. We are on perfect good terms, but all or anything might happen to either, & neither would dream of telling the other, a state of things I do not call friendship. But on this & such a matter I dwell as little as possible. I have to live alone & do so though ungracefully.... So I stay at home, & oppose the morbids. I can tell you that I miss Helena Cortazzi though — now & then. The Reids are good & friendly people, but of them even I see little. Campbell of the 46th (Simeon's cousin) is a really nice fellow, but all these people are mad after snipes & woodcox now, & abjure all intellect & repose. Edwards, my last year's companion, I miss abominably. Bunsen* is a good little chap, clever, but talks like 50 thousand millions of tongues. [C.F.]

28 DECEMBER

Such a big round moon! I have no curtains to these windows, so I see the critter through the blind, but I have had the window frames all listed round with green list, whereby no wind comes in atall atall. Well, I do not ever remember such a December as this has been — only that one shower of rain, & now I really think it seems quite settled fine again for one can't tell how long. But, though fine, it is *wonderfully* cold for Corfu; there is ice in all the shady places a little way out of the town, & the water is rather cold at 5 o'clock in the morning. I do not go out much for I can't get my work done before 4, & then I get a run for an hour or so — such a lot of turkeys one meets on all the roads coming in to be eaten. I get home about 6; & then I write Greek & German for 1 hour, & then dine. I have limited my dinner to soup *or* fish, & 1 dish besides, dropping the pudding or 3rd course, for one doesn't want it. I get tired & sleepy & am glad to be in bed by 10. My man is like a bit of clockwork, & never gives the least trouble. Certainly, the eatable & drinkable of life is cheap here, though so much else is dear — a dish of large mullet for 6*d*., & a woodcock also 6*d*. with potatoes, is a good dinner for anybody, & this year the woodcocks are so large I cannot eat even this one easily. Zantë wine this year is very good, & is only 6*d*. a bottle — which lasts 2 days.

 I go out much less than formerly, not caring to make new acquaintances. On Sundays, Lushington & I dine with each other alternately — if not asked to the Palace. Last night I dined there, for although I never go to levees, balls, or evening parties, Sir John & Lady Young are always very good-natured. Lady Young's stepfather & mother are staying there now; & nothing is talked of by the Corfu world but the Marchioness of Headfort's* diamonds, which cover her up so much that few people have seen their wearer. As for me, I sat next to her at dinner yesterday, but she hadn't got no diamonds; only about 200 big turquoises & emeralds & bangles & spangles & chains & griggly-miggly dazzling messes, a few of which I should have liked to have had for the fun of turning them into pounds & shillings for my Holy Land trip.

 Today a letter has come from Fortescue, which has set me up for a period. Letters are a great comfort to a body. I have written to Jerusalem to know how the country is round about — if not quite quiet, I shan't go. In that case, I should go to Crete in the spring. I am working away at a painting of Mt Athos for Lord Clermont;* & at by-moments I am pasting together all the bits of the outline of the 'big' Corfu, which I shall hang up in my last year's dwelling room. A short time after dinner I wax sleepy, & am getting so now; wherefore I shall leave off. If this cold weather continues I think my old διδάσκαλος — my Greek teacher — will die: he shrivels up & groans, & grows smaller daily. The odd thing to me is that I never cough, & have no asthma; though I don't like the cold at all, as to the feeling of it; but I am in better health now than I ever was in England during winter — the air is so pure & good here. They now say that *last* winter was quite exceptional, & that *this* is the usual state of things. [A.L.]

1 JANUARY   The same perfectly clear & very cold weather. Rose at 5.30 as Papadópoulos [the Greek teacher] came at 6 — so Ollendorf & Plutarch till 8. Then breakfast, & outrageous Sir J. Mandeville. Pasting together the bits of the 'big' Corfu picture, writing exercises, & doing somewhat to another Athos drawing, till 12. Lushington

came in for a moment. A little later came a 'wholesome' & delightful letter from C. 40scue — a vast & unexpected comfort. Then working at Lord Clermont's Athos till 3.30 or 4. Campell came then, whom glad to see. He went to change dress & at 4.15 returned & we walked by the new Parga road, by Condi's & round to the Potamós road home. I back home, & wrote a world of Greek exercises till 7 or so. Dinner. Smoke Melchizedek's pipe, & write to Ann. The Hendersons above have a party & now there is music, cheerful & not too loud. It is a great bit of good fortune that they are so quiet. Bedtime — sleeping: perhaps the happiest new year's day passed for a long time. The more every moment can be occupied the better. The Hendersons above are hard in dance, but I was not much annoyed by it, only a sort of earthquakey bustling movement one was sensible of till sleep came. [J.]

2 JANUARY

Rose at 5.15 but at 6 ὁ διδάσκαλος [the teacher] didn't come, so after having looked out a lot of words, I grew uneasy. After breakfast, & hearing George read, pasting the 'cartoon(!)' of the Corfu picture. But I had somehow resolved to go to Aghii Deka to draw a bit of rock, with Mt San Giorgio beyond, so at 11.30 — I could not get out before — off I set. What lots of *turkeys* coming in at this time. There were some clouds today, but it was very bright, & ice was in all the ditches. A pull up to Aghii Deka & after that I lost my way, & had a particularly tough haul up to the place I was bound for. There — coming about 1.30 or 2 — I drew about 2 or $2^1/_2$ hours, when it grew cold, & I came down, walking hard & stoplessly to town, by 6.30 or so. Bright stars. Dinner, a Melchizedek pipe. I read a great deal of Grote, about Socrates, & some Plato. [J.]

3 JANUARY

O mi i! how cold it is! The weather hasn't changed after all, & I believe don't mean to. It's as bright & cold & icicular as possible, & elicits the ordibble murmurs of the cantankerous Corcyreans. As for the English, they like the cold generally. I don't. Notwithstanding which, I must own to being in absolously better health than for I don't know how long past. Yesterday I went up a mounting, & made a sketch — ἔκαμα μίαν ζωγραφίαν. A majestic abundance of tympanum-torturing turkeys are now met with on all the roads, coming into Corfu to be eaten. These birds are of a highly irascible disposition, & I never knew before 2 days ago that they objected to being whistled to. But Colonel Campbell informed me of the fact, & proved it to me, since when it is one of my peculiar happinesses to whistle to all the turkeys I meet or see — they get into such a damnable rage I can hardly stand for laughing. After all, suppose a swell party in London, say at Cambridge House, if any one person began to whistle furiously at all the rest, wouldn't *they* get into a rage I should like to know? . . .

Reflections on daily life, etc.: what you say to me is exactly true, but infernally difficult to follow out, i.e. 'That the freedom of the inner man consists in obedience.' Doubtless whenever the time comes that a man so willingly practises obedience as to find no annoyance from the process, he does so with a good will, & therefore a choice, & that is freedom. For my own part at present I find stuffing every moment with work

'The Monastery of
Aghios Elías', Análipsis, 1858.

the sole panacea (panaceum?) against more thought than is good for one. I only wish there were 28 hours in every day.... I do not read the Testament now — much — leastways in Greek, though I could do so with pleasure. But would you believe it, I have read the death of Socrates & Plato. I was so struck by Φαίδων [*Phaedo*] that I rose at night & worked till I made out the last part of it entirely. How is it that the thoughts of this wonderful man are kept darkly away from the youths of the age (except they go to the universities, & then only as matters of language or scarcely more) because Socrates was a 'Pagan'? I shall have more to say, & think about, concerning Socrates, whose opinion on death I now read for the first time, & there is no harm in wishing that we 2 may some day read Plato together; we both have much similar tendency to an analytical state of mind I think. *Intanto*, my old διδάσκαλος [teacher] persists in keeping me in Plutarch, & also in Lucian's dialogues, & won't hear of Plato. The former, Plutarch, I hate — Lucian delights me as so very absurd & new....

Dining at the Palace 3 days ago, I sat next to Sir John after dinner & he talked to me a good deal. (His way of talking of you moreover is agreeable to me.) His appreciation of Greek character is all the more near the right one, inasmuch as he is longer here: but as you say in your last, the firm hand is want*ed* here, & I add is want*ing*.

I want to speak of a plan which Sir John slightly spoke of — & possibly you may know all about & more than I do: that of making each of the islands a separate government. I know that such plan is thought a good one by more than one person here, & I believe it to be one deserving of great attention, because it may be feasible, & because it will go some steps towards 'breaking the bundle of sticks'. Kefaloniá by itself would easier be managed than Kefalónians always influencing Corfu. And Corfu by itself, its population being very mixed as to religion, & almost wholly Italian in language (as to the upper classes), might more easily be brought back to the use of the Italian or even English in its public affairs, than if it joined to all the other islands. The Greek revolutionary class is a majority — if you combine all the islands — but I should think a minority in this [island] alone. Also, great benefit would accrue to each island by means of more self-government being allowed to it. As for the upstart vetoes & obstructions of these ridiculous municipalities & parliaments, a governor should — as he is entitled to do — sweep them away at once. . . . Here are 10 woodcox, what can I do with them all? . . . I must leave off. I feel like 5 nutmeg-graters full of baked eggshells — so dry & cold & miserable. [C.F.]

3 JANUARY

. . . I went out alone & walked round by the marshes & back thro' Potamós. It rained a little, & was very cold. Thousands of turkeys going in to be eaten. At 6.30 I went to Lushington's & dined. . . . By very hard talking I kept myself alive, but later the miserable self-wrapped manner of Lushington irritated me too much to bear well — not the less so, that going into his room, I saw V.'s portrait there. So I came away at 10 — & really think it will be far better to avoid meeting so frequently. I was going to ask him to dine tomorrow, his birthday, but in some parenthesis he said he was going to shoot in Albania. [J.]

4 JANUARY

Cold as ever — & snowlike — with clouds. Greek from 6 to 8 as usual. But I begin the day wearily & sadly. Lushington is 35 years old today. Somehow I did nothing all this day. Wrote Greek: fidgetted for letters: had bookshelves put up: prepared the paint. At 2.30 Lushington called — but anything sadder or more unsatisfactory than his visit could not be. As for me, I went out at 3, & saw the downfall of the Bastion, & up by the olives to Análipsis. The sea was all deep dark green, white-flecked: the hills very purple & gold. On to One Gun Battery & back to home by 5.30 . . . [J.]

7 JANUARY

Last night I dined at the Palace, & sat next to Lady Headfort again, quite covered up with a new lot of jewels; & this time they were all Afghan & Hindoo — wonderful goldimagriggory spoppomontologies. Bless the woman — she must have a caravan full of jewellery. The evening was pleasant enough, only little Powys there besides, who sings very well, but passes his life in shooting ducks, & preparing for the peerage & a responsible life in England. Do you know there is *no* rain *yet*; & today I must say is abstrusely cold, because it is windy withall. The opposite mountains are all in sunshine, & seem all pearls & amethysts, but we are cloudy here, & the Corfiotes grumble horribly at the cold. I can't say but I should like it warmer, but there is no comparison between this & last winter for comfort; there is a certain respectability in this regular, sharp, fine weather, whereas all that squash & tempest & thunder & wind was confusing & uncomfortable, not to say disreputable for the time of the year. [A.L.]

8 JANUARY No δικάσκαλος [teacher]. But I rose at 5.45 & did a page of Xenophon — a dreary cold raining morning. Worked pretty well all day at Lord Clermont's Athos. At 4, went to the Citadel, & called on the Shakespears — afterwards sat with Lady Reid . . . Home by 6.15. At 6.30 Lushington came. Talk of Socrates, Plato, Aristotle, etc. — a better evening than for some time past with him. [J.]

10 JANUARY I am doing the bilious memories of Xenophon concerning Socrates, by which I am immensely interested. Life goes on here very dummily . . . There has been more of the comfortable & less of the intractable in my daily life for the last 3 or 4 weeks than is usual with one: partly from health being so good, partly from constant extreme occupation, partly from interest in Plato & Socrates, about whom I read a good lot in Bohm's translation. I feel, however, the want of forcing myself to undertake some work of a tougher, or more difficult gnashmyteethupon nature. At the Palace I have been once or twice to dinner, for to the Evening Balls I can't & won't go. Lady Young is always certainly very kind in inviting one, a brute. Lady Headfort comes out each time in new & astounding jewels. We get on very well, having endless topics of mutuality-talk, from Rosstrever & Lady Drogheda, to 'Virginia Pattle', or Afghanistan. They, 'the court' (I suppose Sir John also), are all off to Athens in a fortnight or so, Lady Y. characteristically observing, 'I have always wanted to see the ballroom at the Palace, & there are to be some fine fêtes!' My! won't Queen Amalía be down on them! for Sir John's profundities are pretty well known there.

I am reminded that I told you quite wrongly something of the state of feeling here as developed in representation: nearly all the members of this island are anti-English, the contrary is the case with Kefaloniá. Yet in the main perhaps I was right as to the greater general dislike of us in the latter place. Neither was I correct about the Italian or Roman Catholic element. The Greek screw has been allowed to be put on so much more strongly, with each successive government, that every other consideration is giving way to a settled desire to join Greece, & get rid of the English. The evil that is done can only be prevented from increasing by very different persons to hold the reins: the Greek, public & official, cannot now be got rid of as a language, but when it is used to speak absolute treason a check might be put on it. It is impossible to see this beautiful & fertile place what it is & not feel abundant annoyance — & one has little heart to believe it can ever grow better, unless times change almost supernaturally.

After these ozbervations, which are more temperate & less triumphiliginous than those I last wrote, I shall proceed to state that Shakespear is come, by which assertion I do not mean the author of *As You Like It*, *Hamlet*, or other popular drammers, but the Major of that name of the Royal Artillery, who used to live over me, & whose wife is one of the very nicest, even if not the nicest woman here. They are gone to live in the Citadel, next door to the General.* The General objects to the odour of cooking generally & of onions particularly. Lady Buller has not expressed any opionion on the subject so far as is publicly known: the matter rests in a state of oblique & tenacious obscurity for the present.

Last night I, the Shakespears, & Wyndham, dined with the Honourable Edward & Arabella Gage, very good people. We of this Terrace & this part of the town chaff the Shakespears, who now live so far off, & we ask them to 'set us down' on their way to 'Wimbledon'. It is but right you should know the important life-concerns of the island, & therefore I shall not hesitate to insert the following facts before I conclude this morning's scribble. Madam Vitális, the Greek consul's wife, has purchased a large red maccaw. Mrs Macfarlane's female domestic has fallen down stairs, by which precipitate act Mrs M.'s baby has been killed. Sir Gorgeous Figginson Blowing has had an attack of fever. Colonel Campbell (first cousin of Sir J. Simeon) dined with Mr Lear the Artist on Thursday. On Friday that accomplished person entertained Mr Bunsen & Mr Justice Lushington. Captain R. has purchased a cornopean, & practises on it (Mrs G. invariably calls it a cornicopean) but it is not heard generally, on account of the superior row made by Mrs Vitális's maccaw, Captain P.'s. howling dogs, & about 400 turkeys who live at ease about the terrace & adopt a remarkable gobble at certain periods. Lady Headfort has astonished the multitude by a pink satin dress stuffed with pearls. Bye the bye, I heard rather a good thing yesterday. Lady H. (with an aide-de-camp) has been 'doing' the sights of Corfu, & among others the churches. At the Greek Cathedral a beggar came & importuned the glittering Marchioness, who at the moment was indulging in the natural & pleasant act of sucking an orange. Lady H., after a time, paused & said or implied 'silver & gold have I none' but such as she had (being the half-sucked orange) she politely gave the beggar-woman, who (oranges being any number for a half-penny) threw the fruit in her Ladyship's face, & rushed frantically out of the desecrated edifice. . . .

The day is so cold that I can hardly hold my pen, & feel that all or more than all the population of Corfu will expire, or become icicles. No such cold was ever known here, a keen east wind, the first I have ever felt in the island. Snow on Salvador — & a great deal of sad illness among the natives. Of course the Anglo-Saxons rather like the freezing than no; I don't & yet am well because the air is so pure I suppose. Mr George Cockles, my Souliote, refuses to write his copy. «Ποίος ἡμπορεῖ νὰ γράψῃ, Κύριε, εἰς τοῦτο τὸ κρύον;» ['Who can write, Sir, in such cold?'] But until yesterday we have had wonderfully lovely weather & never yet any rain to speak of, sun nearly ever. Today, however, all is gray & ugly. . . .

While I think of it, here are two anecdotes, this time from the Citadel. Colonel Campbell has a celebrated horse, a stallion, called 'Billy'. I hate the sight of him

Garrison troops marching out of the Citadel (artist unknown).

myself, in as much as he bites & kicks whoever he can. The other day, being loose & seeing a helpless horse in a cart, he pounced on him & began to oppress him horribly, the 2 making any amount of row. This happened opposite Lady Buller's window, whereon the lady, being of a tender heart & a decided manner, opened the window & called out, 'Sentinel!' (Sentinel shouldered & presented arms.) 'Shoot the horse directly.' (Sentinel looks horribly bewildered but does nothing.) 'Why don't you shoot it!' S. 'Lord Madam! it's Billy!' Lady B. 'What's Billy? what do I care for Billy? Shoot it I say.' (Billy all the time tearing & biting the prostrate victim horse.) Sentinel. 'Can't nohow madam my lady, 'cause it's the Colonel's Billy.' Here the General Sir J. came up & tranquillized the agitated nerves, of lady, sentinel, & both horses.

Another anecdote is that Sir Henry Holland* being here, & dining at the General's, Lady Buller said promiscuously, 'Sir Henry, in all your travels were you ever in Albania?' Can't you fancy Sir Henry's smile & quiet: 'Why, Lady Buller, I wrote a book on Albania, because I happened to be there as physician to Ali Pasha in 1812 & 1813.'

I think there are no more anecdotes, but (as Ollendorf may say) there is much ice

& innumerable woodcox.... All last week my διδάσκαλος [teacher] has not been to me, his only child being about, I fear, to die: he has lost 4 before, poor man. So I shall poke on alone in Plato & Xenophon, & wish you were here to help me. Today all the Palace folk were to come, but Lady Y. is unwell, & could not. I dine there tonight, if I don't die of the cold first.... We, *intanto*, abound in turkeys this year, the whole country is black with them, & a sound of gobbling pervades the Corcyrean air.... I meant to have written a lot about the priests & signori, & the good peasantry, & the orange trees, & sea-gulls, & geraniums, & the Ionian Ball, & Jerusalem Artichokes, & Colonel Paterson, & old Dandolo's* palm tree, & my spectacles & the east wind, & Zambelli's* nasty little dogs, & fishermen, & Scarpe's* cats, & whatnot, but I am too sleepy. [C.F.]

Rose at 5.30 — worked at Plato alone — for after all Papadópoulos did not come — which is a horrid bore — & worked more or less all day long at Lord Clermont's picture, which I really think will soon be finished. I weary & worry horribly: nor has Gage paid me the £s he owes, & I can't pay this week's bill... [J.]   14 JANUARY

No *didáskalos* [teacher]. Rose at 8. All things going wrong again. Worked at Walton's picture. Clear, lovely weather, but *very* cold. Walked the Parga road round. Lushington dined with me. While I was up to talking, not disagreeable. Drank too much! [J.]   20 JANUARY

Rose at 8. No Greek. Slept pretty well. Holy Land speculations. Worked very little, touching bits of the Gastoúri & Athos.... At 4 walked out the usual round — alone — yet not so lonely... At 6 I was at home, & dining alone, & reading continually about the blessed Jordan & Dead Sea. Today has been calm — both out & in — but yet this sloth is not good. Tonight, now, at 9 everybody is preparing for the great ball of Lady Young, & I must be one of the very few not going there. [J.]   22 JANUARY

Clearer — but all the Corfu hills thick with white snow: Aghii Deka & Salvador covered. Rose late... At 3 went out — solo — & round by the 'Parga' road. What a wonderful white ridge of mountains! — & Salvador, all dark purple & bright white with a long cloud, to all along the marsh road, how cold & beautiful! Khimariotes plodding along to their adopted olive homes. Then the turn up towards Potamós, & thru' light-trunked olives, all filmy, the pool below, & the far snow range beyond seen through all the leafy dells & airy treetops. Then Potamós, with its lean & straw-hatted gray-trousered men, & its velvet-pelissed yellow-hooded respectable lovely women. And so very, very cold. Εἴς τὴν πόλιν. [To the city.] — Dined solo, & afterwards wrote a bit of Athos journal... [J.]   24 JANUARY

Perfectly clear, & colder than ever. Rose at 8, having read from 3 to 5 or 6. What a contrast to those of last year are these still quiet nights! Yet the cold & indigestion   26 JANUARY make me cross. I finished Lady Headfort's little picture, & sent it, & after that worked without stopping from 11 to 5 on a new painting of Yannina. Gorgeous gold & blue sunset, as I walked out the usual St Rocco & crossroad Kastrádes round — dining alone afterwards, & writing out a page or 2 of that snail Athos journal. [J.]

1 FEBRUARY Perhaps still colder — frightfully cold for the poor Corfiotes. Did not paint. Wrote at intervals to C. Fortescue, Dickenson, Hanson, Walton, Mrs Empson, Mrs Hornby, Bicken, Drummond, & Clover. A nice letter from Miss Dennett. At 5, after Shakespear, Stuart & Ponsonby had been in, the former buying my photographic apparatus, walked the short round & at 6.30 dined alone. Great cold. [J.]

FEBRUARY This is certainly a most irregular climate. It seems as though it was to be always bright winter, & up to this very day it has been so. But now it is the old 1856 to 1857 tempest, roaring & rattling, & pouring; & all the house trembling. But when I remember how for 8 or 9 weeks last year I never slept at all to speak of, I cannot but prefer the cold of this winter, though I have not liked it. As for the Corfiotes, they have suffered greatly, no such winter has been known for 20 years for severity, & numbers of the old & sick die off while, generally speaking, the English are in robust health. My old Greek master has never been since the 12th, except 2 days — 15th & 16th — though I have paid him his £1 by way of charity....

My present intention is to leave here on March 1st by the boat to Alexandria, which I shall reach on the 3rd or 4th; then I shall either go by the French boat to Jaffa & so to Jerusalem, or across the 'short desert' to Gaza & Hebron. Of this, I cannot tell till I get to Alexandria, & will write thence. Once at Jerusalem, I shall stay there till early in April, before which season the roads are not good, nor is the climate settled, in the high country of Judea; & then I shall make rather a longish tour about the Dead Sea, & Jericho, & after that, if at all possible, to Petra & so back to Jerusalem. This will bring me into the beginning of May when, after some little tours to Gibeon etc., I shall set out to Samaria, Tabor, Galilee, Gennesarett, Carmel, Sidon & Tyre, to Beirut — by the end of May I suppose. Lastly, a tour towards Damascus, Baalbek, & a good bit of the Lebanon, will hardly see me back here before June is nearly over.

Such is my scheme; & as to improving myself professionally & otherwise, I believe it to be a good one, though I may not be able to carry it out. You will be delighted to hear that I take an enormous box of medicines. I buy a tent here, & some leather saddle-bags. George is to have charge of the canteen & cooking, & is to look after my drawings etc.; for with the constant attention I wish to pay to what I came to see, I have no extra time to bestow on what a domestic can do quite as well as myself....

I am writing now on the 3rd — 8 p.m. — & strange to say the wet & wind only lasted 24 hours, & today has been as wonderfully bright & fine as ever. But the olives have come down with a run. The roads are in places quite black with those shaken down, & it is sad to see, from the foolish, slow, improvident ways of these people, how nobody picks them up, & how they all get trampled into squash on the roads. For you know the roads are all bordered with great olive trees here, & are consequently part of this large olive garden. About 1,200 Khimariotes have come over to pick up the fruit (& I believe that every Khimariote has brought over 1,200 fleas), & these wonderfully filthy, ruggy, muffy, huzzly, bussly creatures seem as thick as the olives themselves all about the town.

The Khimariote coast of Albania from Corfu, dated 1858.

All the 'Court', as we call the Palace people, were to have gone to Athens yesterday, but the tremendous south wind makes that impossible; only big steamers can stir. I dined last night at the Artillery Mess with Bunsen, & Lushington, who had to come to my door for the fly, was nearly wet through in one minute. Yet today has been like a beautiful, sharp October day. I so often wish you could see the *oranges*! On Sunday L. & I walked over Evrópouli, where there are great orange gardens all the way down to Potamós, & the beauty of the colour & golden fruit was indescribable. I certainly will try one day to do a picture of orange trees & distant Albania. Woodcocks have become at last so vulgar & common, they are not presentable any longer. Lushington & I have forbidden them excepting *cold* for lunch. Seriously, you cannot live on woodcocks, & I for one should be ill if I tried to do so. Nobody knows where the pigs — i.e. the wild boars — are gone this year; it is all ducks & woodcocks, & no pig! . . .

On Wednesday, Thursday & Friday last, I was really very unwell indeed. I could not keep my feet warm, & a very violent diarrhoea rather alarmed me so far as to make me take things in time. Lushington, who is after all a thoroughly kind friend, came & gave me some very good medicine, & between that, & brandy & hot water, & sitting by the fire, I have come alright again. But the houses were *so* cold. And I really think I have done myself no good by eating so much game. Woodcocks are therefore prohibited, & I stick to meat & rice & sherry & water. [A.L.]

4 FEBRUARY ... Suddenly took it into my head to begin *8* small paintings, & actually got outlines of Corfu, Corfu, Zagóri, Filiátes, Philae, Constantinople, St Paul & Ivíron on to canvass. The Shakespears called, & he paid me for the photographic machine — 15*s*. The Zinc man packed & nailed my box of paintings.... [J.]

5 FEBRUARY Colder, clearer, brighter, bluer, if possible; certainly colder. Worked at Ivíron but was soon ill — whether from internal cold or cold feet, or what I cannot tell. Diarrhoea 5 or 6 times, till at 2.30 I got uneasy & wrote to Lushington. He came of course himself, & then went down to his boat at once for a draught, which did me good, & I went out with him — we went through Potamós, & on towards Gouvia some 2 miles, then back, overtaking Sir J. Reid & Boyd near St Rocco. Intense cold tonight. Wrapped up & dined by the fire on rice, & brandy & water. Hot water & fire in bedroom afterwards. [J.]

7 FEBRUARY Rose at 9. Did not go out. Lushington came in at 12, & at 2 we walked by Virós round to the Kombítsi monastery, & then on up to Evrópoulos & to Potamós, & back. It rained a little, but the day was still cold. The walk was passably pleasant. I dined (it was my turn to dine with him) at L.'s., & during dinner it was pleasant enough: after dinner he examined my medicine chart, but I suppose grew bored & finally seemed to wish me at the Devil. That however may not be the case, yet he is an unlucky man in his manner — & one certainly wishes one had never known & liked him, so little can his ordinary mode of expression be understood. [J.]

11 FEBRUARY Very beautiful, clearycloudy lovely day. Rose at 7 & worked pretty well all day at one of those 8 small paintings — Constantinople. Lushington wrote. At 4.45 I walked out — the middling round. Very blind I am with these glasses at twilight. Dined alone at 7. The cessation of extreme cold is a great blessing. The Hendersons overhead are quiet folk generally which is also a great blessing.... [J.]

12 FEBRUARY Colder again. Rose at 8.30. Shocking lateness. Did not paint, but arranged drawing 'material' for Palestine — & other *roba* — till 12 or so. Then, went to Taylor's & paid his bill, at Page's for medicines, & to the Spectacle man, & Citadel, etc. etc. etc. — so home by 2, & lunch. Packings & arrangings again. Noise downstairs — the Muto! At 3.30 or 4 went up to Análipsis — always beautiful — sketched twice & walked over the hill & down to the One Gun road & so home at 6.15. Colder. F.L. came to dine at 7. Agreeable evening. Mrs Gage has a son. The Youngs are gone to Athens ... Much talk with L., but it is dry & chalky work. [J.]

28 FEBRUARY Coldish — gray — not raining. Went to church. To Shakespear's to see his φωτογραφς

At Análipsis,
12 February 1858.

[photographs], home, & made Αλφαβετς [Alphabets] till 2 — then walked out with F.L., & Beechey the dog, thro' Potamós to Gouvia, & all the Kourkouméli road — the wild lichen & moss-covered olives so beautiful — to Afra, & so to Alepoú, & to the χωρίον [village] at top. Khimariote people on road — then queerlings — & begging: ἕν ὄβολο — νά ζήση! [one obol — for life's sake!] Dined at L.'s, but wearied myself with talk; & when after dinner, in that cold room, he took a good cigar himself from a box at the other end, but offered me none, & when caps came ³/₄ of an hour after, I grew black & silent, & went away at 9.30. [J.]

Rose at 7.30 but unwell. Irritacious by numerous noted bothery. Dark & gloomy morning. *Cats*. eh! bah! — X [epileptic fit] but tho' a misery, with certain natural consolations. Could not work nevertheless, so 'ordered' & packed & arranged. At 3 came F.L. who *would* buy 2 of the 8 — δηλαδὴ [that is] the 2 of Corfu. Then

5 MARCH

διδάσκαλος [teacher] No. 3, who was very disagreeable. Later Mrs & Miss Ormsby & Major Moore of the chin. After them, Elliott, a good little fellow. At 5 I walked the middle round — stormy sky & windy — & returned by 6.30. At 7 came Lushington & dined. A pleasant evening: much talk on many matters . . . He went at 11. Καὶ τώρα θέλω νὰ ὑπάγω στὸ κρεββάτι μου [and now I want to go to bed]. [J.]

6 MARCH   Bumble bumble bumble buzz! Boo! Boo! Boo! buzz buzz! bumbleboo bibbleboo bibblebumble babblebobble buzzlebomble buzz! For the life of me I can't think where all these immense moths come from. The first spring day — out they rush, & make such a noise you can't imagine, though where they come from is a wonder. Half my life goes in seizing them & putting them out of the window. I have ejected 32 this morning since breakfast, each as big as a small mouse, & making a noise like 20 bees each one of them. They are distracting animals, though quite harmless, & I greatly object to them on the whole; meanwhile before another set comes out I will write a bit. Such a lot of people keep coming to see 2 little pictures of Athos, & 2 of Corfu, I have just done. . . . Possibly I may eventually espouse a Jebusite lady, or a Hittito, or a Hivite, but I have not yet finally determined which. I have just bought a lot of knives & scissors for the Sheikh's wives. I start by the next Alexandria boat, on Saturday this day week, the 13th; get to Alexandria, I hope, on the 16th or 17th . . . I am beginning to look quite packed up — the 5 pictures are gone away, & by degrees everything is getting into order. [A.L.]

7 MARCH   Immense high wind — tremenjous. Wrote & arranged. Came Frank afterwards, & we walked to the Kourkouméli road, by Gouvia. There, he having brought a revolver, I was taught to fire off a pistol — the first firearm I have used. [J.]

9 MARCH   The Palace party are come back — they had horrid weather & an earthquake. Corinth is totally ruined, *not one* single house habitable. People all fled. Vialimachi down flat on the ground. These earthquakes are dreadful. Boyle, who has just come

back from Naples, fills us with horrors! Amalfi, Sorrento & such lists of lovely old places, all gone! down on the earth, & every inhabitant killed or maimed.

I am off on the 13th & hope to catch a Jaffa boat: otherwise I must wait a week at Alexandria. Lady Juliet George goes with me — & I am all pretty well packed. My 5 pictures for the Academy go away this week & are to arrive in time before the end of the month. At Jerusalem, I shall hope to hear if Lord Clermont's painting is safe. . . .

O! here is a bit of queerness in my life. Brought up by women — & badly besides — & ill always, I never had any chance of manly improvement & exercise, etc., & never touched firearms in all my days. But you can't do work at the Dead Sea without them. So Lushington, who is always very kind & good, makes me take a 5-barrelled revolver; & I have been practising shooting at a mark (I can hardly write for laughing), & have learned all the occult nature of pistols. Don't grin. My progress is slow, but always (I trust) somewhat. At 103 I may marry possibly. . . . I've left you all Leake's *Greece*, in case of my being devoured by Arabs or fever. [C.F.]

Called at 6 by Yanni . . . Weather frightful, pouring rain, & wind. No steamer . . . O! wind! wind! wind! & Frank Lushington still writing letters — but he will not gain his point — the demon of red tape has arranged it long ago. Sleepy. At 3 with the Boyds . . . No steamer. Violent wind. At 5 Frank & I walked on the One Gun road; returning it rained hard & the steamer was signalled. There was time to dine quickly & have a cigar. A pleasant hour. Pouring with rain. At 9, or 8.30, I went down — for it was absurd for Frank to come — solo, thro' the quiet Jews' quarter to the harbour. There were George, & Spiro. Row over the harbour, & alongside steamer to Bombay. Nearly fell into the water, & so did Spiro — I not seeing the steps. On board, & later, writing this. Heavy rain, & no appearance of starting before tomorrow. So begins my Syrian tour . . . [J.]

13 MARCH

JUNE 1858 – AUGUST 1858

18 JUNE   Behold me once more back in the island — & about to leave it again, perhaps shortly.... I have brought all my Judean & Coele-Syrian drawings back safe, & have gained in energy, physical & moral, by this tour into the most interesting land I have ever travelled over, besides filling my mind with scenes enough to last a longer life than mine is likely to be....

One portion of disagreeable matter must be added, I hope the last. You know that Lushington applied for a reinstatement in the old judge's salary, Bowen's own having been raised £200 under pretence of its once having been higher. This, Lord Stanley refused: Lushington's statements had marginal notes by Bowen, & the latter was backed up by Merivale doubtless. I do not blame Lord Stanley as I don't see how anyone could well understand the filth of Bowen's character by intuition.

This however — I mean the refusal to raise the salary — was NOT Lushington's motive for resigning, as he has just done. Sir James Reid resigned immediately afterwards — & his salary had never been touched. No, the reasons are very different from those assigned here. I would not have any friend of mine under the tyranny which this miserably black wretch exercises here for untold money, & all are right to go hence who can. I do not intend to go into much of what has happened, but I will tell you a thing or two. Do you know that Bowen has made Sir J. Young make his blackguard old father-in-law Vice-Governor of Ithaka? Do you know one of the Romas sons married Mr Daniel of Montenegro's sister? Every effort is being made by the Greeks to use their wretched tool as much as possible, & you will soon see the effect of these matters. Mark me, Bowen will now set to work to abolish one of the 2 English judgeships (taking care to appropriate some of his salary), & if the madness of statesmen, or rather their indifference, allows him to stay on here, he will be forced to cause every English influence to cease, & he will end by aiding the Greek party in rooting out every good honest man — a work too congenial to his own base nature not to be zealously undertaken.

I will now, once for all, tell you that Frank will never speak again to the foul assassin Bowen, nor will I ever meet him in any society. My indignation is just, & I know that communication with a man who unscrupulously blackens all who offend him must be hateful to every soul. I am not prepared to say with some that Bowen would violate his own mother & flay his father alive for the smallest personal advantage, because I think he would not run the risk of discovery & hanging, but I will tell you truly that during the 3 years I have had the unpleasant opportunity of seeing this beastly caricature of humanity, no imaginary compound of hellish spite, & cold-blooded lying & calumny, of dirty chicanery, of hideous vulgarity & utterly contemptible vanity — no novelist's panaceum for such a character could ever approach the original.... One more remark: if (though the idea is too absurd) these lengths are given to the Greeks in order that they should 'rise' & defy the English you will soon see the nonsense of such a plan. The Greeks are using the 'sieve' Bowen to squeeze bit by bit all power out of English hands — & well they manage it. Meanwhile, all good men, if they be not tied to the plan by links they cannot break, will avoid this unfortunate place.

My own plans are not for an immediate going away from here unless European war should break out, when I shall come to England at once. Frank Lushington goes in a few weeks: I need not say how I shall miss him — whenever I have thought him less friendly than I supposed he should have been, I have invariably found he was acting rightly & uprightly & that I myself had misinterpreted him now & then. He is one of the best unions of mind & principle I have known. I wish you knew him: do try & do so when he gets to England — there are few better worth knowing on every account. [C.F.]

O that this blank of life would break into some varied light or shade! [J.]   21 JUNE

You will be sorry to hear I have had a bad eye, a sty, only more like an abscess. My brain is confused between cause & effect, & I don't know if my being a pig has produced the sty, or whether the sty makes me a pig. But I know I am a pig . . .   5 JULY

Poor Frank: I never in all the years I've known him heard him say so much as this of any human being — 'I have never known so bad a man.' He has had a difficult time here, & I rejoice at his going — for his sake. . . . This place is wonderfully lovely. I wish you could see it; if you came I could put you up beautifully, & feed you on ginger-beer & claret & prawns & figs. . . . If I go to Jerusalem, I shall have to ask you a good deal about the matter, as I am inclined to be 'impetuous' overmuch, & might start a periodical, 'The Cursed City' as a title.

P.S. — The King of Greece landed here 3 days ago: & went up to see Sir J. & Lady Young. He was received immensely by the Corfiotes, as you may suppose. [C.F.]

. . . I have had — a thing quite unknown to me — styes in my eye; altogether, I suppose from the change of life, I have not been very well. For here it is most abominably hot, & there is no shade near the town, so that all exercise is impossible until it is too late to go beyond the walls. And I do not like yachting, for there is no air & one only sits swinging & flapping, so I scarcely go out at all. The uncertainty of plans, & the discomfort of not arranging oneself regularly, are all small annoyances, & I would certainly never, by choice, pass any summer months in Corfu. . . . All this makes me anxious to get away & unable to work; another week or 2 will probably decide my plans. [A.L.]   10 JULY

Today brought me letters, from Holman Hunt, written from Alfred Tennyson's. He cannot come out at all, so that is settled. And so far I am fixed also — i.e. that I do not go to the East but shall, in all probability, pass my winter in Rome. . . . I can go on   12 JULY with my Arabic & Greek there as well as if I were at Jerusalem, where I should only have gone if Hunt could have been my companion. In the spring of 1859 I wish to return to the Lebanon & to remain there the summer, & then winter at Jerusalem, & in 1860, if well & able, to work out the rest of the Palestine illustrations. But this is so far ahead, & it can only be done by peculiar arrangements, that I should much like to come to England first.... I shall probably be on the south coast, Sussex somewhere.... Poor Lushington is anxious to get away, for the next 2 children — his nieces — are ill, & I know they will follow Eddie; & his second brother is ill also, & Emily Tennyson is far from well. So that if he goes away earlier from here, I may do so also. I mean to send my drawings, books, etc., by sea — some things I shall leave here, for a day may come when I may wish to return (I mean such things as tables etc. made on purpose for drawing etc., & yet fetching little money if sold), busts, & other matters which of course one never would have had could one have foreseen what is happening here. If I go to Rome, I mean to keep George at his usual wages for two months here, & after that decide if he is to come there. I can't do without some servant nowadays, & I don't see the sense of taking a new one when this man is good.... All this shows ... that I am still very unsettled. I go on with my Palestine drawings, & also at 5 paintings, the commencements only. How odd it seems now — to know every corner of outer Jerusalem so well I could draw it with my eyes shut. Lushington & the Shakespears are going out for 2 days to Crevazzuola, & want me to go. But I can't — I wish I could.... But it ain't done, so it's no use to wish at all. Only I wish the fly would get off my paper. I am very sleepy ... [A.L.]

31 JULY All my things are packed — 10 great cases — & go off to Liverpool whenever a steamer turns up; but the Zantë currant season renders them uncertain, & by this bit of ill luck I may arrive in England a month earlier than my property. I start, with Lushington, on the 10th, & we get to Trieste; & if no worse news tomorrow of another

The island of Vlakherné, 6 August 1858.

of his brothers, & his oldest niece — who are I fear both following to rest — we shall take 10 or 12 days on our route by Bruck — Salzburg — Munich — etc. If otherwise, we shall go quickly to England.... My present plan is to go... to Rome in November, & pass the winter there. George I leave here, but he will meet me in Rome. I think it best to keep him, though he has several faults, because he is so steady & honest. His brothers have a great loss in Lushington as a master. And the captain of Lushington's yacht, poor Luigi, is entirely miserable by the change. Nor am I at all cheerful in leaving this place (by far the most lovely of all I have seen in the world) for the sake of the trees & beautiful scenes. But it must be done. [A.L.]

All the little time I have away from painting goes in Greek. Would you believe it... I am nearly half through Οἰδίπους ἐπὶ Κολώνωι [Oedipus at Colonus] — yes, & understand it well too. I am almost thanking God that I was never educated, for it seems to me that 999 of those who are so, expensively & laboriously, have lost all before they arrive at my age — & remain like Swift's Stulbruggs — cut & dry for life, making no use of their earlier gained treasures: whereas I seem to be on the threshold of knowledge, & at least have a long way to the chilling certainty which most men methinks seem to have, that all labour for light is vain & time thrown away. [C.F.]

2 SEPTEMBER
LONDON

NOVEMBER 1861 – MAY 1862

11 NOVEMBER
AT SEA
. . . Came on board the Austrian Lloyd steamer, *Europa*. Passengers: Greek Consul at Saloníki; Baron Alten — Hanoverian, going (rather a day late) to congratulate King Otho on his 25th wedding day; 3 Frankfurt merchants — going on a tour to the East; a Prussian Graf von Henchel — just like an Englishman & rather like Frank Lushington speaking English & having trouble in America — going to Corfu for health. And several other *anonymi* — a Greek lady *par example*, whose parting from her children was antique a demonstration — & so we left Trieste at 2. Dined at 4 — & all merry. But at 5 came a violent south wind & it was the Devil! Oh! Oh! Oh! Night of torture! [J.]

17 NOVEMBER
Horrible night! Gray morning! 'Conveyed' myself on board, & sate miserably. For 2 or 3 hours the sea was quiet enough for me to read A. P. Stanley's *Eastern Church* & talk with Graf Henchel — a most agreeable fellow. But I could not eat or sleep, & so was *à la mort*. [J.]

18 NOVEMBER
Wind always against us. Ill & suffering from head & nerves horribly. The company are all pleasant . . . Towards 2 or 3 p.m. (when we *ought* to have been in Corfu) great wind began, & the good *Europa* went up & down *assai* [a lot]: yet she never shipped seas . . . I have never been in a worse gale — only the sea in that *canale* is *ristretto* [restricted]. At 12, 'utterly outworn', I lay down & slept. [J]

19 NOVEMBER
ROYAL HOTEL
CORFU
I woke at 4 — as the anchor was thrown down opposite Paramythiótti's house — in Corfu harbour. The steamer, or pumps — '*chi sa?*' — seemed to say: Dŏ nŏt fŏrgēt, Dŏ nŏt fŏrgēt, Nēvēr fŏrgēt — interminably. I could but (Whittington-like) seal the fancy, as to dearest Ann, & the recollection of her care of me, & to the necessity & good of remembering that there is a superior power who guides & rules all, & to whom gratitude is ever due, be that guiding apparently painful or not. And that what we feel to be wrong in us, tho' we know it to have been unavoidably there by circumstances, yet have we to remedy as far as we can. At 6.30, or 7, ashore — George, & also Spiro, came to meet me — & went (after seeing another hotel) to Royal Hotel, where I got 2 rooms. Wash & breakfast. Taylor's *poi* — where was Boyd, with whom walked. Search for houses, with George. *None*. Later, heard that a family was going from Casa Paramythiótti, & went to see the rooms, finding Fillipo (J. B. Edwards' servant) there, & suppose it better to take them. Saw Kirkwall; Graf Henchel called as I came back: then Wolff,* the successor to Bowen. The weather clouds, & I, having lunched, now prepare to go out. Sent George with a note to Mr Bolland's offering to take the rooms till January: & walked out with Graf Henchel von Donnersmarck to Kastrádes, & up towards Análipsis. We stopped at the Villa

Cortazzi, & walked into the gardens. Gray & cloudy as the day was, yet the loveliness of that place was wondrous. Then to Análipsis — the old olives, the village, & the top of the hill! Graf George Henchel is a delightful & intelligent companion. As we came down we met the old priest who stopped & talked. So we returned at 5.

Dined: a young middy, & (I suppose) a surgeon; after, 2 other marine ossifers . . . Much amusement out of all, only one can't write it down — & if I could, isn't there a piano going close by me? But the essence of this Corfu society is the knowledge that it is constantly changing — that knowledge preventing any of its constituent parts doing otherwise than amusing itself without any reference to the rest. [J.]

22 NOVEMBER

. . . At 1.30 with Count George Henchel by Mandoúki, to Potamós, with the little Aghion Pandeléimon above. Graf Henchel is a delightful fellow. He has been twice married — the 2nd time to his 'deceased wife's sister'. Home by 5. Dressed: a bore; at 7 Palace. *How* strange all this Palace life! — & how awfully a bore! — where after was some piano-cum-whistling. Away by 9.30. Δὲν λέγωμεν τίποτες [we didn't say anything]. [J.]

Casa Paramythiótti (indicated by an arrow), Corfu harbour.

26 NOVEMBER

Cold, perfectly bright, & *how beautiful*! Breakfast. After which went to Paramythiótti's & by degrees unpacked a lot with George — only the glass of the long Corfu picture, & one of the lamp glasses, were broken. Count Henchel called, but I suppose I shall not see him much more — *vu*, my application. At 1.30 walked out, all by Alepoú — τὰ σκαλιὰ μ' ἐμποδίζουνται [the steps impede me] — & so by the happy valley to the

Effrosíni (Foffy) Kourkouméli, daughter of Demétrius Kourkouméli, who was to become Lear's friend.

bridge (near which I met, I suppose, Mme Kourkouméli·& her daughters, very pretty girls anyhow), & so on by those most amazing olives to Afra & Kourkouméli church where I came on Kourkouméli himself. He was not cordial, & barely civil — & not to be wondered at is that. Gave 3 fingers, & said 'Ouf', when I observed I had seen some ladies & thought them his but could not see. '*Con tanti grand occhiali?*' ['With such large spectacles?'] After which I walked *innanze* [ahead] & quickly. O! those olive groves! By Gouvia, & so to the upper Potamós road, & to Potamós where I always find the peasants pleasant, & then by 5.30 to the hotel.... [J.]

27 NOVEMBER
CASA PARAMYTHIOTTI

As brilliant & clear as earth can show. Rose at 7. Paid Turlock (Royal Hotel) bill — a very well-conducted & quiet hotel — & walk on the Parade with Boyd... To the Casa Paramythiótti, George also. Bolland there, but they are going. While they went out on one side, we spread gradually in the other, & so on, all day. Taylor sent chairs etc., & before 5 we really got the whole house into something like order.

At 7 dined at Carter's. Count Henchel & 9 English there — a very pleasant party. Home by 8.30. George tells me Spiro is unwell. Evidently, one has lived in Corfu 5000000000 years — if not more. Slept at Casa Paramythiótti for the first time. [J.]

28 NOVEMBER

The same glorious weather, & not quite so cold.... Arranged & unpacked all the morning. Count Henchel came — but I could not have him here much, seeing he walks & whistles. At 2 called on Lady & Sir C. Sargent, they seem nice people, & have a jolly little boy, & a pleasant niece.... At 6 dined at Carter's — Count Henchel, the 3 men of yesterday, & a surgeon of the 4th. Ate too little & drank too much. [J.]

All without — the sea, mountains, olive woods — are as lovely as colour & calm atmosphere & cloudless sky can make them; but within I confess to being blank & weary & sad to a shocking amount. And perhaps a lesson may be learnt from this state of things, that the outside is not what we should so much think of — but then how the Devil is it to be otherwise with a dirty landscape painter? Knowing me, however, as you do, you may suppose I do not give way to this. [H.H.]

1861
[DATE UNKNOWN]

Perfectly clear & bright again — all amethyst & gold. Worked at the Florence & Turin outlines all day long, & nearly completed both in pencil. Grew horribly weary & tired. . . . Against my will went & dined at Wolff's — Count Henchel & one of the Miss Kourkoumélis only. Horribly bored at dinner — the good-natured Count's insequent talk & Mrs W.'s namby & pamby smallness — & also W.'s fluffy zigzag talk. After dinner came in Strahan, & Mrs W. played most tiresomely. Came away at 10.20, as they were sitting down to cards.

30 NOVEMBER

Henry Drummond Wolff,
Secretary to the Lord High Commissioner.

Really, were it not solely for the winter — & the voyage, & the dread of London Darkness etc. — I would send the fact of expense gone to to the rightabout, & leave Corfu at once: however, I suppose it is better to be patient for 3 months. So ends November 1861. [J.]

After I left Trieste, I had an abominable passage hither; once we were on the point of putting back, but finally we got here 20 hours after our time — on the 19th. Everybody was overwhelmingly hospitable, from the Palace downwards, but as the balls, & small monotonous whist- or tea-parties are wholly out of my line in this very

1 DECEMBER

137

very very small tittletattle place, & as moreover night walks from this side of the city to the other don't suit me, not to speak of late hours & a multitude of new & uninteresting acquaintance, I decline all visiting on the plea of health & antiquity or what not. The Wolffs have very amiably asked me several times — they seem very & justly popular — but the only point at which Greeks, Germans, French, Italians, & English in such a place as this can amalgamate being balls & the smallest of gossip, this tone of social life bores me even more than total loneliness, tho' that is very bad for me I know — only the alternative is wusser. The Sargents seem nice people, but they live remote. The Colquhouns* are remote & less nice — by report. The Palace is dull: no lady — the dinner there of 12 was as all dinners are. The General is going, & what I am sorry for, Lady Buller, she being one of the nicest women here.

What I find queer here is the extreme Toryism of all parties, except Sir C. Sargent. (You will remember that the swells here are so by a Tory ministry.) Yet it sounds queer to hear the revolution in Italy spoken of sometimes with horror, sometimes as merely an absurd phase of politics soon to pass by; though on consideration, you can easily suppose that any such a word as 'nationality' must be odious to the ears of all Government parties; & you can easily conceive that the R.C.s — native & English – have a tower of strength in the Pope's consul — & that they believe in the speedy extinction of Victor Emmanuel, & the restoration of the Roman States to Pio IX. There is a movement among the Jews* also — for 'representation' (!) at which both Greeks & R.C.s foam & scoff.

Meanwhile the society is far less amalgamated than in former years, when such old resident & reputed families as the Reids, Gisbornes, Cortazzis & others, made a nucleus of social life, or when so intellectual a man as F. Lushington had a table & house. And so the aspect spiritual of this little piggywiggy island is much as a very little village in Ireland would be — peopled by Orangemen & papists — & having all the extra fuss & ill-will produced by a Court & small officials — more or less with or against a resident crowded garrison.

The aspect material meanwhile (with which I have most to do — tho' unhappily no man can be quite independent of the others) is, so far as climate & country goes, lovelier than ever. Yet seeing it has never rained since April last, & that it is now daily perfectly clear & fine, the wise anticipate 3 months rain at once & continual. For myself I must get through this winter as well as I can, the loss of my dear Ann, & also of Lushington as a resident here, being a great weight to bear. . . .

The whole affair of 'Ionianism' appears to me absurd & ill-conditioned: an impossible end tried for by impracticable means. Clark, the good chaplain, is still here; but I shan't go regularly to church, & if he sees the *Essays & Reviews** on my table — *me voilà fiini*. Aubrey De Vere has just arrived, which, if I had to see him, would be a bore, but isn't. O! if I could but come back to London, bringing with me the gold & blue & lilac & pink of the air, sun, hills & snow with me! . . . The prison has been revolting lately & Lady Emily Kozzíris* greatly disturbed. Kozzíris seems to be agreed on by all hands as more incompetent than ever. [C.F.]

Perfection-weather — *al solito* — & the band-music, the whistle of the man-of-war, the plash of the harbour sea are not unpleasant. . . . Did not go out at all . . . But prepared to dine, when at 6 p.m. came in Oswald Middleton, who is ordered off to Kefaloniá on Saturday, whom I am very sorry for. I ask him to dine tomorrow. Dine: oh! what a noise overhead! & write. Terrible row upstairs: if, as in 1855, I had not fixed myself so, I could find my heart to go away. [J.]

2 DECEMBER

. . . I should not stay another year here — *certes*. If I could only get time enough I would do all my destined topography, & then try to settle once & for all in England: near Highgate if I could. O my dear Ann! [J.]

3 DECEMBER

. . . Colonel Maude from upstairs came: a really nice pleasant fellow — & lo! he is one of Aunt Kate's Maudes, & has stayed at Winwick & at Knowsley. He obligingly came to ask me to a 'little dance' on Friday — & hearing I could not go to it, said he hoped anyhow a system of pot-lucking could be brought about between the 2 floors. [J.]

4 DECEMBER

A bitterly cold day — all through. The west room so windy I give it up & breakfast in the studio or middle room. . . . At 2.30 went out with my sketch book in Yanni's 'Coliseo Nuovo' as George calls it, & drew below Análipsis, walking afterwards to One Gun. Dined at 6.30, & penned out my sketch afterwards. Heard George read – & make a fuss about the stench in the kitchen from the drain, which is serious. The amount of bore here is formidable, but I have gone in for withstanding it & fighting it out. [J.]

5 DECEMBER

The 'bore' increases. All day long preparation for a great dance are going on above, dragging furniture etc., & even the sleeping room over mine is to have the musicians! So I go partially mad. . . . Dine. But the noise upstairs is horrible — & I really turn over all sorts of ways to go — or be quiet. I imagine I must sleep out. At 8, unable to bear more, went out to the Boyds', but they were dining out. Returned, & called on Mr Craven, the 2nd padre, on the 3rd floor — he having called on me today. Found that Mrs Craven had just been confined. The Paymaster of the 4th was there. After sitting till 10, came away. The Maude — or Maudit — ball had begun, & sleep belowstairs was out of the question. So I packed a few things in a knapsack, & taking George with me to Turlock's, got a bed there. Pouring rain & south wind at last. [J.]

6 DECEMBER

Pouring rain & dark. Slept ill — bed uncomfortable. At 8.30 came home, & breakfasted. Began 2 small drawings of Philae & Corfu, but the whole furniture upstairs is moved, & I should think 20 soldiers & 10 horses there. Headache & feverish, & find work wholly *impossible*. What to do? It seems that the Bollands are unable to stay in their new house, & wish to come back here. So, as far as that goes, I can cut off, with only the loss of expense in sending my things out, buying some here, & loss of time. About 2.30 called on amiable Mrs Boyd — & detailed some of my

7 DECEMBER

miseries: also heard Charley Boyd read some of my 'Nonsense' . . . [J.]

8 DECEMBER   Wonderful to relate, the weather is perfectly lovely again — cloudless, the mountains snowy. Went to church: crowded: a bore; Clark's sermon ditto. . . . At 3, walked out, meeting Boyd & Baron d'Everton,* & so to the Casino* — the De Veres out: & on to Análipsis, where, on the platform, fell in with Sargent & Wolff to whom I expatiated on the view & with whom I walked to the One Gun & back to town by 6. (I may be mistaken, but Sargent's *accueil* seems to arise from caring for oneself — Wolff's from a general principle of diplomatic or official bethesametoeverybody-hospitality. It is odd enough that W. reminds me of his predecessor at times — a kind of fluffy shiftiness. Of course he is a gentleman, which Bowen was not in any degree.) . . . If I ever return to Corfu it will be to portray all I can of it, & go — not live here. So I came home. Blew up G. for sleeping in his clothes. [J.]

12 DECEMBER   . . . At 1.30 I went solo to Análipsis, where I drew till 4.15. (I remember such weather in 1855 — & indeed, it lasted, more or less, all that winter.) Walked all along the cliffs to One Gun — what opal views of Nikópolis & St Maura! what gold-sunset-through-leafness of the groves of olives! Fell in with Middleton & Major Cox & walked with them to Kanóni. While talking with them there came Sir H. Storks, Lord High Commissioner,* whereby our conversation ended. I took leave of him to go with them, but he 'would signify' I was to walk with him; & so he walks as far as the town. And I don't remember a more unbumptious, & yet a more thought-speaking & intelligent Governor anywhere. Moreover, he spoke kindly to the peasants everywhere — Τί κάμεις; Καλά; [How are you? Well?]. So I got home by 5.45. Wonderful pure light! & dined (G. had done some tripe but it looked like a lot of lizards, & I couldn't eat it). . . . [J.]

15 DECEMBER   Here I am again in the 'Little Isle' . . . I am writing by a clear window & with the clear mountains perfectly reflected in a mirror-like sea dotted all over with sparklesail-boats, & powdered far on each side of the 2 big men-of-war lying close to my door with an infinity of white specks (millions to wit) of what you might guess to be lotus flowers or sea mushrooms, but in reality are the seagulls, placidly waiting for their dinners from the big ships' kitchens. I don't remember to have seen such a month of purely beautiful weather at this season: day after day the same, the same rose & crimson evenings, the same lilac & silver mornings. Once only it clouded & was abominably cold for 2 days & then came pouring rain which everyone said would last for 3 months at least — but lo! next morning all was wiped up & smiling once more. However, we must have lots of rain bye & bye of course. At my first coming (I arrived on the 19th November) I was extremely bizzerable here; apart from F. Lushington being away & the Reids & Edwards & the Cortazzis — all of which facts I was prepared for — there was no one else hardly left in the whole island, & nobody having been here above 2 or 3 years, nobody cares for nobody . . .

Then I could not get lodged (for of course a large painting room is a *sine qua non*) & I was going on to Athens: & I got altogether moped & cross & disgusting. Even when, by a lucky chance, I popped into the 1st floor of a new house on the Line Wall with a *perfect north light,* I was bored to death by the *noise* of Corfu houses, which are so built that you hear everything on all sides & above & below: people over me gave a ball; people under me had twin babies; people on the left played on 4 violins & a cornet; people on the right have coughs & compose sermons aloud. So I nearly went mad till by degrees I got furnished & to work — & such a lot of work as I have cut out might be a proof of complete insanity to those who do not know that unless I work I am wretched. Florence, Turin, Mt Blanc, the Dead Sea & the Mer de Glace, Spezia & Massia & Corfus endless, beside Philaes & Olympusses occupy my minutes & leave me but little grumble time, the more that light here is always a No. 1. Then, everybody seems to think I had come here to amuse them. Everybody asked me to dine or play whist: everybody 'hoped I would let them sit & look at me painting'. The grates wouldn't burn, the drains would smell. Even the regular & undemonstrative George was put out, for his brother (Spiro) was ill, & his youngest boy also. And before I could get to work Christmas English bills began to come in, & against all this desolation & bother, I had only better health to put in antagonism, & hope for the fewtcher.

But at present I am somewhat livelier. One of the twin babies is dead & the other poorly. The violin people have gone. The people overhead are quieter. The grates burn better & the drains 'smell' better. Spiro & Haralámbi-the-small are recovering. And as yet there is little wind & next to no cold. So, unless you hear to the contrary, you may suppose I am progressing. Aubrey De Vere is here — he mooneth about moonily. Some friends of Mrs Brookfield (the Decies) also are here; but I have finally fixed *never* to dine out except on a Sunday. Frank's successor, Sir C. Sargent, seems a nice fellow, but I eschew intimacies. Bowen's successor (old Wolff's son) is also good-natured. Mess dinners abound, but the Palace is dull — at least after good-natured vulgar roaring helter-skelter Lady Young. *En revanche,* the Governor is a better Governor & hath brains & a will. He has asked me a second time to dine today — & I hope he won't begin to ask me to dinner often, as I avoid swells; but I do not know how to prevent popularity unless I invent some new plan not yet hit on.

Meanwhile, the island is, if possible, lovelier than ever, & I cannot conceive more fairy-like scenery, or more perfect Greek landscape. My life is going to be thus — as far as I can. Rise at 5 or 6 & do Greek till 8. Breakfast & teach George till 9. 9 to 4 work hard as possible. 4 to 6 walk (the sun don't set till 5 here); 6.30 dine. 7.30 to 10.30 penning out topographical drawings. If so be I get any tin, I shall devote April to May to doing a fresh piece of Peloponnesus illustration — probably Elis or Maina [Mani] or Epídavros, or I might, could & should & would go to Crete; but these things depend on other matters so much that it is in vain to arrange B 4 ☞ In June I expect I shall be back in England for the Great Exhibition,* & the showing there of my two large pictures, Corfu & Lebanon, may do me some good as to commissions.

Whether I shall go to Palestine in the Autumn, or in the following Spring, remains also undecided. . . .

Oranges are a halfpenny a piece — but it is a *vergona* [shame] to gather them, they look so lovely. Owls are plentiful. Flights of gray gregarious gaggling grisogonous geese adorn the silver shining surface of the softly sounding sea. We are all talking about the 'American Outrage'* — tho' to judge by my letter, one among us does not think it much anyhow. That, however is a mistake, for I think lots, nor do I cease to feel my sister's death at all, & I suppose I never shall now. . . . I have decided to go to the Palace in dirty boots; to eat my fish with my fingers; & to spit in the tumbler: on which I shall never be asked again. [E.T.]

17 DECEMBER The present ephusion of my pen will be written in better sperrits, because I have got to work, & am working hard; moreover I got letters from Frank Lushington yesterday & also from the printer of the *Book of Nonsense*, who tells me that Routledge & Warne have brought it out & that over 500 copies have been already sold. Please do what you can to encrease the sail by axing & talking about it. . . .

I like the Lord High, who has asked me to dine twice (& again on Christmas day, which I refused), & once walked back from the One Gun with the landscape painter. What I like in him is that he has a will besides brains, & has a soldierly & straight-forward manner quite trustworthy, & withal a proper setting forth of dignity. The Court is called dull, but at least it is not like that of the Young dynasty, which was wholly a dilettante affair — & one always felt that the whole set were there for Lady Y.'s 'amusement', & G.'s benefit. Sir John's vacillating manner & softness — mustard & mulberries in a hash — are well replaced by the present Governor's qualities as far as a 'worm' can judge, & I think he is well looked on by all — certainly as a man of business there is but one opinion of him. . . .

I wish I had more time for Greek: if I had my way & wor an axiom maker & lawgiver, I would cause it to be understood that Greek is (or a knowledge of it) the first of virtues: cleanliness the 2nd, & Godliness — as held up by parsons generally — the 3rd. O mi hi! — here is a noo table, sicks feet too by 3 feet hate! I shall dine at one end of it, write at the other, & 'pen out' in the middle. . . .

P.S. A. Tennyson has written an im: & also a small pome. [C.F.]

19 DECEMBER The nearly full moon opposite my window at 7, then the gradual plum-rosiness, & lastly at 7.30 the first crimson of sunlight on Salvador is a sight not to be forgotten. . . . Worked very well, from 9 to 3, at the Florence. But Mrs Maude jigs etc. & an organ in the street nearly drove me mad. Then came Count Henchel (he says there is a report that Prince Albert is dead) & now it has clouded from noon — it is raining & gloomy. . . . It really seems to be believed that the report of Prince Albert's death is a true one: undoubtedly one of the most terrible events possible just now, at least as far as we mortals can see. A telegram came to a Greek merchant here, & was taken to Sir Storks at the opera, which he left directly. It is said the Prince died on the 16th.

At 6.30 dine with Craven, the chaplain on the 2nd floor — a bluff gruff soldierly sort of priest. There were young Storks — & one Major Buchanan, a really nice fellow. After dinner, we bashed the piano etc. for a time, a vast thunder & lightning & rain & hail storm the while. And came away at 10.15.

Poor Queen! It seems really true, this terrible news. The Lord High C. has put off his ball for tomorrow. I cannot think the poor Queen will ever rally from this loss. [J.]

Rose at 7. A delightful half-sunny, half-pearly gray day, warm enough to have the window open, a woodfire within. After breakfast & hearing George read, worked at the architecture of the Florence picture absolutely almost without stopping from 9 to 5. I could have seen a few minutes longer by the bright reflection of the sunset but thought it better to rush out, which I did...   21 DECEMBER

The Prince is really dead — most sad to think of. He died on Saturday the 14th. And poor Queen Victoria is a widow. Sadder days still I fear are in store. What man can have done his duty in all ways as son, brother, husband, father, & public man in the highest station, more & better than Prince Albert? ...   [J.]

The 5th Sunday here — & would I were away; yet I bethink me, Sundays, when I am settled anywhere, are always 'sad & strange'. However, the day is once more lovely to a fabulous degree.   22 DECEMBER

After breakfast wrote to Middleton of Huyton, & read & wrote, determining not to go to church till next Sunday, till 1, when George came back with his 2 boys. Nikóla, the eldest, is a fine lad with good expression & eyes. Little Haralámbi is very pretty but I think very delicate, & I do not think, if he does not get stronger, that he will live. But what is life?

'O life, O earth, O time!'

Now — 1.30 — to go out, or not? There are times when this loneliness is too dreadful almost to bear — yet it is less so of late & yesterday I was much better. There are so many causes now also for dejection, over & above those of old, that on the whole I think myself better. However, at 2 I walked over the new 'Parga' road, to the Potamós ditto, & then by the Gouvia marsh road up to the Potamós *giro*, which I took. The glen scenery — or rather glades of olive woods — so filmy & sparkly & truly wondrous, & almost inimitable; & so also the higher olives above Potamós & then the sea & snow mountains; & the thick groves of Evrópouli; then those black kerchief'd dames of Potamós, & so slowly, & sadly, to the Alepoú road & across by the poplars to the Aghii Deka, & so '*home*' by 6.15. George turned out a dinner of macaroni, duck & sausages, & I asked questions of Souli, but he is abstract & *testa di legno* [block-headed] as he says of his son Nikóla. The Maudes are tolerably quiet in these days. But I by no means feel that it is profitable to go on long, even so long as 3 months here. [J.]

A gray day... Did not go out at all.... Dined. But George had a fit of grumbling,   23 DECEMBER

143

having been obliged, owing to a fête of St Spirídon tomorrow, & Christmas day after, to go hither & thither for heaps of things. After a time he comes into decent humour, for he is always amenable to reason if kindly urged to him. However, he went on growling again — & went out at 8. I set to work at penning out, & finished the Temple Corfu view began on the 5th & 6th. But as at 10 G. had not come in, I wonder what is come to him. At 10.30 I have done my work — & just then I hear the Souliot enter. I really do half think it would be better to cut Greece for the present — altogether: for poor George as well as for myself. For he can get no other master while I am hereabouts, & I do not think his staying with me is for his benefit. [J.]

24 DECEMBER   A miserably sleepless night. Morning gray. After breakfast I work a little at the Florence olives. But I am *mortisimo* in body & soul. Yet looking back — even as far as 6 years old (at the clown & circus at Highgate*), & then to all since — how can it be otherwise? The wonder is, things are as well as they are through constant fighting. Gray, & showery at times. Worked from 2 to 5 at the Turin buildings & trees: all ill. A weary day — but when have I not been weary in winter time, or indeed anywhere when settled? — or indeed, anywhere? . . . Dined. The Maudes seem always away nowadays — & often the 'stilly night' is the order of the day. [J.]

25 DECEMBER   What an odd Christmas day! To begin with, a hard north-easter, & Salvador (when seen for mists) covered with snow 2 thirds down! Sent George out to his home, & wrote to R. Fowler, & worked at Turin — very decently. At 3, Hutton, a nice fellow, & Lawson, ditto, came, & stayed till 5. At 6 I dined — on macaroni & cold beef — & penned out . . . till 10.40. [J.]

30 DECEMBER   Same lovely weather — but cold in the shade. At 9 went out — principal shops shut by order of the L.H.C. owing to Prince Albert's death. Took 4 rooms at the Hotel San Giorgio for Miss Goldsmid* from the 20th — at 10*s*. a day if they stayed a month, 12*s*. a day if less than a fortnight. . . . George not returning, I wonder what has occurred & go down to the post, getting an *Observer* of the 22nd (meet Count Henchel — going off to Alexandria). . . . At 2.30 George comes in & says Spiro is taken violently ill — I fear bronchitis or diptheria — 3 doctors are with him. I greatly fear he will not recover this time. . . . At 6.30 found G. had returned. Poor Spiro is in the same state. Dined at 7 — & afterwards G. went home, & I suppose will sleep there. [J.]

1 JANUARY   Weather perfectly lovely. Ἀς δοκιμάσωμεν νὰ ἀρχίσωμεν καλὰ τὸν χρόνον. [Let's try to start the year well.] George came at 7.15. Spiro is a little better. Worked at Florence till 11, pre-colouring sky, foreground & city. Put by my work, as calls must be made today. Also Taylor's bill of £59 overcometh me. From 11 to 2 calls on Decies, Luard, Sargent, Wolff, Bridge, Stockly, Barr, Sir G. Buller, Sir H. Storks, Peel, Boyd & Loughman. 2 to 4 penned out. . . . 4 to 6.15 walked by the new Parga road — & the usual round. The mountains wonderfully beautiful, peach-rose, & sea dark purple

gray — north wind. Met Sir C. Sargent who tells me Spiro is better, & asks me to dine on Sunday, which I wish to do. Dine at 6.30, & dress, & pen out 1856 sketches till 9.30, up to which time the Maudes, who asked me upstairs, are still at dinner — a serious bore, as I had rather go to bed. I must now send George to his mother's. [J.]

Stormy — west wind — & high. . . . By 2.15, reached Spiro's — dirty & wet, for it rained. Spiro is somewhat better, but I by no means feel assured of his total recovery. There were all the family except Yanni & Christos. Tatianí was there — a woman with such grace of form, & fine make, & a beautiful face. Fancy George never having said a word of his wife — the ancient dodger! Returned by 3. Church at 3.30. Craven preached — & not badly. Afterwards called on the Decies, & ate lemons. 'Home' by 6 & dressed, & to Sir C. Sargent. Pleasant evening — only Aubrey De Vere is too absurdly dreamy & abstracted-boshy. Sang A. Tennyson. Home by 11. [J.] 5 JANUARY

The morning was gray, & stormy, & raining. At 10 it cleared, by a vast north wind: sea furious — boats all ashore. At 1.30 steamer from Trieste to Alexandria came in, but is now — 2 p.m. — still going round & round — for no pratique boat can go out. I hurried up to Mrs De Vere's to decline dining there — being really all cold & unwell. . . . The sea was a little calmer at 4, when a boat got the mail off. . . . George went to his mother's: he is all put out by Spiro's illness, & by the little possibility of arranging better here in Corfu, & it is plain to me they all wish to go & settle at Athens or Patras. [J.] 7 JANUARY

Calm again, & lovely — all day: but *cold*. Wrote to Lady Waldegrave & Fortescue till 10.30. Painted, from 10.30 to 5, at Butrínto. At 5.15 walked to Kastrádes & back by 6.15. 6.30 dined. 7.30 to 10.20 penned out 3 Egyptian drawings — Thebes.
    Werry methodickle, we are. [J.] 8 JANUARY

Wonderfully calm & bright — but cold particular. George, returning at 7.15, says Spiro is now going on so well that he will not sleep there anymore. . . . At 6.30, walked by the Parga new road round, & called at Spiro's & saw him. He is up, & walking, but *very weak*. Dined at the Herberts'. A very delightful evening, though I suffered at dinner from the fire behind me: & also from poor dear Aubrey De Vere who at times is a bore. Home by 12. [J.] 9 JANUARY

The woes of painters: just now I looked out of the window at the time the 2nd were marching by — I having a full palate & brushes in my hand: whereat Colonel Bruce saw me & saluted; & not liking to make a formillier nod in presence of the hole harmy, I put up my hand to salute — & thereby transferred all my colours into my hair & whiskers, which I must now wash in turpentine or shave off. [C.F.] 21 JANUARY

. . . At 2.30 came the Trieste boat, & with a glass I saw Miss J. Goldsmid & her party. 27 JANUARY

145

But the vessel was declared in quarantine by some Ionian bother, & it was 4 before they got out. Called at their hotel & saw Julia Goldsmid. Walked from 5 to 6.30 — by Kastrádes, & the sea, home. Dined. Penned out till 10.30. Dreadful night, from a rat gnawing a hole through from the drain into my bedroom. Ill. [J.]

29 JANUARY   If possible, lovelier still. Yet it must needs be that I stay in to work: those 4 upper Análipsis subjects try me dreadfully — only, if I leave them I could not well enjoy going out, knowing how impossible it will be for me to move from Corfu unless they be done & sold. So I have to reflect on the destiny of millions, who cannot even enjoy the scenes indoors as I do. A keen sense of every kind of beauty is, I take it, if given in the extreme, always more or less a sorrow to its owner, though production of good to others. This coming of Julia Goldsmid does not aid me either, but rather the contrary.

Bye & bye, after several interruptions, Maude came in, & what with talking, & one's work going wrong, & the thought of dining up there with the Forts & Cravens, I grew over irritable, & now could 'cry bitterly' as J.E. said. It is seldom nowadays that I am so 'utterly cast down'. Weariness of life — & loneliness! Rushed out at 5 blinded & weary, not seeing the hills nor sky. Met the nice Decies, who stopped, & Sir H. Storks, who stopped also. Round by Kastrádes, & called at the Kokális ... & home.

Dined at the Maudes.... By great effort I got thro' dinner & evening — but with greatest difficulty. This weary work *won't* do. Fresh row between Maude & Paramythiótti about the dogs, which Maude ought not certainly to keep in the cellar. Down in my room by 11 & penned out Kalamía drawing till 12.30. 'Trouble on trouble — pain on pain' — the drain smell is beginning again. I shall not be able to live here anyhow, if anywhere in Corfu. [J.]

30 JANUARY   ... Kind note from Mrs Decie; the Decies inviting me every Sunday: particularly good & kind, since they are wholly free from want of any visitors.... At 7 home. Dined. After which, Maude's 6 dogs below annoyed me horribly, & wishing to retreat to bed, the drain began again — so I grew half crazy with disgust, & hustled the mattress into the next room floor — sitting to finish the Kalamiá drawing in a rage.

10.30, I really half resolve to pack up all, & finish what I can in London — going a tour in the islands till it is time to go back. It does *not* seem possible to exist here. *Vedremo domani.* [J.]

1 FEBRUARY   ... Remove all things out of the back room, & the bedroom things into it, turning the bedroom into a 'showroom'. Read Turner's life. Count G. Henchel v. Donnersmarck came — returned from Alexandria — & brought letters from the Saunders. He is a bore. Everything is a bore. Did not go out. Dined at 7 — & penned out till 10.30. The wretched Mrs Craven has played 75 variations till I was nearly crazy — & now the Maudes are making a mad pothouse above me. [J.]

2 FEBRUARY   The Prince of Wales is to be here in 2 or 3 weeks — I suppose only passing. Arthur P.

Stanley I see by the papers is to be with him — who, though no courtier, is exactly the man for such a place: & his nomination to it greatly pleases me. Alas! for my visit to Jerusalem! shall I ever get there? (I should not like to go with the Royal party tho' — nine league boots — & all restraint.)

Sir H. Storks is particularly kind to me. He is a *well-bred* man & fitted in all respects for his place it seems to me. I discover by degrees why the military don't like him: he is only a Colonel in the army — *ergo* Generals & Colonels don't like to be under him. But, so far as I can learn, their small provocations have been only necessarily interfered with by him. I never saw society so disjointed & dishevelled as this is nowadays.

Miss Julia Goldsmid has come — with a friend — Mrs Naylor. (I got them rooms in a new hotel, the other part of which is taken by Kozzíri & Lady Emily.) Miss G. had determined, I find, not to go to the synagogue here, & had she not done so, I should have deterred her if possible from going there. For as the Jews here are all of the lowest orders, the advent of a lady might have brought 'Confusion on the little Isle'. O Lord! I must take Mrs Naylor to church this afternoon.

I dine at Wollf's today which may or may not be 'a bore'. Mrs W. is a clever little woman — *very*. (I remember you used often to bully me for being 'easily bored' by people: but, when one reflects, you yourself are most singularly hedged in & unapproachable by all but a very limited set & class — (no fault of yours: I only wish I could be so too). 'Moral' — you, aboiding various disagreeables in men & things, cannot justly blow me up for disgust at *not* being able to avoid said disagreeables. As a point of illustration, Lord Ernest Bruce is here — deaf, & to *me* a frightful bore. But to the unsensitive, he, being a Lord, & 'affable & talks so much!' is 'a delightful man'!)...

At present my only wish is that these accursed rats were away, & that Colonel Maude wouldn't bump his chair over my head so. The old General [Sir George Buller] is going to leave Corfu, & the new, Sir J. Inglis, is just a-coming. Count G. Henchel von Donnersmarck — his name is not quite long enough — has come back: he is the delight of most — as he talks unceasingly & in a completely monotonous voice; to me he is the deadliest of bores, tho' not bad as a man I daresay. Is not perpetual talk — idea-less prattle — the utmost of bore?

I am feeling to begin to wish *not* to come to England this year: but 2 months will decide. Keeping up rooms in London & 2 long journeys are certain expenses, pitted against what are very uncertain gains. There is a man in a boat here under the window who catches fish all & every day with a long 5-pronged fork, a waistcoat & drawers being his dress. Why should I not do the same? [C.F.]

4 FEBRUARY

Paradise weather all day.... Paradise without, for I cannot move. Began to work on Corfu D — the little one — but worked ill. Fear of noise (which presently came in 4 artillary men carrying up wood) & disgust of repetition of subject made me work badly — & besides, I was unwell. At 2 lunched. At 3, most weary & sad, yet with a persistence I had not in old times, I shall try to work again. O! these 4 Análipsis pictures! Worked on till 5. Internally, a very wretched day, but outwardly calm & purple-bright Paradise. Dined at 7 & penned out till 10. Lapsista drawings. The Lord be thanked, the Maudes are out — so stillness rains [sic] above & below. But it is hard prison-work, albeit there is much to be thankful for indeed. (After writing this, read some journal of this day & other following days of 1861: one surely ought to be content!) [J.]

6 FEBRUARY . . . My life will not be long here — I mean in this world — I think. But that does not depress me. The state of this life — while I live here — *does*. . . . [J.]

8 FEBRUARY Cloudy & sunny at times: once or twice a half shower of rain, being calm & open-window no-fire weather. Worked at Corfu A — trees & foreground — but tho' no one came, little things interrupted me. First, paying Paramythiótti's rent: I asked for the refusal of the upper floor, but got no answer. Then there were noisy street cars — & looking out for the Post Ancona boat, which came not. At 2 — salutes — the new general, Sir J. Inglis, landing. A new ship-of-war came in. Then the General's packages to stare at — & the 2nd Regiment & band twice past. And at 5 — sunset beautiful — a second set of salute guns — I conclude for Lord & Lady Buller's going. *What* a life has her's been here! . . . The sun comes round Fort Neuf now at 4.30, whereby, later in the year, this room will be useless. Things must be as they may: go, or not go. Dined at 6.30 & penned out till 9.30, but the room was useless for another cause: the awful noise of the Maudes. Went to bed angry & half thinking of going away. [J.]

9 FEBRUARY Pouring rain, & thunderstorms: high south wind all day. More angry still that there are neither letters nor papers. $\Delta\iota\alpha\tau\iota$; [Why?] In a horrid rage. Looked out Tennyson illustrations for his poems. . . . A deadly doleful day — dark pouring gloomy — & I gloomier. . . . [J.]

10 FEBRUARY Worked — but not much — at Corfu A: trees. Count George Henchel von Donnersmarck came, & his brother-in-law: a better bred man, & a gentlemanly fellow. Afterwards, just as I was getting to work again, came someone else, & George announced '*il Capitano d'un bastimento*'. So I went angrily to the front room, & was none the less angry at seeing a large dog in it — when lo, Geoff Hornby!* So we talked, & at 4.30 walked, & went to the *Neptune* at 5.30. The noise of the Maude people today was *dreadful*: they seem to throw down tables & chairs for fun . . . [J.]

12 FEBRUARY . . . Unless the Maudes & Cravens go, I am off. — Walked a little way to the One Gun. A half-drunk sailor on a grey horse insisted on shaking hands with me — 'I know you're an Englishman by your jib!' — & wanted me to go & 'have a drop of something to drink' with him. [J.]

14 FEBRUARY

Very fine, & north wind. Coldy. It is not possible to rise before 7.30 in that little dark room. O Corfu houses! Worked . . . from 9 to 3.30 — but irregularly as the Alexandria steamer came in early, & worry abounded. Letters (but no papers, which enraged me) from J. B. Edwards, Mrs Clive, & Emily Tennyson, the last enclosing A.T.'s most exquisite lines on Prince Albert. Copied them out for Mrs Decie. [J.]

15 FEBRUARY

. . . Worked, not over well, at Corfu A. Steamer in — & neither letters nor papers. The Cravens called — bores both — tho' I suppose good people: 'Have you called on Lady Inglis?' 'No.' 'Are you going to . . . ?' 'Perhaps yes or no.' 'Why so . . . ?' 'I don't wish to go out.' 'But you are under martial law here, & everyone is bound to call on the general, etc.' 'We suffer fools gladly, being wise ourselves': I am sure I do not suffer them gladly, so I cannot be wise. [J.]

16 FEBRUARY

I have been looking carefully over all A. Tennyson's poems, & noting out all the landscape subjects once more — which in all amount to 250. Sometimes I think I shall make the last effort of my life to illustrate the whole of these by degrees — & finally, having constructed a gallery near London, receive shillings for the sight of my pictures, & expire myself gradually in the middle of my own works, wheeling or being wheeled in a narmchair. *Intanto*, do you see the *Book of Nonsense* on all railway bookstalls? [C.F.]

16 FEBRUARY

I have been going through every one of A.T.'s poems — *Princess, Maud, Idylls* and all, having lost my former list of landscape illustrations — in order to get up my ideas on the subject of Landscapes once more. In all, I have put down 250. In the poems 153, *Princess* 24, *Titonus* 1, *Maud* 32, *In Memoriam* 23, *Idylls* 17. Shall I ever live to paint them? It is to be doubted. Meanwhile I am working very drudgeful at various necessities, & wish I were a chimney-sweeper or a teapot. . . .

This house too is unquiet, for there is a family named Maude above me, which I wish I could send 'into the garden' if there were one; & although one of the twins is dead yet the other, having I firmly believe swallowed the violin (which has been mute of late), hath a hoarser & catguttier voice than in aforetime. . . . O my! here the sun is so bright. Only a few, a very few, winter days have happened; then there were storms — thunder & lightning & rorin' of the angry elephants. I do not know if I shall come to England this year. Alfred would not like this place — it is so crowded & small & silly & buzzy. I however, who live in a chamber on a wall, overlooking the sea, seldom go out, or if I do I avoid the garrison gapings & gawglings & run away to the distant olives, & return at dusk. Perhaps in mid April I may coast along from here to Arta — & draw coves & harbours. . . .

Monday 17th. It is really an awful shame that the Poet Laureate hath only an ancient & polykettlejarring instrument in his house. Neither is it moral, for it sets a bad example to others, & flouts the musical deities. Oh dear I feel so sick! Geoff [Hornby] will have me come on board to dine today, & the wind is rising; I declare I won't go if it is rough. Please think of, & suggest, various subjects for Alfred to write on. Would William Tell be a possibly feasible one? Sith he always says he must know the scenery of the subjex, & surely Grütli would be a wonderful scene — not to speak of all about the lake, Uri, etc.. Bless me, this place is in such a fuss! Here's a big man-of-war — Turk — & a little Turkey steamer besides. I must say I like the Ottoman flag — the broad & long one — coloured crimsonflashing manyfolded traily fally floating banner, with the gold crescent shining out of it. Then there are 2 Greek steamers, bringing down the 2 sons of King Ludwig of Bavaria, one of whom is to be the successor of the King of Greece. The Greeks don't like having Bavarian kings. I wish I could send you heaps of cyclamen, which are lying so thickly about the trees. Yet see how vicious a practice it is to spell ill — for perhaps you suppose I mean 'sickly men', & that I am lamenting an unforseen mortality on the island, & wishing only that I could send the invalids to England. Not at all. I mean the beautiful flowers, I do. Also there are snowdrops & violets & anemones. . . .

To go on with the fuss, there are 3 men-of-war here & a gunboat — all ours — & a steamer — the *Osborne* — gone to fetch the Prince of Wales. He is to be here on the 20th & 21st but nobody knows exactly how or when or where or why or which or whosoever or what. I must go & paint goats. Bother goats — & goats' ears & noses. Bother goats' ears & noses. [E.T.]

17 FEBRUARY   Very fair early. Closed at 12 — rain, more or less, from 4 to 11. Worked ill & very little at Corfu A. Worry for steamer, which brought a letter from Holman Hunt. Wrote to him, & thus did little work. Did not go out till 6, when I called on Miss Goldsmid. Then to *Neptune* — a very disagreeable boating. Dined with dear little Geoff — how very absurd, remembering the gardens of Knowsley & Woolwich. Captain Clifford — 'cleverer' man than he seems but for a wearisome 'humour', & a queer countenance. The doctor, parson, & Commander Appleford are silent at dinner, which was very good tho'. Foreboding the boating back. At 10.30 came away.

No ships for me — if I had my will: that phase of life is shut from me. Home by 11 — but as George had lighted a fire, & the people under my bedroom were giving a dance, violins etc., it was no use to go to bed, so I sat up & penned out the last Zagóri drawings. Bed at **1 A.M.**, when I imagine the last fiddling is extinct but am not sure.
[J.]

18 FEBRUARY   . . . Last night (or morning) noise went on till nearly 6: so I could not sleep & rose at 8.30. [J.]

22 FEBRUARY   . . . At 6.35 home, & when sitting down — beginning to eat fish — a smart wrenchy-shock of earthquake, at 7. All the bells rang. Yet George was uncertain at the moment as to if it was not someone trying at the door! Upstairs, Mrs Maude understood it at once, since there, so much higher, the windows etc. jingled. That poor lonely little woman! [J.]

23 FEBRUARY

There is nothing much more difficult to do than write a long letter when one is in no happy mood. But the nature of these houses is such that every noise made above & below is distinctly heard; & if you will only think how one organ distracts *you*, consider how 5 pianos all going at once must worry *me*. However, there is one hope left, that when I get into the 3rd floor, which I have just taken, I shall be quieter. Nevertheless, since I arrived here at the end of November 1861, I find I have written exactly 76 letters, so that I really cannot be blamed for indolence, although I am not able to apply often to long epistles. Bother. When one is an angel, how one will keep pulling one's quills out of one's wings & writing continually with fresh pens, painting all the while, making love, going to millions of different places, up mountains & down valleys, studying hundreds of languages, & always eating & drinking in the delightfullest modes of quantity & quality of foods & liquors. [H.H.]

24 FEBRUARY

Gray all day: spitting rain at times. Painted inertly & ill at Yannina. Always the fussy waiting for post bothers. But it didn't come. 'Fat' came at 2, & said he & Mrs F. were coming to see pictures: but they *didn't*. Meanwhile, at 3 — what was far far better — Geoff *did* come — that child is a trumpy-brick. We two walked out, to Alepoú. He is telegraphed to go in March to Candia [in Crete], & would I could go too ! But, δέν εἶναι δυνατόν [it's not possible]. How we talked. I perhaps πάρα πολύ [too much]. We met the Prince also, riding with 3. After he passed, we heard (for they trotted on): 'Lear?' — 'Yes, Sir, Lear.' — 'O, I saw him at Rome' — a very facile & expedite explanation. At 6 when I returned, Craven asked me upstairs to dine — bother: I said no, so I dined alone . . . [J.]

14 MARCH

Gray — gleaming — calm. Ill, from sleeplessness; & no sooner had I begun to work on Florence, unwell & hardly able, with all my attention & application, to proceed as I wish, the horrible-silly Maudes began their noises above, she playing some dozens of bits, not 3 minutes each, from various operas, all out of tune, & between whiles pushing her chair awry & scampering — her brother whistling or knocking chairs down. Then came in George — no letters & only a paper of February 10!

So this last straw broke the camel's back & I put all on one side & vowed to go, packing 2 boxes — all my books — that instant. Resolving to walk to Garoúna, another steamer comes in at noon, & I wait, & at 1 p.m. send George again. One letter, from Ellen, who is very kind in writing so regularly. So I walked straight up, but slowly, to Aghii Deka. What unsurpassable beauty of distance & of foreground! Beyond, I went 1 mile & returned. All the 7 miles I did in 16 minutes each — as was becoming. Dined at 7 — cold beef. All the books, ordered of Bickers, have come — a pleasure. Penned out a little. Above is a shrieky shrieky music (a dog howling all the time) — enough to drive one mad — tho' it is *scientific* enough. But it is *certain* that *this* sort of life will not do. [J.]

16 MARCH

. . . Went to church at 11. . . . Clark preached about those dreadful old bores Jacob

Kastellános,
19 May 1848.

        & Esau. Also the church was crowded — a bore — so I shall not try the morning again. Home by 1. To Miss Goldsmid — & with her & Mrs Naylor to Garoúna. Wonderfully lovely place & beyond, to the bay, walking at times: also to Kastellános. Pleasant drive — *quâ* drive — albeit I hate drives, & Sundays are sow [*sic*] odious here. [J.]

20 MARCH   Gray early — but lovely after 10. Rose at 6.45. Breakfast, & at 9 off with George to the Hotel St George, & at 9.30 with Miss Goldsmid & Mrs Naylor to Palaiokastrítsa which we reached at 12.20. Very lovely bay & rox. We lunched in the monastery — & afterwards saw the bones of an old whale & prowled about the sands till 2.45. Very beautiful place. Recollections of 2 other times here. Drive back much worried by coach-movement, & nerves by restraint. Bad. Walked from Potamós road — & home by 6.15, seeing Craven on the way. Dined with Miss Goldsmid: a pleasant evening — yet — yet — yet. Home by 10.15 [J.]

24 MARCH   ... Sent 3 green frogs & 2 trap spiders to Mrs Naylor. It grieves me to see so little of Miss Goldsmid — but what else can I do? ... [J.]

25 MARCH   .... Painted — at Yannina — till 12, when Mrs & Miss Raquenau, good Mrs Boyd, & their friends came, & later Boyd — they are persons it is a pleasure to shew pictures to. Not well all day. At 3.30 went to Análipsis & drew till 5.30 or 6 ... Then ... walked back by 6.45. Ah! the surprising-endless beauty of Análipsis!
    Upstairs to Craven's. Mrs C., & he, I. Along of nurses — well & good — &

Análipsis, 25 March 1862.

babies καλά [well & good]. But later, when it came to personal scandal . . . I blazed up, & said I would not hear it. But we 'ended friendly.' But *what* a life of matrimony! O criki! 'Let us alone.' [J.]

Being unable to paint, walked about — suffering no end. Painted somewhat at the small Corfus. No letters. At 3.30 to Miss Goldsmid, & at 4, with her & Mrs Naylor, Captain Hillier, the maid & Cagiati, to the Captain's boat, & on to the steamer. Unpleasantly rough. So. She is gone. It is a twinge: – – – . Came home — & read papers, & at 5 I went out again. Dreadfully nervous. Steamer — seen from Análipsis — seems to go quietly. [J.]   7 APRIL

Rose at 6.30. Quite cloudy all day, & warm. Towards sunset N.E. winds & a little rain. Painted the skies to small Corfus & seas etc. Mrs De Vere came, & later Oikonómos & G. Paramythiótti. At 2 walked slowly to Potamós & drew at Pandeleímona till 5.30. Saw dwarf Dionýsios, & returned to dine at 7.30 . . . Penned out till 12. Had arranged to go to Palaiokastrítsa on Thursday, but *cui bono* in such weather? [J.]   8 APRIL

Potamós, 8 and 23 April 1862; 28 January 1864, 3 p.m.

All excursion-plans are absurd. San Salvador has not been visible for days. The weather is just like November — but warmer. Worked at Grenfell's Philae — not very well. Nervous & irritated. By 2.30 I had worked every bit of the colour out of the painting, & apparently spoiled all my work: certainly this *mestiere civile* [genteel profession] annoys me more & more, & I am just now miserable enough, but *I won't* give way: *piuttosto* [rather] I'll begin another Philae.

At 2 the weather cleared a bit & the gulls sat on the calmer sea. Then I thought I would dine on cold mutton having first attempted a translation of Alfred Tennyson's Will — «Θέλημα». O bother. After witch [*sic*] sate reading R. Burton's *City of the Saints* — & walking up & down till 6.30. A beautiful sunset, but with clouds. At 7.30 supper — absurd — a 2nd dinner of eggs & rice. And penned out till 10. Queer day. Queer life! [J.]

13 APRIL Fine, but pale, & somewhat misty. Wrote till 12. At 12.30 came the procession of St Spirídon — & most beautiful it was. I hardly remember any more striking assemblage

of colour & form than the grand priest concourse, banners, etc., against the blue hills. And the peasants' dresses were delightful. . . . At 4 walked to Potamós & to new parts of it, what olives etc. And so to Dionýsios beyond, & back — what wonderful peasant dresses! Two on a horse! Nicer mannered people exist not — nor I fancy better. At 6.30 went up to the Casino where were the De Veres only. Little Mary De Vere in her nightdress was really as like a small angel as could be. Would one have been as happy as one fancies if one had been married & had had children? Left at 10.30. The moonlight, frogs, fireflies, cypresses, quiet, mountains — but how little of this life is attainable. Home by 11.15 [J.]

14 APRIL

Wolff knows as little of me as may be, beyond that he & Mrs W. have been very good in asking me there, & that I have not gone. You can well guess that sudden intimacies with a crowd is not *al mio gusto*. He is a good enough little fellow, but too *repandu* & superficial to please me greatly, though not more so than is just the thing for his place here, & they are very properly highly popular. He cannot do without society, & it is not easy to find out at first how much men like you who ask odious & vulgar people just as they do oneself — some by way of having someone to break the life of monotony here than for really esteeming one. After a while, however, they asked me in a different way, & were really very friendly, but he is right in saying I have not been in good spirits. The occupation of my life — a daily journal to my sister Ann — is gone; & constant losses of friends do not enliven. . . . The people I have seen most here were the Decies (now gone), Geoff Hornby, & Miss Goldsmid — also gone now — the De Veres, & young Luard. Isn't that enough for a man to know — besides the Palace — dining out twice a week? The crowd of people wholly indifferent to me I will not make up to or know. As it is, perpetual interruptions have spoiled my winter: a noisy home, & much suffering from nerves of head, have prevented *any study* of languages & I have had but scanty exercise — no company to be had for such purposes. Thus I can't profess to be lucky — I ain't, & am half wishing I had not put by £100 last year, since I should have it now. . . . I wish you had been a 'bloody painter', as I heard a sailor say the other day. [C.F.]

15 APRIL

At 5 or 6 a.m. I had hoped for fine weather — but it became the same dark terrible gloomy scirocco. However, by 9.30 all was ready, & at 10 I set off, leaving George to follow. I went up to the Casa Kandóni,* & returned Ida Pfeiffer's last travels, which have immensely interested me. So on by the busy fields below Potamós & through the town, & passed poor Dionýsios. And so to the road, which I shall never be able to draw & yet never enough admire. Then at the Gouvia or Kondokáli 'Inn' I stopped — at 11.30 — & had an egg & some water: the people were all civil & kindly as usual. George & the cart came up at 12.20, & we went on to the 9th mile, & at the Grand Junction Hotel stopped. Αὐγὰ γεμισμένα [stuffed eggs] & garlicky sausage — but really good wine was the order of the day. *Osteria* life is always a delight to me — I cannot quite tell why, except that it began from Roman days. Afterwards, at 2.30, I

The monastery, Palaiokastrítsa, 15–19 April 1862.

walked on alone, & at the 10th mile, alas, was joined by a χωρικός [villager], who talked no end, & insisted on walking on with me. He called Sir H. Storks ὁ πρῶτος πολὺ κάλλιστος ἁρμοστής [the first most excellent Governor] & said he had been to his place — Makrádes — where later he asked me to come to a Panagýri [festival] this day week. Finally he said, «Ἂς ὑπάγωμεν σιμὰ στὴν Ἀγγλίαν» ['let's go soon to England'], & declared he would learn English directly. At the 12th mile the rock & olive scenery is immensely fine — & peak also but less so in such a day of clouds — but it was not easy to draw. Bye & bye — it was then 5.30 — the double bay came & the vast rocks of St Angelo, & so on & on to below the convent — at $15^1/_2$ miles — a wonderful scene of calm sea & massive savage promontory. Of course found that George had all the house very tolerably ready, but he had broken a lampshade to my disgust: it fell from the cart where he had insisted on keeping it all day for security. At 8 cold mutton & a bottle of beer were refreshing, & later coffee & a cigarette still more so. [J.]

16 APRIL
PALAIOKASTRITSA

Finer — clearer — & so all through. The day was not done when I went to bed, for the new frame-bed was uninhabitable, & we had to put a table flap. This however was so

Kastro St Angelo, Palaiokastrítsa, 16 and 19 April 1862.

hard that I got hardly any sleep all night, & could not rise till 7.

Drew Lakónes — outline, & then St Angelo, when 1o! 3 carts of furniture & a carriage, the last holding Mrs Lyall, Mrs Bridge & Mrs Creyke who have supposed they had taken these 2 cottages. Luckily the convent rooms were empty & I got them established there. Then, at 1, I drew the 'shadowed coves' & 2 other views till 4, then 2 more small, & at 5.45 came up again to the hill. The view is vastly grand & lovely at sunset — & seems to me far more so than of olden days. The Lakónes & other peasants are delightful in manner, but the small boys bore — 'one farden'. It is now 7 — ὥρα τοῦ γεύματος [supper time]. Dined: & penned out till 9.30. Then bed — but alas! the frame-bed borrowed of the convent was buggious: so I had no sleep, & nearly went mad. A fearful night. [J.]

Very lovely day — north wind. Thank God — slept well: the bugs being all kilt. Rose at 6, & at 7 a cup of coffee, & drew above & below till 9, or 9.30, when I came up to breakfast. The beauty of colour & reflection in the convent rocks & bay at early morn is summut wonderful. Anyhow I am constantly feeling how better I *recollect* of all

18 APRIL
PALAIOKASTRITSA

Palaiokastrítsa, 15 and 16 April 1862.

these beauties — or rather, how gray skies, bustle-life, & varieties, efface their reality-impression.

    After breakfast drew again, & at 2 went to the bay, drawing in colour, but failing frightfully. Drew on in pencil till 5.30, when Creyke & Bridge & their wives passed me — & I walked on & met Mrs C. & Mrs B. with whom I walked up the hill. The glory of southern skies — tho' one has had little enough of it latterly. I am certain, whatever good I may get by 'colour from nature', I get more by pencil — seeing my inability to struggle against physical painter-defects. Some very grand studies abound here. Dinner at 7.15 — a cold half fowl, rice & potatoes, & some 'wine of the country' the bill of fare & very fair. Penned out till 9.30. Bed. Slept pretty well — nay — well. [J.]

20 APRIL
EASTER SUNDAY
PALAIOKASTRITSA

Rose at 7, & breakfasted at 8.30. Sate by the open window & wrote to C. Fortescue — or walked about the small platformy house gardens till 12. How glorious was that blue level of sea! & the πρινάρι [Holm oak] & salvia, & the white butterflies — a quiet of bygone days, which, tho' I deprecate dwelling long on their memory, *will* be remembered sometimes. Abruzzi — & 1843. Do you ever think of me Donna ....? I hope not. Yet your lot in those few bright days was brighter than it ever had been, & I

Palaiokastrítsa, 16–17–18–19–20 April 1862.

fear ever could be. And you — of Costella days? Where are you & your babe — ? A dream world.

At 12 called at 'the convent'. Mrs Creyke is unwell. Sat with Mrs Lydall, who is a nice good Englishwoman, μοῦ φαίνεται [it seems to me]. Then drew at various points — the 'citadel-buffetted tempest-crowned' St Angelo. And at 3.30 drew till 6 at the Lakónes view. At 6 Captain C. & Mrs Bridge, a nice good woman too, went στὴν πόλιν [to the town]. Καὶ ἐγῶ [and I] walked a bit on the road, below the stately rocks & proud olives, returning to dine at 7. George provides a (melancholy) duck: but George (who dined by invitation with the Ἡγούμενος [abbot] today), always does his best.

And now: *how* still! *how* silent! — even the bubble surf so far below is scarely heard! Palaiokastrítsa memories, if I live, will live with me. [J.]

I have been wondering if on the whole the being influenced to an extreme by everything in natural or physical life — i.e., atmosphere, light, shadow, & all the

20 APRIL
PALAIOKASTRITSA

varieties of day & night — is a blessing or the contrary; & the end of my speculations has been that 'things must be as they may', & the best is to make the best of what happens. I should, however, have added 'quiet & repose' to my list of influences, for at this beautiful place there is just now perfect quiet, excepting only a dim hum of myriad ripples 500 feet below me, all round the giant rocks which rise perpendicularly from the sea: which sea, perfectly calm & blue, stretches right out westward unbrokenly to the sky, cloudless that, save a streak of lilac cloud on the horizon. On my left is the convent of Palaiokastrítsa, & happily, as the monkery had functions at 2 a.m., they are all fast asleep now, & to my left is one of the many peacocktail-hued bays here, reflecting the vast red cliffs & their crowning roofs of *prinári* [Holm oak], myrtle & sage. Far above them, higher & higher, the immense rock of St Angelo rising into the air, on whose summit the old castle still is seen a ruin, just 1,400 feet above the water. It half seems to me that such life as this must be wholly another from the drum-beating bothery frivolity of the town of Corfu, & I seem to grow a year younger every hour. Not that it will last. Accursed picnic parties with miserable scores of asses male & female are coming tomorrow, & peace flies — as I shall too. Even now there are 3 families in the convent, & picnics were perceived yesterday in the valley.

As for me, I work pretty hard, & have secured drawings of this singularly lovely place — should I publish or write on Corfu, for without Palaiokastrítsa such a work would be nil. I left Corfu on Tuesday, walking here (16 miles), sending on George with beds, canteen, etc.; & he got 1 of the 2 cottages they let here to summer residents all in decent order by the evening. Yet Wednesday & Thursday were high-wind days, & unprofitable in that this is only the 3rd of the Lotus-eating kind. Tomorrow I hope to finish what I have begun here, as well as to get a good drawing of a loaded mule for my Mt Athos picture: & on the 2 or 3 next days I hope to go to Doukádes, Gardelládes & other places near here, so as by degrees to work out my Hellenic topography with fear & trembling, then return to Corfu, & remain there till the end of April, packing up & sending off — before May — the *load* of unfinished work I have gone on with through the winter, rarely consecutively, owing to the constant noise & annoyance of my life for 4 months. Set off against this, my health has regularly improved: no asthma, & the sprain gradually getting well — nerves & head, notwithstanding, suffering from local causes. It is my nature to be so completely unable to follow out my thoughts on canvass if I am the least bewildered or bothered, that chiefly for this cause I have not finished anything & I must look to a good deal of hard work in June & July in London — or if impossible there, in some far quiet lodging. And when once people here had seen these pictures — incomplete as they are — endless applications were made, although but for 1 or 2 hours, & all my days have been spoilt even by friendly & kind folk! For the setting of colours & easels, the moving of pictures, & the break-up of one's morning train of ideas cannot be done twice.

All these things considered, I am not sure of my thriving here another year, except by a different mode of acting — & I have taken the rooms I have now (being quieter than the first set) on speculation, moreover, owing to them being larger than any I could hope to get elsewhere, & more suitable in most respects. Winter health is a great matter; & if, next year, by the sale of paintings this summer, I can avoid the constant drudgery & worry of the last six months, I may be able to make more progress than of late, both in languages & in visiting the many parts of Greece which have been a dead letter to me this year for want of tin & time. We shall see. Meanwhile, ἀποστελμένα [having sent] all my pictures, I mean to go down to Lefkímo & to other spots in this island, to procure all I can of its characteristics; & then, quite at the end of May — or early in June — to come by Ancona to Turin & England, so as that by the 10th July I have a chance of seeing you.

Meanwhile, I was thinking since I came here of the Clermont house & people at Ravensdale, having been greatly interested by a book I had out, Goldwin Smith's *Ireland & the Irish*. I have heard no one speak of this but by name, nor had I seen a review of it. You alone once named it as among books you had been reading. But I should like to know if I am right in judging it as one of the most clear & good books on a difficult theme, & one written not only with knowledge but with a good & broad spirit. I suppose as he prophesies, the Anglican Church must go down — there at all events — though I never before knew the realities of wickedness through which it has been kept in its place so long. I should much like to talk over that book with you someday. I wonder if attachment among the people spreads towards such abiding solid good landlords as Dr Clermont.

A great drawback to these islands is the once a week post: there is a tension & a vacuum for 6 days — & a horrid smash of disappointment if the 7th brings nothing. And the interim is to be filled up by — what? Races & garrison balls, calls & dinners? Nay — but by abstracted study & quiet patience, the real remedies, only that, as I

Corfu Garrison races.

have before explained, these are so difficult to carry through....

I shall — or should – have a chapel of my own. Belfast Protestantism, Athanasian creeds, & all kinds of moony miracles should have no entrance there; but a plain worship of God, & a perpetual endeavour at progress (which reminds me of Tennyson's little poem, 'Will', which I have been trying to translate [into Greek] & part of which I send you). One thing, under all circumstances, I have quite decided on — ἀποφάσισα ἀκριβῶς: when I go to heaven — 'if indeed I go' — & am surrounded by thousands of polite angels, I shall say courteously, 'Please leave me alone! You are doubtless all delightful, but I do not wish to become acquainted with you. Let me have a park & a beautiful view of sea & hill, mountain & river, valley & plain, with no end of tropical foliage, a few well-behaved small cherubs to cook & keep the place clean, &, after I am quite established — say for a million or two of years — an angel of a wife. Above all, let there be no hens! No, not one! I give up eggs & roast chicken for ever!' — which rhapsody arises from a cursed infernal hen having just laid an egg under my window, & she screeches! O Lord! how she screeches & will screech for an hour! Wherefore, goodbye. No more, dear friend, for at a screech I stop. [C.F.]

21 APRIL
PALAIOKASTRITSA

Did not sleep well. Δὲν ἐκοιμήθηκα τόσον καλά, ἂν καλὰ καὶ δὲν ἐξεύρω τὸ διατί. [I didn't sleep well, even though I don't rightly know why.] Rose however at 5.40 & at 6.20 drew one more view of the castle St Angelo. Returned to breakfast at 8. After mooning about (boles all wrong) drew a mule, barrel-loaded, at the convent door: but biting fleas, & crowing cox disturbed. I have resolved to go however tomorrow — for many reasons: want of money; a feeling of imprisonment; & having come to the end of one's visit here. At 12.30 — conversed with Dr Roberts — drew on the beach, 'shadowed coves' — then at 2 walked on, filling up other outlines to 2 miles distance, returning at 4 to draw the rock scene — which took to 5.40 — when I was 'utterly outworn'. Palaiokastrítsa, beautiful as it is, wearies me as only a mass of foregrounds after the first general views are taken: tho' it is so devoted to great swells, & so un-countrylike in its ways, though so un-townlike in its position. So I go! And leaving Doukádes & Lakónes to other times. If indeed such times come — for I truly weary of Corfu.

Towards sunset, talked with Dr R. & Mrs Creyke, also with Mrs Lyall who is clever & oddly-pleasant. Mrs Creyke is fairy-like & with many charms. I do not like to see her or any doctor sitting on rox after sunset. Meanwhile a placid female dog, having brought forth 4 puppies, & they being destroyed, she now screameth & howleth. Καλόγεροι [monks] are there here, but after Sabas* & Athos how can they interest? Γευμάτισα [I dined] on boiled fowl & *anginares* [artichokes] & read Holy Land travels: I would fain see the East once more: just now ὅμως [however] I am covered with fleas, & sad. [J.]

22 APRIL
PALAIOKASTRITSA

The female dog 'owled a good deal, but as George says, *'ha compassione'* — so she was forgiven.

St Symeon, 22 April 1862 — 'all purple grays'.

    Rose at 4.30, & dressed, & packed. Breakfast at 6, &, leaving George to settle all, set off walking. Had it more extended distance, few views could be more fine than that looking to the Doukádes & Lakónes rox at early dawn. I left the Palaiokastrítsa bays & rocks & shrubs with a kind of regret: absolute regrets there are none of, nowadays. Walked on, drawing at 3 places, & at 9, near Doukádes George & the *carro* overtook me, & went on. At 11 I reached the *osteria* of the 8½ mile — but it was full, so George bought some wine & cold fowl to the shade of a nolive tree & so I lunched — a large dog μαζί [as well]. Then they went on, & I slowly — very: revelling in the heat of the day & the shadows of the olives & the grass & ferns. All along by Gouvio — & the Potamós flats, & up by Condi's house, & thru' Mandoúki, & so on to 'home' by 2.35. Where, of course, I find the rooms in perfect order but the post was closed — & a good deal of botherary from the last row & firings of pistols at Easter.
    Washed & dressed, & sat still, & wrote notes. At 7.15 George presented a dinner of roast lamb & pease — worthy [of] an alderman. A curiously active & patient fellow

is G. Kokáli. Penned out till 10. George is gone to his mounting 'ome. 10.30. *Πρέπει νὰ ὑπάγωμεν στὸ κρεββάτι.* [We must go to bed.] And so ends the Palaiokastrítsa 'outing'. [J.]

26 APRIL   Rose at 5. Set off at 6 with D. Oikonómos — hottish walking, but slow, to Kinopiástres, where I was introduced to Sig. Villetta: it is curious to remember how I sat to draw *outside* the house years ago. After sketching an outline of the pearlblue mountains, breakfast — tea, trout & eggs — was ready, & very pleasant, in the garden, below the pergola. Then I wandered about, seeking places I might draw in: certainly Kinopiástres is a lovely place. Then I called on Mr & Mrs Mexa, living in one of the Villetta Villas, & then at 12 with Villetta, & Mexa (Oikonómos went to sleep) we went in search of some pine trees — those which of old Frank Lushington & I used to walk to — but we only discovered them after a long & hot & messy walk, returning by 3 to Kinopiástres. Mexa conversed sensibly about the 'Protection'; he likes the English but cannot understand their policy — of which perhaps they have nil. At 4 we dined — all 4 of us — & very well. Oikonómos came out strongly with the *κρασὶ* [wine] — as a Zoroastrian or what not. Once in a way this sort of thing is pleasant; & anyhow Villetta's hospitality & kindness is extreme.

At 6.40 we, Oikonómos & I, slowly walked home, that very queer bird talking always, & *τόσον καὶ πόσον!* [so much and how much!] Speaking of his aristocratic Epirote mother's society, he said she never entered into his plans — «*καὶ ἐὰν τὴν λέγω ὅτι μοῦ χρειάζεται νὰ ἔχω γυναῖκα*» ['and if I tell her I need a wife'], 'she will not understand me, but rather if anything opposes me.' Very hot walk & innumerable fireflies. [J.]

27 APRIL   I returned here on the 22nd — much the better for my stay *εἰς τὴν ἐξοχὴν* [in the country]; but the place — Palaiokastrítsa — is becoming unbearable from the number of visitors & picnics, & I am glad I have *done* it. I have since been working at Grenfell's 'Philae', which had, I had thought, come to grief; but it is now turning out better than before. I am very anxious to have that, the Florence, & Athos, all pretty nearly ready by the time I get to England — say June 15th — so as to have some tin from them — of which commodity little is now left me. Bother — my mornings here now are delightfully calm & quiet & pleasant, only I have had to show pictures to several parties, bother them. The country is looking lovely, & I mean from May 1st to proceed to gather views in all the south of the island. Yesterday I was at one of the loveliest paradise places; but I had to leave & dine with a Corfiote proprietor, & was not left quiet.... The hospitality of these people is wholly beyond praise. There was some conversation of a small interest — & from men who have had for long years every feeling of regard & respect for English character & even some ties of affection. But it seems to me that even the extremist Anti-Radicals are becoming weary of the present state of things. If it is urged to them, 'Differing as you do with Dandolo etc. etc. — why do you not manifest openly a counter feeling?', they reply, 'What support

do you give us, or what inducement to do so? The increasing malignity of the press — albeit proceeding from a minority — places us more & more in jeopardy, & your protection is merely for the use of the island & not for our benefit. True, there is no truth in the more violent statements of the address, but, on the other hand, do you promote our welfare as you should? Do you not prohibit the building of houses beyond the city etc., & yet at the same time upbraid us for want of energy etc. etc.? Are there not Condi, Kandóni, etc., who would instantly build houses & hotels but that you by your fortification laws prevent them? Is there any remedy but the commencement of a wholly new city, & would you permit that? From all which, & more, we believe that you have a settled policy not made known to us, whereby you do not choose that we should thrive as a colony, but only keep us as a garrison held for your own purpose & for an indefinite time. This "indefinite" feeling — this uncertainty of state which hangs over all — is our curse, & your warmest admirers are beginning to think such protection is no real protection, & to feel that however they are opposed to the anti-English party, there is a great foundation of truth in what they say against you.'

And no doubt there is, tho' I do not join either yes or no in these discussions, except to blame the violence of the other side, & to praise Sir H. Storks, who is without doubt a most able man. The very best guarantee we could give to the Ionians that we really act for their welfare is to permit them to build an increase to their city; or if obstacles are thrown in their way by one of their party divisions, to compel an alteration in their municipal laws, or by some other mode, of which everyone knows — where there is a will there is a way. There can be no doubt that at present a restless & worrying spirit preys on all the people; nor is it to be explained — if a cession of the island is determined, tho' to take place at a distant date — why such an event is treated as impossible. If the contrary is determined on, why is a feeling of permanence not cultivated? When I see you perhaps I can say more on this matter. That the Ionians have reasons in supposing that they are to be joined to Greece is to me beyond any doubt: whether it would be good for them or not is quite another question.

The weather is perfectly enchanting now: so warm & bright always. I wish I was married to a clever good nice fat little Greek girl, & had 25 olive trees, some goats & a horse. But the above girl, happily for herself, likes somebody else.... [C.F.]

29 APRIL Fine, but misty early. Rose at 7.... Abschewed [*sic*] work, as it is impossible to do anything while so unsettled. Whereon *resolving* to send off the pictures, packed & screwed in with G.'s help all the morning 16 cases. Nice letter from Sir G. Markoran — I am to go to his home at Strongíli.... At 4.30 or 5 went up to Kandóni Hill where I drew till 5.30. Saw Mrs Wolff, but she did not come back. Home by 7.30, dined. Penned out till 10.30. [J.]

2 MAY Rose at 5 & 'packed'. Breakfast at 6.30. Set off μοναχός [alone], leaving notes at Bridge's & paper at the Sargent's, & going down to Kastrádes, where I 'conferred' 2 hats on Nikóla & poor little Harálambos — who I wish was stronger. Good old

Kandóni, 29 April 1862.

Vasilía Kokáli [George's mother]: 65.

 I walked slowly up to Aghii Deka, & drew a bit: & at 1, waited for George whom I saw coming up with the car [*sic*]: & at 1.30, had some eggs at the ξενοδοχεῖον [inn] outside Aghii Deka, during which facts, M. Grasset, & 3 French gentlemen, all fresh from Mauritius, came up. One of them knows Cockburn intimately. At 2.30 walked on, some of the most beautiful views of Corfu, & under the most beautiful phases of light & shade . . . 'to be seen'. After the turning to Stavrós, there were some novel & fine views of Aghios Mathaíos & other places — but at the 10th mile from Corfu the land grew weary & wildernessy, & at the 12th mile, when the car stopped & we were told that the few dirty ruined houses above was Strongíli horror arose.

 There was howbeit no help — so I had the things all placed in the 'Casino Markoran', but it was deadly gloomy, the more that it was heavy-cloudy & began to rain. From 4.30 to 6 I wandered with Markoran's man — he is a very dirty man — & finally drew a pretty nook of palms, olives & cypresses — for there is really nothing to call for general drawing.

 Came up at 6.30 & at 7 had a good dinner of cold lamb & pease. [J.]

Gardíki, or Palaiókastro, 3 May 1862.

But I got little or no sleep at least till 3.30: partly fleas, partly noises. However, at 5.20 rose, & G. had a regular breakfast by 6: & at 6.30 we were off — Spiro Assoníti preceding as guide. Damp & low ground, olive woods with roots but meagre arms, patches of green, & myrtle & *prinári* [Holm oak], cistus, & passed-away asphodel. There were semi-dry ditches too & a tortoise or 2, land & water. We went near Zigono — a χαλασμένο χωριό [ruined village] & by 8 reached Aghios Matthaíos, a finely placed village. The Head Police received Burr's letter joyfully, & gave me a peasant to guide me — I decided first — to Pantokrátora, a monastery high up. A very pretty & hot pull! — & welcomed with a cup of coffee & some *raki*: after which I drew on a higher point still — the view of Lefkími, Albania, & other 'islands' very beautiful, & opposite Fano & St Angelo etc. We got down to Aghios Matthaíos at 12, & then had eggs & beans at the *stathmós* [stopping place], at 1.30 set out again. The scenery is very beautiful — broken rox & superb olives, & so round the Aghios Matthaíos mountain to Gardíki, or Palaiókastro — a castle like [?]Bodeino or any 12th century gray ivied walls, but with immense olives about it. I drew on a hill till 3.30 — the long plain & sea foamy, a beautiful scene, but the vast olives are for studies not sketches, & I grew

3 MAY
STRONGILI

Stavrós,
4 May 1862.
(Section of the
painting opposite.)

Legend below boy seated at right:
Τὸ ἡσυχόν καὶ φρόνιμον
παιδίον τοῦ Σταυροῦ.
[The quiet and discrete
boy of Stavros.]

disgusted ... Returned by another route, to the δημόσιαν [public] road near Vraganiótika — & about a mile from Strongíli I sent back the Aghios Matthaíos guide with 2s. 6d. having given him his dinner also. Lud! *How* he talked — G.'s silent nature is no end of blessing. At 'home' by 5 & at 7.20 p.m. about to dine. Which that γεῦμα [meal] was surprising — curry & Ps. G.'s assiduity is untiring. Bed at 8.45. ·[J.]

4 MAY
STRONGILI

Slept vastly better — not to say well: & rose a little before 5. Plain coffee & bread the order of the day: & George & I were off before 6. A pleasant shadeful walk ... the olives *are* wonderful, the interminable perspective of the silver light-catching trunks contrasting with the deep shades on the green & fern below. Soon at Stavrós — where a perlite χωριάτης [villager] showed us to the *topos* [place] where ὅλοι οἱ Ἄγγλοι [all the English] were wont to go: & no lovelier view can be seen, so much so that I rank it first of all the distant Corfu views, as regards the seeing all & everything. At 7 therefore, with a circle of very well kept in order boys, I sat down to draw, & afterwards a 2nd & 3rd view, so that it was 1 before I left off — 6 hours of it. Then went to a *bottega*, & had some capital eggs & bread & cheese & wine: good people —

staring constantly. «Φυσικά» ['naturally'], saith G. There were some extremely handsome women & παιδιά [children]. At 2 we came down, & walked slowly, with interludes of Bertoldino & other matters. Home by sunset: this place is too damp to be out afterwards. A toughy fowl (to G.'s dismay) & new potatoes were the dinner: alas vile wine — whereby indigestion & sleeplessness. Bed by 8.45. . . . [J.]

Falla, near Strongíli, 4 May 1862.

Below Vouriatádes, 5 May 1862 — 'olives dark below — hoary above, hill — graylilac green, fields & sheep bright through olives'.

5 MAY
STRONGILI

Rose at 5 — a very sleepless & comfortless night, dogs barking etc. etc. Off with G. & Spiro Assoníti — a cloudy threatening sky. Across the olive woods — wonderful scenes of long-armed light-foliaged trees — like Calabria in 1847. But it soon poured down torrents of rain, also hail & thunder, & we stood up ¼ of an hour. But it soon abated & we walked up to Vouriatádes, apparently a dreary village & the people thereof gloomy & odious — 2 or 3 gave directions as to Ano Pavliána, but followed us — a difficult track, & one so slushy & steep I could hardly manage. However at the top is the village & Mr Charlton's house, a charming place of neatness & roses & gardens, & a γραμματέας [secretary] who soon gave me some coffee & eggs, & offered dinner later. Whereby I drew 3 or 4 times — but it was cold, & at 12.30 had eggs & wine: 3 little children, 3d. a piece, but I wrote a note to Mr C. promising him a drawing. The view over Lefkími to Paxos is beautiful. At 2.30 we went away — a morning of good luck; & came down by Kato Pavliána to a high road, & so to Vouriatádes again. Then through the olive woods — goats & sheep, & so — clouds again gathering — to Strongíli about 5 or not so late. Then it rained a good lot. And afterwards I drew from the window.

Now it is 6 & fine again. Boles is bad, & all wrong today. After all this, did the accounts with George. Feverish & unwell, nervous to a horrid degree. No sleep at all.

And (at 11.45) I fancied I heard steps, & a trying of the door: & which presently turned out a fact by a violent shake & force of the outer door — which however held — & the *ladri* [thieves] ran down the steps. So considering the bad air, & . . . my being so unwell, I ἀποφάσισα [decided] to go [to] George who awoke also, rose, & we did not go to rest again. [J.]

From 12 to 4 we walked about, G. smoking. This place, in an unfrequented spot off the road, is not good to dwell in. At 4.30 we packed — by 5.30 Spiro Assoníti was engaged to find 2 horses, whereat we packed & are off by 6 — certainly a *beautiful* vegetable valley, & full of fine bits — but ill to dwell in. I think I shall go to Lefkími as soon as possible. We were in Corfu by 9.50, at my door. . . . George, as if he had no trouble at all, made a good lunch for me at 11 — after which I slept till 5. [J.]

6 MAY
STRONGILI

At first I was rather alarmed about the 'medium' affair,* for the mere going to those impostors & the attraction of continued conversation about them does a deal of harm, when those who go to see & return to talk are people of position whose example is sheepily followed by thousands of fools — from Belgravian fools downward. But if you, Kinglake,* Wolff & others speak as plainly as you write to me, then I believe good may come of these people being visited. That they are gross impostors, 'trading' (as a good letter in the *Times* said some weeks ago) 'on the affections & credulity of mankind', I have no doubt; yet many do not think so; & it should be the part of those who are wise, & who can suffer fools gladly (which I never can) to enlighten the assy-masses who can't help themselves — God not having willed them much brains, & priests having muddled the little they have. . . .

A more gritty vexation is that I have done so little in Greek or in Greek topography this winter. Nevertheless I shall bring away the most part of this island I fancy. . . . Tomorrow I go out again to Lefkímo, & by the time I return thence I trust to hear how my pictures look at the Great International Exhibition — seeing that 2 Royal Academicians had the hanging of them, I should tremble for their fate, were not one of the Commissioners — Fairbairn — my friend. [C.F.]

7 MAY
CASA
PARAMYTHIOTTI

Fine day. Rose at 4.30. Packed. Off by 6.20. Light carriage. . . . Very clear & lovely weather. Walked on — horses resting at Strongíli. On to 19th mile, & lunched very pleasantly close to Aghia Triáda. At Lefkími by 1. Dr & Mrs Samsóni kindly folk. Coffee. Walked with them to the river. At 3.30 . . . went to Aghios Nikólas & Aghia Análipsis, but could not draw. Returned: washed: waited: wrote. The doctor came at times & talked. At 7.30 supper befell — & very pleasant too & good withal, macaroni, *triglia* [red mullet], eggs, παλαμίδα [tunny], etc. Small only boy — 15 months old. Under-doctor — Samuéllo — intelligent: student in Paris & London. At 9 I begged to go to bed, which was (apparently) clean. [J.]

8 MAY
LEFKIMI

Arkoúdillas, 9 May 1862.

9 MAY
LEFKIMI

Slept well. No fleas. G. in an anteroom. Rose 4.30. Coffee. Off 5.30, with G. & a guide Dimítri. Heavy mist on all places, plains & hills: wild paths, & flat desert-like spots; sandy walk by roadside. Inland to Aghios Prokópios — a picturesque little monastery, beautiful olives. Hills near sea, Cape Lefkími solitary. Goats & dogs. Cape Lefkími — drew. . . . Fine ravine. At monastery of Arkoúdillas by 9.30. Wonderful grove of cypresses; drew a good deal: lovely day. Lunch, & drew. At 2, after various sketches, began to go homeward. Walked down the hill by beautiful zigzags to Aghios Prokópios — a wonderfully pretty specimen of rural Greek monastery. To the sea thence, & bathed, & so by sand & hilly modulations, back to Melíkia & the Casa Kori by 6. This home & family reminds me of Abruzzi days. Dr Samuéllo dined, & nothing could be more pleasant than the whole matter — save that they asked me to eat too much. Moreover I was too tired to be as polite as I ought to be. Bed at 9.30. The doctor goes to town tomorrow. [J.]

10 MAY
LEFKIMI

Slept well, yet I think some heaviness proceeds from the air. At 5.30 (why do they put cinnamon in their coffee?) G. & I & Dimítri, a well-behaved obliging χωριάτης [villager], went out. Lovely lots of green sward & fern, with beautiful olives — characteristic bits of Lefkími scenery we passed, & so reached the cypress tuffy hill of

Lefkími, Leohório — from the chapel of Aghios Taxiárchis, 10 May 1862.

Aghios Taxiárchis by 7, or 6.30, where I drew 3 or 4 times. The cypress tree is here *amisuratamente* [immeasurably] existing; & thousands of tiny little cypress treelets peek up everywhere. At 9.30 we went 'cross country' to Aghios Nikólas where we lunched — but χωρὶς νερό [without water]. So I remain under the shade of a giant *schinus*, a lentisk lace. There is everywhere a flood of gold & green & blue. This, & the breeze, blowing freshly now & then, remind one of days in many lands before *that* knowledge came which tells us we have so little, & so much conjecture. On Swiss, & Como hills in 1837 — in the first years of Roman & Amalfi life '38–9 — the long Civitella sojourns 1839–40 — Abruzzi '43–44 — Sicily & Greece '48–49. I do not now suppose that kind of happiness can ever come back but by unexpected & unsought snatches; so I do not strive after it, nor mourn that I cannot have it. Only now & then, the whole long stream of bright past life glitters before one as it were in a distant valley, & I can seem to mark all its windings & shallows, & the lights & shadows on its far distant shores. Just now the lilac range of Albanian mountains with the few pale but defined clouds

Aghios Taxiárchis, 10 May 1862.

above, the blue sky & far deeper blue sea, the long almost blue plain of distant olives, & the still dark berryful cypresses close by — all bring back old memories. (What excessive contrast there is between the blooblooness of the sea & lilac hills, & the rich raw Sienna green of those cypresses!) Afterwards, drew twice, & then to the hill of Análipsis, & drew till 6: after which fogs begin & outdoor life is fever. This Análipsis view is the most pleasing hereabouts, & were there well-drawn figures, it would be beautiful, at sunset especially, when the mountains, by means of many detail-shadows, lose much of their wall-like form. 'Home' at 6.20 . . . [J.]

12 MAY
LEFKIMI

My 50th birthday. Rose at 4.20, off by 5.15. Long winding paths through olive groves, then dips & struggles into quite wild places, stuffed with all sorts of underwood, through old olives growing tangly all about. Frogs there were also, & rushes. A man passing, & asked the way to Spartero, said, «Διατί ἐπιθυμεῖς νὰ πηγαίνῃς στὸ χωριό μου;» ['Why do you want to go to my village?'] 'I shall not tell you.' Small miserable collection of huts, & tavern . . . & I see no fun in going back by them: so having drawn the northern distance above the last village but one — Dragótina — & great groups of vast olives higher up, we arrived at Spartero, 20 little houses scattered here & there — κατοικίες [dwellings] — & say them wretched: the people only half polite. Nonetheless there is superb scenery all about the place. We took a boy to guide us to Aghios Prokópios (the best place to pass the rest of the day in) — ever-winding paths thro'

Lefkími, 10 May 1862.

thickets, a few scared cattle, a church (in a wilderness), & thus by 10 or 10.30 reached the grove of the Holy Prokópios. Lunched & drew in the wide grove till 1: nothing but a very elaborate study of this wood — even if that — could convey an idea of this beautiful place: the quiet, warmth, & semi-shade are delightful. The elements — trees, clouds, etc., silence — ὅλη ἡ φύσις δηλαδὴ [all nature that is] — seem to have far more part with me or I with them, than mankind. After death perhaps I shall be a tree, a cloud, a cabbage or silence in the next world: but most possibly an ass. In these Prokópian holy glades are but 3 very manifold colours: the warm pale green of the floor, with long shades, the gray uniform freckle-shimmer of the roof, with dark brown gray of the supporting pillartrunx. At 1, or 1.30, into the monastery, & drew till 3 — awfully tortured by fleas, & obliged to stand in the sun all the time. As soon as I got to the sea I bathed — killing 11 fleas first. At 6 reached the Casa Kori, paid Dimítri 2 dollars, a shilling, for his day's work — he merits it well. Sat in the gallery with Dr & Mrs S. till dinner — Dr Samuéllo also. 7.30 dinner — *alquanto troppo*, & I was horribly bored by a flea. Bed by 10.15. Kindly good folk. [J.]

Costumes of Lefkími.

13 MAY
LEFKIMI
HLOMOS

50 years old. Sky rather overcast. Rose at 4.15: coffee, a dollar to old Sotíri, & then good-bye to good Dr Samsóni — a kindly man leading a hard life of work for the benefit of others. The way in which all the family adapt themselves to the unpleasantness of Lefkími is highly praiseworthy. What can I send them? . . . toys for their little boy, who I fear will die, as have some 3 before him. I have even remembered my old days in Abruzzi while here. Morning fine, & we went on to Perivóli, where I drew tho' it has few charms. Then through uncultivated wilds of olive & *prinári* etc. etc. — below Marathiás which G. says was pulled down in '18 or '19 when all the people died of the plague. (Pigs are not allowed by the *governo* to this day, on account of their disinterring propensities, throughout Lefkími.) Next was Argirádes — rather a pretty village; I decide on coming back to it, but on seeing the rough long road however to Hlomós I gave that idea up wholly. Hlomós itself is ugly, but the views there are wonderful. The wind however was so that nothing could be done out of doors. Sig. [?]Lavnarino's house, when opened by a highly morose &

unclean man, is good, but full of fleas: howbeit we must endure it for a night. No sheets — & a vast rattling of windows. Swallows twitter all around. (Little girl near Argirádes tying up great red poppies in a wreath — 1st May, quo' George: *dunque* is the Mayday festivity a Greek one!) At 3 the day is wholly gloomy & disgusting, so I drew from the window of the forlorn nasty country house — moth-eaten chairs etc. G. & I went up to the top church, Taxiárchis, & I drew a little here & there, & then returned, ordering a horse for tomorrow. No wine — no nothing.

What a night! A hurricane of wind, & a world of fleas. I walked up & down from 7, having no appetite — & unable to lie down from incessant torment by vermin all night long. [J.]

14 MAY

At 4.30 got coffee, & at 5.30 set off — man & horse. Of course, the very best view from Hlomós is just beyond the village: it was however too windy to draw. We soon got to Messonghí & later passed Capodístria's house (where Frank & I once landed, & whence walked back). Tired, sleepless & cross: scirocco no end. Was angry at G.'s account of the peasants in that murder affair,* & spoke harshly. He also was angry — having a bad eye & being tired. So I set off alone, & walked straight into Corfu — reaching home at 10.45. [J.]

18 MAY

Always scirocco — thick & warm, not windy. Rose at 5. Later, packed all my books... Tremedously oppressive scirocco all day — no mountains visible. *Cui bono* this remaining here to draw? The *Marathon* is to come tomorrow. [J.]

19 MAY

Yesterday I went to church. Lord! Lord! what an idiotic sermon did good Craven preach about the next world, as how many excellent men believed that we should not recognize anyone in the future state, *because*, if we were to do so, we should *also* perceive our friends — alas! great numbers of them! tortured in the gulf of fire below — as it is plain from Dives twigging (he did not say 'twig') 'Lazarus in heaven above'. Why are men allowed to talk such nonsense unsnubbed in a wooden desk, who would be scouted in an ordinary room?...

Wonderful to relate, I have packed up, & decided to go by the Liverpool steamer *Marathon*, which is expected tomorrow — by Zantë & Malta — & to England about the 10th or 12th I suppose.... So here's for the island valley of Avilion... [C.F.]

20 MAY

Rose at 5, same scirocco. Packed. Wrote many letters. Got ticket. Paid G. 3 months' wages — & Paramythiótti 2 months' rent. Good old Vasilía came — & afterwards Spiro. Got £40 from Taylor. Yanni Kokáli also came, to whom I gave a good knife & pair of scissors. Their mother was sad enough, or to use George's few words, *non poteva parlare* [she was not able to speak]. At 3 G. made me dine on pigeons & pease, & had it not been for a great rage that I fell in about paying the Zincaro, who would not send in his bill, all had gone smoothly. '*Anch' io*' — said G. — '*me arrabio*' ['I, too, am furious']; & that is saying much. At 6 we went on board the *Marathon*, a famous large screw

177

Liverpool steamer, & I had a cabin to myself. George soon went back — poor fellow: doubtless one of the truly best men I have ever known.

We are to start at 12 — or 1. After the long dreadful scirocco the mountains are really clearing, & becoming divine: somehow the beauty of these Epiros hills is enough for one life... [J.]

21 MAY The sun was not yet risen on the Casa Paramythióti when I woke, & we were leaving Corfu — going out north of Vido about 4.15. The mountains were lovely but I slept again till 7 — then rose. How gladly one would linger in the beautiful calm & opal colour of that coast, & yet to pass months in it would seem hardly to compensate for the pain of the weary island prison life.... [J.]

'... much the bird of the English'.

NOVEMBER 1862 – JUNE 1863

At 2 off Sassona, & at 3 Linguetta; & thence awful rolling & misery till 7.30, when we got into smooth water off the end of Corfu. On deck, with the De Veres & Mr Baillie — the 'extinct Duke'* — & watched all the points as we entered the narrow channel. Breakfast, after which we were off Vido, & anchored at 11 — a 53 hours' voyage, & happy is it a no worse one. George soon came aboard (not well apparently) & we went ashore. No trouble with the *Dogana*, & at 12 in Casa Paramythiótti. How very queer! Unpacked & arranged till 4. Then called on Stockly & Luard — but Luard is at the Creykes — on the Sargents, & dine at Carters. [J.]

23 NOVEMBER

Rose at 6.30. Breakfast, as exactly as possible as of old — ἔχομεν μεγάλην τάξιν [we have a strict regime]. Afterwards called on the De Veres, Cravens, Luard (who, poor fellow, is ill & going home), Mr Baillie, wrote name at Palace, Taylor, Boyds, & had hair cut — all by 12. After that, bothered & arranged room etc., but it poured with rain. Hired a piano; & so at 4 — it was too wet to walk with Mr Baillie though it was a little less rainy — walked to Kastrádes, & meeting with Sir C. Sargent, with him for an hour or so. He is absolutely violent against Storks . . . Returned at 6 to dine — as usual well, with George's good care: stewed beef, soup, potatoes & sausages etc. — & fussle bustle at the window when more violent rain began, & George opened it: in came a robin — πολὺ ὄρνις Ἄγγλων [much the bird of the English]. . . . [J.]

24 NOVEMBER

Rose at 7. Fine — i.e. no rain — but gray (& after all the demonstrations of the moon I believe we are not at fine weather yet). The contents of the 2 boxes of yesterday I arranged before breakfast. And afterwards, began to draw outlines of drawings 'to be made' — to the amount of 30! . . . At 2.30 I set off, straight on end, along the ancient road, up to Kinopiástes . . . Walked back by 6. George's dinner was pleasant, & welcome. . . . My piano is a blessing. The waves plash, plash, but I think we shall have more rain. Up to now — 10 — I have written out a lot of words from A. P. Stanley's *Eastern Church*. But must now go to bed. [J.]

26 NOVEMBER

Day fine, but cold, & clouds at times. Very poorly — ill. Cough & asthma violent. But I got to church, where Clark preached an excellent sermon. I was however in great pain all through. Came home & wrote to C. Fortescue at times — at times awfully ill with violent cough, headache & asthma. Took quinine, jujubes, squills, blackcurrant lozenges & specacucumber — 'in the multitude'. At 3.30 walked with Sir C. Sargent to One Gun Battery, struggling to keep above water. Done up when I got home at 5.30, but fought out the battle, dressed, & to the De Veres. Miserably ill at first, but got better about 9. . . . De Vere is a delightful fellow, & Mrs De V. a simple-hearted duck. Home by 10.30, ill enough, yet better than this morning. Hot water etc. [J.]

30 NOVEMBER

179

31 NOVEMBER I myself only arrived here on the 23rd. . . . I *didn't* 'go pretty straight to Corfu' — *au contraire*, the road being broken up by torrents near Nice, I was obliged to go in a steamer to Genoa. (There was such a fat cardinal on board, & didn't I get likenesses of him under the table!) Then I went to Ancona, but the Italian boats were postponed for a month, & so I had to wait for the small Trieste boat, which, coming, could not start for bad weather. If I had not had my rooms & drawings at Corfu I should have given up going — & suffered so horribly in the passage that I do not know if this won't be the last time of these long journeys. . . . Of course I found George & the house all right, & next morning the exact supply of bacon, 2 eggs & 3 pieces of dry toast as if I had never gone away. The weather, *intanto*, has been constantly raining–cum–gleams & with vast thunderstorms. But it seems to be taking up now. But in the meantime, I caught a very bad cold on Friday night — coming from the Palace ball — & all yesterday my 'bronchial asthma' was very bad indeed. Today too I am very far from otherwise than downright ill — & fear fever as well as other bothers. Can't go to church — which may be put down to Dr Colenso* or not.

Through the week I have prepared many beginnings of water-colour drawings, & shall not touch oils till January. Whether I shall have success in selling the subjects time will show . . . I have also been going on with my long-projected illustrations of Tennyson, so there is work enough cut out. Concerning this place, its beauty is, if possible, greater than before. The Lord High has asked me to a ball, & to dine on Friday next. Folks here — the natives — think of nothing else but ὁ διάδοχος τῆς Βασιλείας τῆς Ἑλλάδος [the heir to the Kingdom of Greece]. . . . I can't write consecutively for phits of coffin. . . .

All Greece seems voting for Prince Alfred;* & could that happen, the very best salve & guarantee for future peace & former ills would happen: but I fear it can't. Only, I suggest, let Prince Alfred rush here & be suddenly crowned (your Government disowning it like the Nice & Savoy affair) & who can alter it? Thereafter, too, guarantees might then be given to Turkey for behaviour etc.: I half suspect it will end so. . . . Of society — more another thyme. Of balls — of moons — of fish & other vegetables — & of all future & past events as things may be. I have got a piano. Also a carpet. Also a tame redbreast; also a hearthrug & two doormats. . . . I am beginning to cough again. Goodbye. . . . Tea & broth abound. . . . Here we hear that should Prince Alfred finally be elected, & then be refused by England, Gladstone is likely to be the next favourite! Fancy Mrs G. Queen of Greece! I shall write to Mr G. & ask him to make me Πρῶτος Ζωγράφος [Head Painter] & Grand Peripatetic Ass & Boshproducing Luminary forthwith. [C.F.]

2 DECEMBER Rise thoroughly poorly & chilly & depressed to a horrible degree. Worked at 5 of the 30 drawings. Nervous irritation horrible all day. Had some lunch at 1. At 2 came a note from Colonel Wynne, putting off the dinner at the R.A. & R.E. mess & saying that Vernon died last night. Poor old Granville Vernon! Brought 8 of the 30 drawings into a 2nd stage. But at 4 came Napoleone Zambelli & says an officer has committed a

horrible suicide: poison first, then cut his throat. Can this be Edward Vernon? N.Z. stayed some time; he seems really to think Prince Alfred may become King of Greece. Did not go out. 2nd note from Colonel Wynne: the funeral is at 8 tomorrow, which I suppose means at the Citadel — & with the cough I can hardly go. . . . George's 4 or 5 months of idleness are bad for him, & this year must be the last of it. Moreover, I have thought all day long that travel *must* be given up. At times I have a dreadful vacancy of mind which is horrible. Just now — 8.15 — I am better. [J.]

3 DECEMBER

Having so lately written to you, you will be surprised that I send another letter so soon. But it is on a miserably sad subject . . . Vernon died here on Monday night, & was buried this morning at 8 . . . One great blessing is the poor fellow was quite mad, & could only have lived as a lunatic or idiot.

He was on parade on Monday as usual. But it was observed that he was eccentric & restless. After the parade he went to the Colonel, & said he had something dreadful on his mind, but could not as yet tell him what. About 3 p.m. he sent his servant for some eggs into the town, & then went out & wrote some incoherent cheques & orders for money, for large sums, & with the addition, 'be quick for I am to be hanged at 4 p.m.' & 'I am mad'.

At 3.30 he went to Colonel Wright & to his horror told him 'he was to be hanged at 4, as he had committed s⎯⎯ with a dog'. He then went to his room, & a discussion was immediately held as to the propriety of shutting him up at once under restraint. But while this was occurring, before 4 p.m., his servant returned & found his door locked, & blood running below the door — on breaking open which the unfortunate Vernon was found with his throat cut on each side. He was sensible, & got into bed; but on the surgeon's saying, 'the wound is not fatal', he said, 'I have taken care of that, & have eaten corrosive sublimate & sugar of lead.' The stomach pump was used, but to no effect. It was after found he had taken enough corrosive sublimate to kill 20 men. He nevertheless lingered in extreme agony till 9 p.m. On his brain a tumour was found, so that there was at once a verdict of 'insanity'. He spoke of some papers — & some were found — all full of the frightful delusion he was a prey to. I have these details from Baring* & others who know them. There seems no doubt that the constant drinking of spirits brought on the disease, partly if not wholly. The stomach was entirely burned away by the corrosive sublimate, so that his tortures must have been too dreadful to think of. [C.F.]

1862
[DATE UNKNOWN]

. . . But you will expect me to say something about myself, & that . . . is the hardest go of all. For, firstly, I am less & less interested in myself, having come to regard the remainder of life as so much time to be used up to the best of my power — & then the end. And, secondly, there is really so little to say that I do not know where to begin . . . [H.H.]

4 DECEMBER

Finish, but gleamy & cloudy at times. Slept rather better, & rose at 7.30. . . . Drew at

181

some 6 or 7 of the 30 drawings from 9 to 5, broken by lunch & by half an hour of pleasant De Vere's visit. Did not go out. Dined at 7. Before & after a little of all things. Translated a page of Leake's *Morea*. Did a little Homer; & after dinner, to my surprise, actually penned out a whole Palaiokastrítsa drawing. Poor George has a dreadful cold, & went to bed at 9. I now go, at 10.30. An odd routine of life, but καλά [good] if only one be occupied. [J.]

Corfu from Kastrádes, showing the monastery of St Theodore the Tiro, 6 December 1862.

6 DECEMBER   A day not wholly without discomfort, yet one to be thankful for. Rose at 7.20, George — ill of cold — calling me. Arranged, but slightly, 30 other drawings, & measured all of them & the previous 30, so as to decide if I shall send for frames or not. This took me to 11 or 12. Then I walked out to get the outlines for 2 or 3 of my drawngs more accurately — πλέον ἀκριβῶς. Drew till 2 p.m. by the Casino gate, thanks to the cold very uninterruptedly. After that, drew again near Análipsis, & walking slowly along the Battery road to get my 4th drawing, lo! Colonel Bowen! So we fraternized & went back. A quiet amiable man — & how long is it since, at Lord Coventry's, I used to see him: 1838. Leaving him I returned & drew my last sketch, & so came back by 4.30 . . . Voice failing, but on the whole, since the cessation of rain, I am wonderfully in better health today — 'more well' indeed than I have yet been since I came. Came back by 5 & found 4 *Daily Telegraphs*. But by the time I had 'cleaned myself' Stefanízzi [the Greek teacher] came. An hour's lesson — came to 7. I don't know if I gain or not much. Then dinner, short & quickly despatched. But it was 8.30 or 8.45 before I had done, & 'what with one thing & t'other' I am unable & unwilling to begin to pen out laboriously. So I have written this, & am going to bed — & indeed it is 10.30. The waves break, break — & the quiet of this house after last year! [J.]

Did not sleep well, but only towards morning — 6 or 6.30 — got real sleep. But rose at 7.30 & immediately after breakfast & hearing George read, worked at the smaller 30 Tyrants till 4, carrying 15 of them on a stage. Then I thought it better to go out than always to work. So I walked out . . . by the Parga road, & back. What colour! . . . Home by 5.30. At 6 Stefanízzi. He is impatient, & though a learned man not so good a teacher as poor Papadópoulos. Dined at 7.15. A small fowl. From 8 to 10

12 DECEMBER

Corfu from Kastrádes, a worked-up water-colour of the sketch opposite, dated 1863.

penned out part of the large Palaiokastrítsa drawing. Spiro's boy is dying. It is very sad how this good family suffer. [J.]

Colder & less sun, dry. Worked at the smaller 30 Tyrants. An odd life, never going out. George returns at 1 or 2, having been going for doctors. Spiro's hand is better, & the child after 6 days has opened its eyes & has had some milk. I wish it may live — blind wish, but natural. Day clouded at 4 & became darky, & I was tired. So at 4.30, wonderful to say, I left off work for half an hour & played on the piano. George had gone out for a doctor for the little boy — did not come in till 5.15, & then angry, since 'Serno' the doctor had refused to go for a dollar, & wanted a carriage paid also. Beast. Finally he is to meet Koskino at Spiro's at noon tomorrow — the 3rd doctor not liking to give a medicine to the child on his own hook. Φαίνεται [it seems], the doctors having left the boy so completely, & he having lived in spite of them, they may do no good now by returning. Spiro is better. Greek from 5.20 to 7. Dined & read papers. Penned out 8.15 to 10.15. Calm is the night. Whatever may be ahead, we had no such calm quiet last year I trow. [J.]

18 DECEMBER

22 DECEMBER ... Opinion seems general that the 7 Islands are to be given up, & a kind of dismay prevails. [J.]

25 DECEMBER A merry Christmas day — τῶν ὁποίων [of which] this is my 50th. Wonderful beauty of early morning, Salvador nearly crimson, Likoúri all snow. It was almost impossible to leave the open window, so glorious & pure & bright was all. Nevertheless, πρέπει νὰ δουλεύσῃ ὁ ἄνθρωπος [man has to work]. So after breakfast & hearing George read (Spiro's boy, I fear, will die after all, poor people), I drew till 2. Then, making some letters for darling little Mary De Vere, I walked out at 2.30, to Potamós & beyond — the poor dwarf Dionýsios — & so on by the Potamós flats — how wonderfully lovely was the distance — homeward about 5. Entering, near the Porto Reale, a great crowd, all very merry & 'zito'ing — the English *sopratutto* [above all]. And, as night came on, a general illumination. But why? As yet there is nothing sure. At 7 to De Veres. Mary De Vere well again. Later, singing. Utterly friendly — & I think the pleasantest Christmas day I have passed for many a day. Home by 12. [J.]

28 DECEMBER The same Paradise weather. Long as I have seen these mountains yet their beauty today was so wonderful that I fancy it new ... George says the little boy is dying, nearly cold. They have taken him away & have gone to Kastrádes. Poor Spiro — how unwise to have gone to San Rocco at all. Not that I think the poor child would have lived anyhow, yet these removals have given more trouble. George said, very truly, '*Si l'uomo far male senza rimedio all'uomo, e male davvero; ma quando Iddio far male all'uomo, anche senza rimedio, z'e ancora questo di buono, che Iddio lo fece il male e Iddio e giusto, cosa z'e di bene dentro.*' ['If man does something bad to man and it cannot be remedied, it is truly bad; but when God does something bad to man, and it too cannot be remedied, there is none the less this good in it, that it is God who has done it, and God is just, so there will be good in it.'] [J.]

30 DECEMBER George came in at 8, just before breakfast, saying, '*Spiro e venuto a piangere con me: moreva il picolo in sue braccie alle sei ore stamattina. Venite a vederlo.*' ['Spiro has come to weep with me: the little boy died in his arms at 6 o'clock this morning. Come and see him.'] So I went, poor fellow. [J.]

31 DECEMBER Gray & damp, & at times a few light showers; but warm & pleasant — a 'nice summer day' στὴν Ἀγγλίαν [in England]. Drew — uncertainly — the smaller 30 Tyrants, Pisa, etc. They are an odd sort of drawings, in as much as they recall vividly other places & times, yet have no 'upward aspiration' as vorx of hart. Possibly they may be all unsold. Nevertheless these 60 *must* be done, even if to be unsold.

At 3.30 walked to One Gun Battery to make the annual traditional sketch. Saw heaps of people — that round a bore always because of this. Also His Excellency, who stopped & was amiable: it has to be admitted, his manner is always delightful. ...

George has buried the little boy today, & he is calmer now, not so awful cross.

Poor people, it is a sad close of the year for them. Penned out the last of all the 30 drawings made at Palaiokastrítsa in the spring. So for once we have our drawings penned out in the year they were made. And now — I go to bed. (George has been sawing a new lot of wood at intervals, to save a professional sawyer — cost 8*s*.) 'The year is going: let him go.' Yet, though I do think this 1862 has been better than 1861, I wish 1863 may be far better. [J.]

1 JANUARY

Whether I shall get to Palestine in the Spring to finish my tour there, goodness gracious only knows. If not, I shall get to the other islands & bring out some work on the whole 7* in the Autumn. Nothing can be lovelier than this place, & although there is a good deal of variable weather, no severe cold has yet occurred. And then the exquisite beauty of the loaded orange trees & the never-ending grace of the olives are for a landscape painter a constant source of delight. A great blessing too to me is always to have light, & this winter the house I live in is perfectly quiet (except a piano well played by the Italian Consul below me). Everybody is very amiable & hospitable to me, but I lead a quiet life as I can, being strongly convinced that a regular application to some kind of self-improvement by way of work is more successful to ensure comfort than any great variety of social fuss. Wherefore I live like a clock: dining out regularly on Sundays always — as I send my servant home on that day & cease from cookery, & I also dine out on Tuesdays, & Saturdays if asked. On Mondays, Wednesdays & Fridays I have a Greek master & pen out my sketches till midnight. Thursdays someone or other comes & dines with me. And all the day — 7 hours daily — goes in hard work, for if I don't work now I can't bye & bye have my excursions. Endless yachts are here with unmitigated swells — Dukes & Earls — & other peerful travelling parties; but not having anything in my study as yet, they don't greatly benefit me at present. [L.W.]

1 JANUARY

Very little work — 1 or 2 of the smaller 30 Tyrants advanced a stage. At 12 or 1 came the young Duke of St Albans . . . The Duke bought Marathon, Athens, Athos, Corfu & Olympus, to my surprise. He is still shy, as at Rome, but far more manly than then, & very unaffected & pleasant. . . . [J.]

3 JANUARY

A busy day. Sent George to buy a lampshade, leave a book at the Palace, see to a sideboard for sale, pay 1 or 2 bills, & get dinner for this evening. Meanwhile, I drew hard all day, getting all the smaller 30 Tyrants into another stage, till 4.15, when I walked out a little way . . . [J.]

6 JANUARY

George tells me Christos [George's brother] nearly died last night. [J.]

7 JANUARY

Very warm & fine all day, light clouds. But I did not go out at all. *Anzi*, I worked hard at the Spezzia, Constantinople, Baalbec, & 2 Dead Sea drawings of the larger 30 Tyrants. Hard & odious work, but it *must* be done. . . . Christos remains the same, only weaker. It seems Spiro has taken the rooms at San Rocco for 2 or 3 or 5 years. It is very dreadful-sad for the rest of this poor family, but, as George says, Spiro is *padrone*. If the miseries of this family were in 'high life', *what* a novel might be made; but being as they are, who cares? Their steadfast helping each other will last   if other world there be — beyond this. [J.]

11 JANUARY Should not . . . impudence & ignorance be represented in white ties? Why should Craven — preaching from a text about Moses, 'your sins will find you out' — declare that not taking the Holy Sacrament would *certainly* make a man miserable here, & *probably* hereafter? Yet poor Craven, though a sad goose, is a good & laborious man, while his wife resembles the mother of the milky herd & produces an ecclesiastical baby regularly every 10 months. I shall ask him to dine with me on Thursday next. . . . Bye the bye — talking of fools — there is an old man here partly so by nature — partly by drink — a seafaring man who has formerly been in the Balearic Isles. He has taken a kind of monomaniac fancy to my Nonsense Book, & declares that he *knew personally* the Aunt of the Girl of Majorca! I hear it is more than humanity can bear to hear him point out how exactly like she is, & how she used to jump the walls in Majorca with flying leaps! . . .

Concerning the concession of the Isles, I do not see that it could be done till there be a certainty of a solid & strong government in Greece, which amounts to saying it can't be done now. Yet it seems to me, that could the English Government get the other powers to agree that such a definite arrangement should be made whenever the proper time arrives, a positive statement of this sort may do much to make governing here more easy, the principal cause of their botheration being thus removed. Surely they might govern them without a parliament here at all, on the grounds that the fate of the islands would be settled, & only a question of time as to when carried to an ultimatum or τέλος [end]. Wolff is not yet come. Μοῦ φαίνεται [it seems to me] a secretary who is away 9 months out of 12 is not a very requisite functionary. In fact Storx is more a ruler than any I have known here, & the manner of the Judges' dismissal* is, as far as I can see, the only error of his sway of 3 or 4 years. . . . The weather is at present lovely & the views over the harbour are of the most clipfombious & ompsiquillious nature. . . . Here's somebod a nokking at the dolorous door. I must stop. [C.F.]

14 JANUARY . . . At times I say, would I had been educated. But that is folly. Far better to work than regret. [J.]

15 JANUARY The same perfect weather. Hardly a cloud in all the sky: every crag & wrinkle of Salvador, every gull & goose, every sail & boat, reflected clear & calm in the bright sea from 7.30 to 6 p.m. It is not possible to imagine greater beauty of nature. A contrast to this is the utter weariness of employ — these 60 drawings. Shall I or shall I not be able to get through them? Anyhow, I worked at nos. 11 & 12 of the smaller

Tyrants, & also 13. But the prospect of not completing them by February is really dispiriting. Never say die. . . . [J.]

16 JANUARY

. . . The state of inner man today has been always tossing to & fro. The beauty & loveliness *out* of doors, the ugliness *in*: & a kind of serene happiness not usual here — yet as it were impertinent, for cause there is none for it. Ball at Palace tonight, but I go not. [J.]

17 JANUARY

. . . Worked at nos. 15, 16, 17 & 18 of the smaller 30 Tyrants — slow process, but persisted in as I didn't think it was in me to do. Did not go out at all. . . . The belief really seems that the English go hence & soon. [J.]

19 JANUARY

An unco' miserable day. Got *no* sleep — violent tempest, & a window open about 2 a.m. George up, & all sorts of fuss. Awful wind all day — awful. . . . Utterly unwell: indigestion & asthma. Worked a little at the smaller 30 Tyrants . . . The wind so awful I thought the windows must come in, & prepared to go to the next room, but the wind fell. . . . [J.]

25 JANUARY

Very perfect lovely weather. . . . Walked by the half Potamós round & back by Condi Lane & Mandoúki — sauntering by Kastrádes till 6. At 7.30, Palace.

Dinner good & pleasant, but I was shy & queer, by degrees better, & the evening was on the whole pleasant. Talked a good deal with Evelyn Baring.

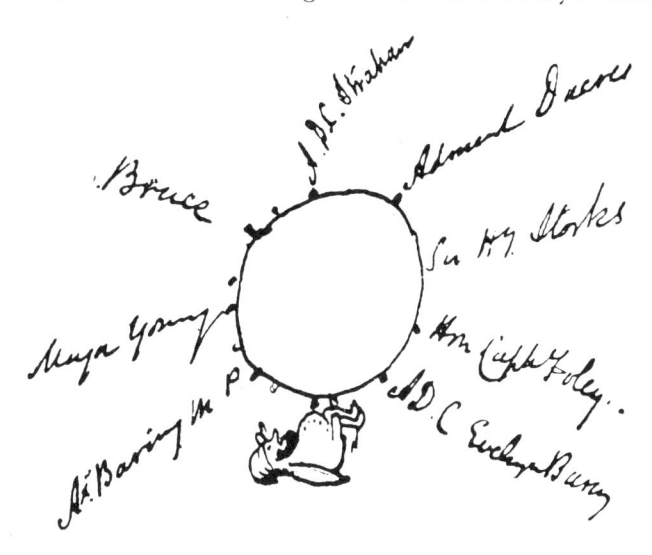

A 'paradigmatical illustration of . . . Sunday's dinner.'

> . . . What a lovely night.
> Bloo vos the waters, bloo the sky —
> Seem'd like a notionung an eye. [J.]

187

28 JANUARY   Calm & brightish all day long. To me this whole winter seems Paradise . . . [J.]

30 JANUARY   Same lovely weather. Finished no. 11 & nearly no. 12 of the larger 30 Tyrants. But worked ill & interruptedly, expecting letters by the mail. Came letters from 5. . . . What with reading letters, & thinking thereon, I could not work well any more, & at 4.30 walked out . . . returning by 6.15. The moonlight & calm were certainly amazingly lovely. Stefanízzi 6.15 to 7.15. But I am uneasy. George was out until just before I came back, & his manner was 'vastly uncivil'. He has some bother I do not know of, & goes again to Kastrádes. Meanwhile I penned out from 8.15 to 11.15, when he returned, but very sulky & queer, & I see him a good deal altered, poor man, in many ways. [J.]

31 JANUARY   Same Paradise weather. Worked at 11, 12 & 13, all of which I finished; but no. 11 is a long & tiresome affair: Spezia with foreground vines. So — January is nearly gone, & I must say I have never passed one so serenely for many many years. Something is to be put down to the better climate, somewhat to the better health, somewhat to less anxiety about beastly money, somewhat to a reaction from the sorrow from dear Ann's going, but I believe most of all to the better state of the 'demon', or rather to his greater absence. . . . Out came poor George with his woe, concerning his son Nikóla, whose master shuts up his school continually, & N. only goes & plays with other boys & don't go home. My good Souliote, I should think, is not a manager of children — but I dare say Nick is a pickle. George is going to Kastrádes & says N. is to come to a school here. I shall pay somewhat more of his schooling, for attention to the life of a child at that age is all in all. (O bother the cats! also the mice!) How quiet is this house! What a contrast to the misery of last year. [J.]

1 FEBRUARY   . . . The dislike of 'Greex' is singularly futile & weary as a subject of converse. Nor is good Mrs De Vere able to keep out of that current of pride & folly — good as she is — entirely. [J.]

1 FEBRUARY   As for me, I may say thankfully that no month of January in all my life has gone so happily as this, by constant work, & by tolerable health, & by the everlasting calm & loveliness of the weather. I always burn 2 fires, because sitting motionless 7 or 8 hours a day requires that; but I generally have an open window, & the gorgeousness of the mountains has been daily most wonderful. The winter seems all gone for the present, though the Equal-noxious gales will doubtless come in disgustable force. Meanwhile, my large stock of water-colour drawings will be done this week: unluckily my frames have not come out, so I must nail them against the walls. . . . I trust to sell these & still to go to Palestine, unless indeed the Islands shall be given up all at once — no probable event. As far as my wits go, it seems to me that the present move is to enforce public recognition of a distinct principle, viz., that when Greece is established, the end of our control here is at hand. But that it should cease yet, or until a firm government

is put in our place, seems to me very improbable.

    Alack! the summer is going! The wind is going round to the north, & there will be a fuss, tempest, & the golden moon will cease . . . [C.F.]

2 FEBRUARY

Same lovely glory weather. Rose unwell — stomach upset. Finished nos. 14 & 15, so two thirds are done of this awful job. But I was ill & restless & depressed . . . I am weary, O how weary of all things. Had the 'showroom' cleaned out, perhaps to put up these drawings by nail, for the frames do not seem likely to come & I wish now I had not ordered them but had fixed £5 for the drawings each. . . . Scarlet fever among the children here is awful. [J.]

4 FEBRUARY

Absolute glorious calm & clearness all day. Rose at 6.30, & breakfast 7.30, & shut up house & off with George at 8.20, arriving at Virós about 10.15. There we stayed all day, I drawing 5 times, large & small. But the magnificent colour of these dells of orange & lemon trees, with the grayer olive & amethyst hills, are inimitable & wondrous. It was a

Virós, 4 February 1863, 2 p.m.

189

little too cold to be pleasant though. All the peasantry are so civil & agreeable in manner. At 4.30 we walked to the brow of the hill overhanging Giannéta's garden, & then back through Virós. It was now dark, but the moon did not rise till 6.15 — a long narrow unbroken column of golden light, only just at the shore ripply at the edges. George had a good dinner of cold mutton & hot potatoes & sausages, which with Kefalónian wine made a good 'repast' . . . I sat, reading Finlay,* till 10. After drawing from nature, one can hardly work at mechanical stuff — so I penned out nil. [J.]

7 FEBRUARY At night the wind was high, & especially at 3 a.m., when it was hurricanious. But at 7 it was the same gorgeous brilliant calm as ever in these days. Wonderful! Drew at nos. 26 & 27 all day, which I finished — & almost no. 28. So that this terribly wearying incubus nears its end. I was wrong to begin so large a fixed duty, but having begun it I was right to carry it through (not that it is carried through yet, however). . . . [J.]

8 FEBRUARY The evening before, a man, after growling at all 'Greeks' with the contemptuous annoyance of an Anglo-Saxon, spoke as bitterly as he could of a nice young Englishman — an officer — married to a really nice Greek girl: 'He was ceasing to be English entirely, & becoming Greek altogether.' 'But how?' said I. And after obliging my man to confess that Captain ——— was as good-tempered, as attentive to his duties, as fond of exercises, as regular at church, etc. etc. etc., as before he married, he began to get cross, & at last grumbled out, 'Well then! I'll tell you what he does! He breakfasts *à la fourchette* at 11 or 12 — & if you can say a man is an Englishman who does that, the devil's in it.' . . . We are becoming convinced that we are a-going to go, but when, we wot not. On Friday, perhaps the last ball given by the last Lord High came off — & I *ought* to have gone but didn't. (Lord! how I hate the bustle & lights & fuss of 'society' — social in reality as is my nature, not gregarious. Geese, swine, gnats, etc., are gregarious.) . . .

My water-colour drawings are all done but 2 — a really remarkable spot of energy: tho', by reason of sitting still & poking to see them my neck has grown longer & my body fatter, & I am like to this — . . . My plans are still unsettled . . . I think I shall pantechnichize for a good long time — & go about wandering as it were like a tailless baboon. Athens does not appear to me to be a bad place to stick in . . . I can't tell yet, but I think this year will see a change in my life, if so be I live — for I don't look to do that very long . . . [C.F.]

10 FEBRUARY . . . Finished the 2 last of the 60 Tyrants, & many of the tracings. So that, absolutely, the whole 60, & nearly all the tracing of the lot, have taken me 63 days, though I have not always worked equally. A singular spotch of energy. And some of them are good drawings in their way. . . . [J.]

11 FEBRUARY . . . After breakfast, finished all the tracing before noon, & then began to colour the penned-out sketches which I have done since I came back this season. . . . There is a lull

in Greek, but one can't do all at once. At present I think of other paintings also. How quiet is this house! The exquisite playing of the Consul's wife below the only variety for silence. George also is silent & writes. [J.]

19 FEBRUARY

Same wonderful weather, but cold. Rose 7.30, better but unwell. At 9 Sir H. Storks (& Strahan) came. It was a pleasure to show the 60 drawings to him — such interest & intelligence. Moreover he bought 2, so 12 out of the 60 are gone. . . . Worked at the Ponte Pelissier piny ponderous perilous painting. . . . [J.]

21 FEBRUARY

. . . The narrow, sad, circular, bitter Island-life bother breaks out even in so good a woman as Mrs Boyd. The only real way to live here or elsewhere is to make interests, either internal or external, wholly unconnected with the place. . . . [J.]

22 FEBRUARY

Rose at 7.15 & went to church. Talked with Clarke on Colenso. Irritated by his sermon, on the old ridiculous Lot's wife story. Why must he say that non-communicants have some crimes or what nots which prevent their joining their fellow Christians? I am conscious of none, & only always refrain because I will join no church intimately whose dogmas are so loathsomely blasphemous as ours in the Athanasian creed. 10.30 to 1.30 went mostly in drawing numerals for little Mary De Vere, which I then took her: she is a darling little girl. . . . Return to change shoes, & then thence again & with Sargent & Wolff to Potamós, & back by the flats by 6. These 2 men bore me as seeing nothing whatever in the landscape; moreover they jaw, & dispute, & bore. However, we get on pretty well. Day most brilliant, but sadly cold. At 7.30 to the Palace. Evening livelier than at times. But a little too much dirt. Would one were away in $\dot{\epsilon}\lambda\epsilon\upsilon\theta\epsilon\rho\iota\alpha$ [freedom] 'o somewhere!' . . . [J.]

23 FEBRUARY

Same wonderful weather. Rose unwell. But I said, 'bother these difficulties'. So at 9 I went to Taylor's. Then came back to work. Worked at *new* Philae. At 10.30 came Foffy Kourkouméli & Fizzy [Wolff's son] & stayed a time. At 2, I walked by the Condi Lane & Potamós flats to that beautiful view I have so long intended to draw, & there I remained till 5, when I cut across to the Potamós road & drew again till 5.30, then home by 7. . . . [J.]

24 FEBRUARY

Began to work at the oil Porto Trescoglie. But Lady Wolff & F. Kourkouméli came at 10.30 & stayed a time; & when they went came Professor Ansted,* from Sir H. Storks, to know about the island's geography. Willing to do all I could . . . Found all the 60 frames arrived & took them out. . . . [J.]

26 FEBRUARY

Same absolute Paradise weather. Passed all day in undoing & cleaning the new 60 frames, unnailing the 14 already fixed (of the old ones), & arranging & nailing all the 60 drawings in the new frames. Afterwards measuring & knocking nails in the 'show-room', & hanging 1 side entirely, & a 2nd partly. . . . It was 6.15 when I left off work, &

Govíno [Gouvia] Road, 23 February 1863, 4 p.m. (Lear mistakenly put the date of 24 February.)

George was horribly cross, *Quaresima* [Lent] having obstructed his ways. At 7 Professor Ansted came, but dinner not till 7.30; howbeit it was very good. The professor is pleasant in some ways — most ways, but he was not very well, & possibly was 'ill at ease'. He looked over many sketches, but although pleased with them he despairs of reproducing them &, like Mrs Leake, advises 'relinquishing that idea'. If he does too much here he will be ill. I do not see that I can go out tomorrow as I wished as well as finish the 'exhibition' rooms. . . . [J.]

27 FEBRUARY   A day altogether upset & nil. Hung the 60 pictures, knocking nails etc. etc. till 12 or 1. Then did nothing, being ill & cross. At 4 drew Vido from Mandoúki. At 7.30 to the Palace — Sir H. Storks has asked me today & on Sunday — *de trop, selon moi*. 'Let us alone.' [J.]

1 MARCH   About the 20th I finished the last of the 60 drawings, all of 10 or 12 guineas each in price, & last week the frames came, & then, after two days' insertion of the drawings,

192

in Greek, but one can't do all at once. At present I think of other paintings also. How quiet is this house! The exquisite playing of the Consul's wife below the only variety for silence. George also is silent & writes. [J.]

Same wonderful weather, but cold. Rose 7.30, better but unwell. At 9 Sir H. Storks (& Strahan) came. It was a pleasure to show the 60 drawings to him — such interest & intelligence. Moreover he bought 2, so 12 out of the 60 are gone. . . . Worked at the Ponte Pelissier piny ponderous perilous painting. . . . [J.] 19 FEBRUARY

. . . The narrow, sad, circular, bitter Island-life bother breaks out even in so good a woman as Mrs Boyd. The only real way to live here or elsewhere is to make interests, either internal or external, wholly unconnected with the place. . . . [J.] 21 FEBRUARY

Rose at 7.15 & went to church. Talked with Clarke on Colenso. Irritated by his sermon, on the old ridiculous Lot's wife story. Why must he say that non-communicants have some crimes or what nots which prevent their joining their fellow Christians? I am conscious of none, & only always refrain because I will join no church intimately whose dogmas are so loathsomely blasphemous as ours in the Athanasian creed. 10.30 to 1.30 went mostly in drawing numerals for little Mary De Vere, which I then took her: she is a darling little girl. . . . Return to change shoes, & then thence again & with Sargent & Wolff to Potamós, & back by the flats by 6. These 2 men bore me as seeing nothing whatever in the landscape; moreover they jaw, & dispute, & bore. However, we get on pretty well. Day most brilliant, but sadly cold. At 7.30 to the Palace. Evening livelier than at times. But a little too much dirt. Would one were away in $\dot{\varepsilon}\lambda\varepsilon\upsilon\theta\varepsilon\rho\acute{\iota}\alpha$ [freedom] 'o somewhere!' . . . [J.] 22 FEBRUARY

Same wonderful weather. Rose unwell. But I said, 'bother these difficulties'. So at 9 I went to Taylor's. Then came back to work. Worked at *new* Philae. At 10.30 came Foffy Kourkouméli & Fizzy [Wolff's son] & stayed a time. At 2, I walked by the Condi Lane & Potamós flats to that beautiful view I have so long intended to draw, & there I remained till 5, when I cut across to the Potamós road & drew again till 5.30, then home by 7. . . . [J.] 23 FEBRUARY

Began to work at the oil Porto Trescoglie. But Lady Wolff & F. Kourkouméli came at 10.30 & stayed a time; & when they went came Professor Ansted,* from Sir H. Storks, to know about the island's geography. Willing to do all I could . . . Found all the 60 frames arrived & took them out. . . . [J.] 24 FEBRUARY

Same absolute Paradise weather. Passed all day in undoing & cleaning the new 60 frames, unnailing the 14 already fixed (of the old ones), & arranging & nailing all the 60 drawings in the new frames. Afterwards measuring & knocking nails in the 'show-room', & hanging 1 side entirely, & a 2nd partly. . . . It was 6.15 when I left off work, & 26 FEBRUARY

Govíno [Gouvia] Road, 23 February 1863, 4 p.m. (Lear mistakenly put the date of 24 February.)

George was horribly cross, *Quaresima* [Lent] having obstructed his ways. At 7 Professor Ansted came, but dinner not till 7.30; howbeit it was very good. The professor is pleasant in some ways — most ways, but he was not very well, & possibly was 'ill at ease'. He looked over many sketches, but although pleased with them he despairs of reproducing them &, like Mrs Leake, advises 'relinquishing that idea'. If he does too much here he will be ill. I do not see that I can go out tomorrow as I wished as well as finish the 'exhibition' rooms. . . . [J.]

27 FEBRUARY   A day altogether upset & nil. Hung the 60 pictures, knocking nails etc. etc. till 12 or 1. Then did nothing, being ill & cross. At 4 drew Vido from Mandoúki. At 7.30 to the Palace — Sir H. Storks has asked me today & on Sunday — *de trop, selon moi*. 'Let us alone.' [J.]

1 MARCH   About the 20th I finished the last of the 60 drawings, all of 10 or 12 guineas each in price, & last week the frames came, & then, after two days' insertion of the drawings,

Vido from Mandoúki, 27 February 1863, 5 p.m.

measuring & nail knocking, I have made a really remarkable gallery of water-colour works. This next week I have to ask some 70 or 80 sets of people to see this same gallery — but I doubt my success in selling the drawings. Cheap photographs are the order of the day now — & I fancy but few here care really about art. Moreover, I can't allow a reunion of gossip & idleness to bore me, so that if in 2 weeks I do not succeed in sale I disperse the great part of the collection. Among those who most enjoy seeing what I have done, Sir H. Storks is eminent. His delight in looking over the drawings was very marked — & at once he bought one of Jerusalem & one of Corfu. Lady Wolff also examines everything minutely & with an eye evidently used to look at nature heartily. Others will irritate me — Sir C. Sargent to wit, who saw all 60 drawings in 19 minutes, calling over the names of each & saying, '£700! Why, you must give a ball!' Fool! As yet I have sold £120 worth, but have not received one farthing — for great people generally suppose that artists gnaw their colours & brushes for food. . . . Overleaf I will give you a sort of picture of my gallery.

The drums of the 6th Regiment announce the hour of church to be proximate, whither I shall not go, but on the contrary, having made George Kokáli a present of a half-worn suit of clothes commemorative of the fact that this day 7 years ago he came to my service, & having sent him home for the day, I shall endeavour, unless Mme Pinna begins to play, to conclude this sheet in peace. Let me see: I wrote last to you on the 10th February — or 8th, rather. Ever since then the weather has been one blaze of light & loveliness, tho' colder than I like it when unable to take exercise. Could I walk or ride, it would seem the finest of English October atmospheres. Day by day the delicate glory of the harbour & mountain tints have been my delight, & I do not at present see my way to leaving so exquisite a place as Corfu.

North side

South side

West side

1. Athens
2. Athens (Duke of St Albans)
3. Ithom
4. Meristos (Duke of St Albans)
5. Thermopylae
6. Jerusalem
7. [?] (Duke of St Albans)
8. Corfu
9. Tripolene
10. Philates
11. Meteora
12. Parga
13. Suli
14. Gethsemane
15. Kleissoura (Mt Druna Gardens)
16. Janina
17. Argos
18. Athos
19. Butrinto
20. [?]
21. Constantinople
22. Baalbek
23. Jerusalem (Sir Henry Storks)
24. Janina
25. Janina
26. Butrinto
27. Philae (Colonel West)
28. Philae (Stephen [?] M.P.)
29. Thebes
30. Palaeokastro Corfu
31. Corfu/Viro
32. Koroned
33. Pisa
34. Athos (Duke of St Albans)
35. Mt Blanc
36. Corfu/Viro
37. C.S. angelo, Corfu
38. Palaeokastro Corfu
39. Corfu citadel
40. Jerusalem
41. S. Salvador, Corfu
42. Corfu Gastouri (Sir W. Storks)
43. Corfu Citadel
44. Corfu (Ascension Duke of St Albans)
45. Corfu (Khakie) (Mrs Lyell)
46. Corfu (Kastrades)
47. Corfu Zaake
48. Valley of [?]
49. Janina
50. Corfu of Gastouri
51. Jericho
52. Philae
53. Dead Sea
54. Dead Sea
55. Pompey's Pillar
56. Baalbek
57. Cedars of Lebanon
58. Jerusalem
59. Berat
60. Corfu of S. Deca

My health also has been better than for 2 years or more bygone. Much of my improvement mental & bodily I attribute to constant occupation & the vast amount of work I have got through by 8-hours-a-day-application is absolutely curious, even to myself; & moreover I may say that many of these drawings are quite superior to any I ever made, from my projecting more power & experience nowadays. Yet if all do not find owners, I am badly off, for the expense of frames & transit here alone swallows the value of 7 out of the 12 ordered — & as yet there is no visible tin from even these. . . .

A little more about myself. This next summer will I think see some considerable change in my plans. This double journey annually bothers me, & I have many ideas *in petto* for plans, should I live. While 4 landscape painters such as Lee, Creswich, Witherington & Redgrave substantially shut out those they don't like from all Academic exhibitions, I never intend to send work to their shop — so that loophole is closed. How then to live without this 'perpetual toil' — always made more or less uneasy by the complete uncertainty of remuneration contrasted with the complete certainty of responsibility to debts of daily food & ordering of life?

You will therefore probably find me giving up England this year altogether, placing things in a pantechnicon, & then passing the winter here, giving up this place also, & taking to a chance life for indefinite time — since, as every year brings me nearer to a finite goal of rest, it appears to me that there is less need to look out for tin for many years of an old age which I shall certainly never reach. To cough, wheeze, spit & snuffle in England I will not. Bother the Greek affairs, which had they culminated in Prince Alfred as king, & a regular established government, would exactly have suited my book as to settling myself in Athens — an idea I have not yet relinquished. So for the present there is little more to say. Going to Palestine appears to me out of the question this spring: rather I may visit Cerigo [Kythera], Zantë, Ithaka & Santa Maura, & come to England in June.

I shall now change the subject, first making a few observations on a family of geese & ganders below my window, whose proceedings greatly interest me. There are 3 of each sex, but 1 gander has 2 wives, & 1, only 1, & the 3rd is impotent. The latter leads a painful life of insult & persecution, for all 3 of the geese persecute him horribly, & having maltreated him spitefully, continually reject him from their society — the melancholy Ruskin of domestic ornithology. The 2nd gander with 1 wife fights furious battles with the bigamous gander, 1 of whose geese is sitting on eggs in a hole, & close to whom her husband with his other wife watch patiently, until at times when the bigamist requires food or water, & he then goes further, leaving the parturient goose in care of the 2nd wife. No sooner does he leave the spot when the monogamous gander rushes to the forbidden hole, pursued by the 2nd wife of the absent bigamist, who sometimes succeeds in beating off the adulterer: but generally she runs as hard as she can & brings back the bigamist who seizes the adulterer's tail feathers in his bill & drags him out backwards, when a fight ensues, sometimes lasting $1/2$ an hour, but always ending in the total discomforture of the monogamist adulterer, who frequently has the additional disgust of seeing the conqueror seize his wife & ravish her forcibly — she is obliged to consent to the ultimate ganderious functions in order to save her life. All this I shall send to some work on Natural History with plates . . .

To return to humanity. Society here is pleasant to me — if I see little of it. Sir H. Storks has been *most* particularly amiable, asking me perpetually to Sunday dinners. He is doubtless one of the most agreeable men socially — and in his public character I perceive that he is always consistent, never for a moment forgetting that he is the Queen's Lord High Commissioner.

Of the swells — next to those Palatial — the ancient general seems a jovial amiable man. But there is no one here I can walk with comfortably, & I miss Lushington horridly at times. Last Sunday I insisted (as Sir C. Sargent & Wolff wanted me to walk) on not pottering to the One Gun Battery — which is like walking up & down Rotten Row — so we walked round Potamós; it was one of the most lovely of afternoons, & the colour & scenery were enough to delight a dead man. These 2 live ones however never once looked at or spoke of it: their talk was of money & politics only, & made me sick for the 3 hours. Lady Wolff is a singularly clever woman. A Professor Ansted is here — a very intellectual & pleasant man. Sir H. Storks sent him to me from my knowing the island well, & I took him to Pelekas & got him to dine with me. There is also a very curious young man — Lord Seymour* — here: his ways are ways of wonder, but it seems to me I should or shall like him. [C.F.]

1 MARCH   Neither the poor little dwarf at Potamós, nor dear little Mary De Vere will see me today I think; nor shall I dine at the Wolffs' (for their frittery evenings bore me), nor try to do so at the Creykes', nor shall I go to the Palace, the latter because I don't want to get into a Sunday dining groove there, not easily to be discontinued. I am not unhappy though, albeit I can't decide on stirring out. Only I dread seeing the numbers of people tomorrow & all next week, & sometimes I would gladly get even into an academic groove, or be a water-colour member, to save the *viva voce* contact with people I can't care about, & whose conversation destroys my capacity for any continuous work. *Intanto*, I have to be thankful for health, & for much of internal or mental progress, whereas I seem to have been naturally in for a constant going back.

9.30 p.m. What a queer Sunday (as Sundays go in Corfu). Well . . . I sate, & prowled about, looking at the quiet ripply harbour, till about 5.30, when George came in, & also for another hour I walked about. Then dined, tranquilly, on cold lamb & hot potatoes & stuffed eggs. . . . Whereafter, reading Sheridan's life by φίτζ [fits], I now go to bed, about 10. So calm a day I have not known for long. [J.]

3 MARCH   Worked at the oil Yannina, more or less well or ill. The 3 Paramythiótti came: good plain people. I thought it would rain hard, but it cleared once more. At 6, dressed, & went up to see dear little Mary De Vere. And then to Sir C. Sargent's. I really cannot remember ever to have undergone such a monotony of miserable slot & slosh of conversation for a long time. Frivolity & ill-nature, beautifully intertwined. Miss Reeve never spoke one word of common sense. Lady Sargent, perhaps once or twice, but it was

more than half sharpness. I bore all pretty well, for me, till they proposed some game, at which I could not play (& I heard Lady S.'s remarks as to 'he looks etc. etc. etc.'). But when they began to laugh at me, 'looking on with pity & contempt' etc. etc. etc., I rose, absurdly suddenly, & wished them good night & rushed away. Rather 'abruptious' & absurd, I own, & I can't help laughing at the memory of it. 'I suffer not fools gladly', being an ass myself. Can't these people let me alone? [J.]

... Many nobs came early, & at 11 Lady Wolff, & Sir S. Valaorítis* & Lady: Lady Wolff in a *capo d'opera* of talent & prettiness & sense & tact & perfection of manner; the Valaorítis also are extremely nice. ... At 5.30 I went to see darling little Mary De Vere & then for a walk. ... Home by 7.30, dined, & George has gone to see his children, being in a fuss, most allowable considering the fearful amount of typhus now about: 8 or 9 or more children, even up to 20, die daily. Penned out till 11. So happy a 'winter' as this, one thing with another, passed I never. [J.]

6 MARCH

A nice note early from Lady Shelley, & at 10 Sir Percy & Lady S.,* & a pretty little girl came, with Professor Ansted. The Shelleys are a most likeable party, & I am to go there this evening. ... At 6.30 to the Shelleys, going off in a boat with Sir P., Lady S. & 'Floss', who were just arriving from a drive. Their yacht was charming, dinner ditto, they enormously ditto. Most dreamy life! Sir P. put down some notes of my music to 'O world, O life, O time!', & I sang many others. They gave me an engaving also of Shelley, & her volume of memorials — so the day may be termed a white one. [J.]

7 MARCH

... I begin to be vastly weary of hearing people talk nonsense — unanswered — not because they are unanswerable, but because they talk in pulpits. That same morning I heard a 'discourse' on Lot's wife & other unpleasant legends, being, as I find in my journal, the 23rd I have heard on the same subject. Are not the priests of the age blind indeed not to discern that though from the unassailable vantage-ground of custom they may oppress the human intellect for a long while, yet that some day the hour will come for them to go the way of all other priesthoods?

15 MARCH

The battle about Colenso interests me immensely: I perceive that Hampden & Thirlwall are the only 2 of all the silly bishops who have not signed the Memorial to 'Natal'. In the nature of things it was not to be supposed that the bishops were to forward Colenso's views, but they might have done another thing — to wit, let him alone. A broader creed, a better form of worship, the cessation of nonsense & curses, & the recognition of a new state of matters brought about by centuries, science, destiny or what not, will assuredly be demanded & come to pass whether bishops & priests welcome the changes or resist them. Not those who believe that God the Creator is greater than a Book, & that millions unborn are to look up to higher thoughts than those stereotyped by ancient legends, gross ignorance, & hideous bigotry — not those are the Infidels, but these same screamy ganders of the church, who put darkness forward & insist that it is light.

Meanwhile I hear that a measure is to be brought forward in the Legislature to simplify the creed of religious England, & thus by the shortest catechism to abolish all infidel doctrines. The bishops of all dioceses are to prevent the clergy from allowing any person to attend church who does not answer 2 simple questions in the affirmative.

1st. Do you believe in Balaam's ass, Jonah's whale, Elisha's bears, & Lot's wife?

2nd. Do you believe that all mankind who do not believe in these creatures will be burned in everlasting fire, wholly without respect to their wisdom, charity or any other good quality?

Bother . . . I myself should be satisfied for the present if the people could gradually be brought to contemplate the necessity of only portions of the Bible ever being read, or thought worth reading, with the abolition of the damnatory clauses, if not of the whole of the nasty Athanasian Creed — & with the service of the Litany & other prayers, the congregation to stay or not to a sermon as they thought proper.

After nearly 3 months of unchangeable fine weather here the equally 'bnoxious gales are come upon us, said the Lady of Shalott, & winds & rain are our daily food. Rain was indeed very necessary, for the country was extremely dry. No one can imagine the endless loveliness of this island throughout all this winter, if winter it were; but to some natures it was sadly unhealthy, & the number of children who have died is terrible — from 10 to 20 daily — owing to *scarlatina*. . . . My life here has gone on very sklombionbiously on the whole, though I go out very little, not being, as you know, of a gregarious nature. . . . Sir Henry Storks very often asks me to dine on Sunday, & I find the evening there very agreeable: he is so full of anecdote & information that you would suppose he had had nothing to do but *flâner* all his life, instead of being soldier, governor, & what not. To me he seems most excellently fitted for his post here, being always the same consistent man in public life & private.

Heaps of *Gonfiati* [swells] continue to rush about here at intervals: a surprising duchess came to my rooms 2 days ago (Montrose) though I don't think she looked at anything very much. But the people whose acquaintance has most delighted me are the Shelleys, who are here in a yott. Think of my music to 'O world, O life, O time!' — Shelley's words — being put down in notes by Shelley's own son! Then there is Lord Seymour, who seems to me as if he had dreamed a dream & was continually a-dreaming of having dreamed it: *quâ* a Duke's eldest son, certainly an odd mortal, though there is somewhat of interest about him. Also there was Smith O'Brien, who has sailed off to Athens, I really believe, upon some hubbly bubbly errand of stuff. The Duke of St Alban's was here too . . .

At the present moment I have pulled down my Eggzibissyon — & shall send some to England possibly . . . but my principal effort just now is towards the production of 24 views to illustrate the Ionian Islands. [L.W.]

19 MARCH . . . This house is a sort of Paradise this year. Now & then the children below make a noise, but the most beautiful playing on the piano of the Consul's wife is indeed a blessing. The only drawback is that she plays so little, & that the instrument is below

my bedroom. I give up my own next week — a loss, but τί ἐμπορῶ νὰ κάμω; [what can I do?] . . . [J.]

20 MARCH

Soft–soppy–shiny–showery all day. No wind. Rose at 8. Fi! for shame. Worked at Louisa Rawson's Philae from 10 to 5, & very sixsixfully. Wrote to her, saying it was finished. Worked also on the other Philae. Captain Stocker R.A. came at 5, & looked at drawings, to my surprise wanting one of them — the moonlight Yannina. But I don't think that a very good drawing, or anyhow one of my best; & I had rather a young man had one of the very best, because he buys it as an example, or particular pleasure, 'not knowing'. . . . Dined at 7. G. went out for half an hour, but did not return till 9. From 9 to 10.30 I penned out. G. intended to write but slept. [J.]

Nimfes, 21 June 1856, 7 p.m., penned out 20 March 1863.

23 MARCH

The sklimjimfiousness of the situation increases: Sir H. Drummond Wolff has been & gone & bought 2 of my drawings & Captain Stocker is to buy another, so that I shall have enough tin to pay rent & shut up house for 8 weeks or thereabouts. Whereupon I shall first make some studies of what Lady Young used to call 'awnge trees' & then I shall go to Paxos.

> There was an old person of Paxo
> Which complained when the fleas bit his back so,
>   But they gave him a chair
>   And impelled him to swear,
> Which relieved that old person of Paxo.

. . . All my attention is now to be given to a work or worx on the 7 Ionian Islands. But I doubt my doing more than Paxos, Santa Maura & Ithaka this year, as I wish to do them thoroughly, & — *conte che conte* — by engraving, woodcuts, lithograph or what not, must & will 'make a spoon or spoil a horn'. . . . I go hence, as I said, on the 4th April & return towards the end of May. . . . My gallery is nearly dismantled, & must be put up — what remains of it — in Stratford Place, where by June 15 I hope to see you:

> but never more, O! never we
> shall meet to egg & toast & T!

Never mind. I don't grumble at the less I see of my friends, so they gain by it.* . . .
Another Nok at the Dore — Sir Percy & Lady Shelley & little Florence — & to say 'goodbye' which I hate. Lady Shelley is out & out & out a stunner of a delightful woman. [C.F.]

25 MARCH . . . Worked — almost nil. A little at some out-of-window drawings. My piano went at 12. All things rather unhinged. . . . From 4 I began to pull down the pictures, & take them out, which operation lasted to 7. George comes in & says Nikóla has fever, & pains in the throat, & is in a sort of alarm — no wonder, with all these illnesses about. . . . [J.]

26 MARCH Worked a little at San Salvador, but chiefly the early day went in packing — books, drawings, etc. etc. At 2.15 came Captain Wade Browne, & we walked to Potamós & round by the flats, quietly & unhurried. . . . Near to lower Potamós flat bridge a poor *contadino* [peasant] passed, walking hard, but crying miserably. I could not help asking him why, & he said his eldest son died yesterday, his 2nd this morning, & his remaining children . . . were ill with this dreadful sad fever. He said he had no money for the doctor at Argostóli, & was going to Corfu to see what God would do for him. We thought it better to give him 2s. & send him back to see what could be done. . . . At 7.45 sent George to see after Nikóla, & to send a doctor if possible. [J.]

27 MARCH . . . Nikóla Kokáli has been bled & is better. [J.]

30 MARCH . . . Extract from a letter I wrote . . . 'Yet the more I see of this place, so the more I feel that no other spot on earth can be fuller of beauty, & of variety & beauty. For you may

pass your days by gigantic cliffs with breaking foam-waves below them (as at Palaiokastrítsa), or on hills which overlook long seas of foliage backed by snow-covered mountain ridges (as at Garoúna or Gastoúri), or beneath vast olives over-branching dells full of fern & myrtle & soft green fields of bright grass, or in gardens dark with orange & lemon groves, their fruits sparkling golden & yellow against the purple sea & amethyst hills, or by a calm sandy shore below aloe-grown heights, rippling-sparkling curves of sea sounding gently around all day long.' [J.]

1 APRIL

Set off by 6.30 with George to Kinopiástes — very warm. Drew there till it clouded, & rained hard — a storm. But we got shelter in a good-natured peasant's house, his name Stellios. At 1 had my lunch, & from 2 to 4.30 sate about, drawing, or walked about. We then crossed the valley to the new Psorarí road, & went all its length to that village. Nothing can be prettier & nicer than those houses & gardens & balconies etc. & the lovely view beyond. Of a new church I said to 3 women carrying water: «Εἶναι

Kinopiástes, 1 April 1863.

Kinopiástes, 1 April 1863.

ὡραῖα ἡ ἐκκλησία σας.» ['Your church is beautiful.'] To which one spokeswoman said: «'Αλήθεια λέγεις· εἶναι εὔμορφη.» ['You speak truly: it is beautiful.'] The wonderful varied beauty of this garden island is undoubtedly delightful.

We came home by the road below Virós & so by 7 to G.'s home in Kastrádes — & I waited for him till he came out. Alas! Little Haralámbi is worse. The complaint (this awful fever) has attacked his throat & leeches are ordered. Poor G. As he says, it is indeed *duro* to bring up children always expecting their death.... [J.]

2 APRIL Slept ill all night, & could not rise. George came in after 6. Nikóla recovers, but Haralámbi is very ill. Those dreadful 2 swellings on the neck! I think he may not live. George is quiet & says, «Πρέπει νὰ κυττάξωμεν ταῦτα τὰ πράγματα ὡς θέλημα Θεοῦ» ['We must look on these things as the will of God'.] . . . [J.]

3 APRIL George, who sleeps at home now, came at 5.30. Poor little Haralámbi remains the same, but is not worse. Went at 8 to the Vasiláki garden & drew oranges, returning by 11. Found letter asking me to dine at the Palace, so, after taking my ticket to Paxos, I went

at 1.30 & lunched with Captain Phillipps of the 6th, & dawdled after till 3.30. Then I walked by the Parga road & never saw Corfu more beautiful: a sort of plum-lilac hue comes over Salvador & the mountain — a powdery opal purple glory . . . At 6 went to Lady Wolff's . . . Sir Henry Storks came in & says that the islands will be ceded immediately. . . .

Haralámbi is a little better. [J.]

4 APRIL

Very lovely all day. Haralámbi is still somewhat better, & I think he may get well perhaps. But George is to come after me by the following steamer. Paid Paramythiótti £20 for 4 months rent, up to August, got straps, odds & ends, & finished all packing. . . . At 8 went with George on board the Bosphoro steamer, where he left me. There were but few passengers, & the deck was most pleasant, for the bright full moon showed every bit of Corfuland — all the well-known hills, sea smooth as glass: well for me, for I find the steamers never go into Paxo at all, & often no communication is possible. Off Lefkímo light (we started at 10) by 11.30, & Capo Bianco by midnight. [J.]

[Between 4 April and 3 June Lear visited the other Ionian Islands.]

3 JUNE

Sitting on deck all night, nervous & irritable beyond belief, the steamer pitching violently always. At 1, Paxo was visible, & at 2 we were passing those isles, now so well-known. At 3 the sea was smooth below Capo Bianco, the moon sank in mist, & soon the daylight crept above 'Souli's dark rock'. By 4 all the well-known hills were seen, & by 5.30 we anchored below Fort Neuf. Very little difficulty in getting ashore, & none at the *Dogana*, but I had to wait on the stairs, for I had forgotten my key, & had sent George to Spiro — who, however, was here all the while, & had got my breakfast things ready, but had gone to bed again. From 7.30 to 9 unpacked, & washed, & then breakfast. After which I went to sleep. . . . At 5.30 or later went to De Vere's, & saw them, as well as a room full of people. Saw dear little Mary De Vere also, & came away. Called on Middleton — out — &, going to Mrs Boyd, met Boyd, with whom walked till late, & had to run home to dress. Scamper at 7.30 to Palace. Only Sir Henry Storks & E. Baring there. Sir H. not as merry as usual. The acceptance of the Greek throne seems fixed, & one's impression is that the Islands will be ceded immediately, & our occupation end by the end of the year. . . . Home by 10.30. . . . [J.]

4 JUNE

Rose & packed . . . nearly concluding all by 10 or 10.30, when breakfast. . . . At about 3 to the Kokáli house, where I saw all the family, the good old Vasilía, Spiro, Christos, Tatianí & Haralámbi, with Theódoros, really a fine child. Nikóla I am sorry to hear is not going on well. Returned by 4 or 5, calling at the 6th & seeing Harrison & others. Then writing till 6.30 or 7. Dressed, & to the Palace. Being before time, I stood in the gallery, the large dark acacias deep brown against the gray Citadel & the far purple hills. Came a world of strangers. Dinner & wine most illustrious. Balcony afterwards.

[J.]

8 JUNE
ANCONA

You see I am on my way so far, & I suppose I may be in England on Friday & in town on Saturday.... I have wearied awfully of the sea voyage — & do so more & more. Perhaps the whole stagnation of a week or more, besides the actual physical nuisance, makes me determined to put an end to this double 'journey of life'. But where I must live, so as to live *only* in one place, I can't yet decide.... The farther I go from Corfu, the more I look back to the delight its beautiful quiet has so long given me, & I am by no means approaching the filth & horror & noise of London life with a becoming spirit.

Sitting next to the Captain of an Austrian Frigate at Sir H. Stork's on Thursday evening, the German officer said to a subaltern that — the conversation was about the good looks of women — 'I do think the Englishwoman conserve her aperient Galship longer than all the women: even as far as her Antics.' The subaltern withered with confusion till I ventured to explain, 'The Englishwoman preserves her appearance of youth longer than all women — even if she be old. [C.F.]

6 SEPTEMBER
LONDON

I want you to write to Lord Palmerston to ask him to ask the Queen to ask the King of Greece to give me a 'place'. As I never asked anything of you before, I think I may rely on your doing this for me. I wish the place to be created a-purpose for me & the title to be ὁ Ἀρχανοησιαφλυαρίαποιός [Lord High Bosh & Nònsense Producer] with permission to wear a fool's cap (or mitre), 3 pounds of butter yearly & a little pig, & a small donkey to ride on. Please don't forget all this, as I have set my heart on it.

I see by the *Observer* of today that the King of Greece is to come to Windsor or Balmoral about the 15th, & that the vote of the Ionian Parliament cannot be taken before the 2nd or 3rd week in October, after which he is to go to Athens. If I hear before that, that we (the English in the 7 islands) are likely to clear out before Christmas, it will make a great difference to me — for I then should not take out drawings or copies of my new work. So let me know, as far as you may with properriety. [C.F.]

JANUARY 1864 – APRIL 1864

Woke at 6, and rose: exquisite brightness. On deck by 7, & looked once more at Strada Bianca, purple Chika, & white clouds on scornful crags. Get up luggage by 8, & at 10 breakfast, & thereafter we were passing Vido, & at 11.30 anchored. No George coming, I got the man of the Hotel Giorgio to see me ashore, & passing the *Dogana* courteously was at the Casa Paramythiótti by 12. Waiting for some time, ὁ πιστὸς Σουλιότις ἦλθε [the faithful Souliote came]. Little Theódoros seems to have died of tetanus — how brought on I cannot learn. From 1 to 5 worked hard at getting things unpacked & in order. Then washed & dressed, & called at the Boyds', having left my 'Book' at the Palace. The friendly Boyds are in low spirits, as, I fear, are the Corfiotes generally. Spiro called, and is evidently in very great trouble. Went then to Carter's, having ordered dinner there. Middies, & one Skene, a pleasant fellow. After dinner went up to Craven. Home by 9.30 & arranged books. Bad cold in head. [J.] 9 JANUARY

I came here yesterday afternoon — just a week & 4 hours of journey. My travelling companion missed the train at Victoria, so I went alone after all, glad however to be forced to go forth from darkness & weariness and cold. Not that the benefits of it were at first apparent, for the passage to Calais was dreadful, nor could we pass the bar until too late to catch the afternoon train to Paris. Hence, 13 hours of halts at every station ... & consequent obligation to sleep at Paris till the following day at noon. Paris was cold too, but that fact gave me the opportunity of seeing the Prince Imperial who, in a carriage & four, stopped to gaze at the swans in the Tuileries gardens, ice-begirt & crumb-desiring. Lots of little *gamins* stopped also & inspected the imperial child as he did the swans. At night off to Marseilles, where I arrived (deep snow having fallen all night) at noon on the 4th, Monday, & where my travelling companion turned up also, having been in another compartment all the journey. He went south to Naples, but I, fearing the journey to Brindisi, & there being no Genoa boat for some days, followed on by train to Nice, arriving at midnight. Next day, off at 9 in a steamer, going all along the coast most xquisitely, till the wind became a hullabaloo and we could only get to Genoa by 10 p.m., thus missing the night train to Ancona, thereby losing the best chance of hitting the Thursday's boat. Stayed at Genoa therefore all next day — 6th — set off at night again, reaching Ancona on Thursday 7th, just in time to take my place & go on board. 44 hours brought me to Corfu on Saturday 9th (as I said before) & the voyage was thoroughly calm, sunny delightful. George Kokáli was all ready for me, & today everything is so regular & matter of course that I don't seem to have been absent for an hour. The odd pounds extra purchase comfort in home & service very cheaply. 10 JANUARY

Tomorrow I begin to work again — i.e. if a bad cold in my head allows me. Sir Henry Storks sent last night to ask me to dine today, & already of course one has seen heaps of people. . . . Monday 11th. I dined at the Palace yesterday, but was suffering from a regular cold in the head, as I am now. Sir Henry was as ever absolutely amiable gentleman-like, or as someone here says, he 'never forgets that he is the representative of the Queen for one moment'. . . .

Alas, as for Corfu I can say little yet, all the less that 10 shillings worth of letters have just come full of Post Office Orders and cheques from 'silly swells' who *couldn't* pay their subscriptions 3 weeks ago, however I entreated them to do so.

But there is not only great excitement here — great sorrow & perplexity also, & discomfort. And, it seems to me, unless you governing folk shew a little less redtapism to these islands, verily their cession will be a millstone about the neck of the liberal party for long days to come. It is however very difficult to gather or sift untruth from truth, & we are all so in the dark as to what is to take place that it is simply folly to talk or write. Yet it is the first time I have ever seen a community so singularly and uncomfortably placed. My bad cold prevents me from writing more. (Sir H. Storks takes 10 copies of my book, which is highly brick-like). [C.F.]

11 JANUARY Nose & eye cold horrible. Arranging, even commencing drawings, I could not get out till about noon, when I went to Taylor's to order various things. (Taylor has been to Spain, Madrid, Alhambra, etc.) Called at Lady Wolff's, but only saw Fizzy — certainly one of the most delightful boys ever beheld, a very dear little chap. Then I went to Fort Neuf, & saw Phillipps, Graeme & others — the same as in April last. . . . Then I walked out, & on to Potamós, & beyond to the poor Anastásio, & further to the grand lovely view, returning by the same road, slowly. One sees no difference to present between Corfu in 1856 & in 1864. Came home to find no end of letters, and £53 of tin, all in paper. Dined — not very well — & afterwards wrote a good deal. Cold–cold–cold–cold. [J.]

... Certainly it is not possible to see in all this world aught more lovely than San Salvador from 3 to 4 — peach blossom & blue & pink rose, & somewhat like a form of velvet-covered hill. [J.]

14 JANUARY

Cold, black, gloomy. An interregnum of intellest & occupation, for I really can't sit long on account of the cold.... So I sit & lunch by the fireside. A veil of cloud — snowy — covers all. Steamers 'come and go', as little Charley Stanley said many years back.... Dined solo at 6.30, and ἔπειτα [afterwards] set to work at the usual 'penning out', and did 2, yea, part of a 3rd drawing. Once or twice went in to see George writing, which he goes on with *al solito* — & so everything seems to proceed as before the Fathers fell asleep. At 9.45 bed. But I have a fire in my bedroom on these horrid cold nights. [J.]

15 JANUARY

Not so cold, as there was less wind, nevertheless, sunless and cold all through. Did not go out, but worked by fits and badly... Indigestion, discomfort, irritation, & vexation. No steamer — a bore. Dined μοναχός [solo]. I do not go on with Greek, as the penning out of past drawings is so necessary. Penned out till 10 — Samos sketches. [J.]

18 JANUARY

... A certain placidity in this Corfu life is a charm never before attained to except in the early Roman days (at Civitella etc.) & never more to be found on leaving this, I fear — or, rather, I doubt. [J.]

19 JANUARY

... Vido & Fort Abraham are to be *destroyed*. The rest uncertain. [J.]

20 JANUARY

Quite a lovely day all day, & warm — so complete a change. Hitherto I have been suffering from cold as much as at Rome in 1859.... No steamer (of the 21st) in. *But* the lovely calm of the harbour, San Salvador, the colours, the gulls, the boats. Did not go out at all.... Placid days — few now. [J.]

21 JANUARY

... Moonlight — & recollection of other moonlights. But those days are gone, nor do I say, with Mrs N., 'Would those days could come again!' Dined alone, & penned out till nearly 11.... Froude's *Life of Elizabeth* delights me. [J.]

22 JANUARY

Perfection of loveliness all day. Full moon. One of 'those days' — more heaven than earth.... A kind of indifference grows on me. [J.]

23 JANUARY

Awfully unwell — stoppage & pain in bowels. Medicine, but ill all day, hardly able to sit up. Some 'order' must be taken about diet, for, as Bern says, at 50 odd these bouts are not as when one was 30. Major De Vere, Colonel Halliwell & another came & looked at drawings. After which I got worse till at 4 was obliged to go to bed. Feet in hot water, & hot stones wrapped up in flannel eased pain a little, & constant

31 JANUARY

diarrhoea — & had that not ceased I must have sent for a doctor. Some hot tea at times also was a benefit. George was very attentive & good, & got his mattress into the next room to be within reach of the 'bell'.

So ends January 1864. Not so regularly progressing a month as that in last year, but testifying to more return of energy than I should have expected. Leaving London on the 2nd & reaching here on the 9th, I began to work by the 12th; & had I not been so unwell with cold for many days should have worked more than I have. Yet I have all but finished (barring a few hours work) 6 water-colour drawings — £70 worth of work; have finished off previously-commenced sketches in the country, & have penned out some 20 to 30 Kefalónian drawings, besides letters & writing. [J.]

3 FEBRUARY Wonderfully lovely morning. But rose unwell. The increase of chance of war (it seems the Germans will go into Schleswig) makes the necessity greater of decision about what to do here. The medium plan would be not to give up this house at March 6th . . . & to take it on for 3 months if Paramythiótti allows — for I can hardly finish & pack before May. But then — what next? Athens? or a return to London? — the first expensive, the second hateful. The quiet of this house, the cheerful corner room, its green blinds & look-out over the harbour, the large table, good fire, etc., the long quiet study, an even light through all the day, the good order of all things, breakfast, hearing George read, & so on — though I can't pen out at present, for my inside is still bad — are among the scenes & times I fear not to return. Yet if life is so short, & the 'beyond life' so unknown, why regret at all? . . . Inside not at all right yet, but there is far less of that dreadful depression which ate one up for some days. *En revanche* there is more restlessess & worry with better health. [J.]

7 FEBRUARY I shall write today instead of going to church, relaxing my labour from time to time by snatches of the *Daily Telegraph*, Renan's *Jesus*, Miss Rowan's *Meditations on Death*, Newman's *Phases of Faith*, Froude's *Elizabeth*, & Colenso's 4th part. And the better my beloved brethren to set forth the varied subjects which I shall bring under your consideration, I shall first proceed to look through your letter, & reply more or less to the heads thereof.

My 'flight' it seems was by no means too soon: what you suffer, & for how long you suffer in England is hideous to think of — not perhaps at Strawberry Hill or similar houses, but the mass of human beings do suffer, & that terribly. If I were not myself aware of this I should know it by innumerable newspaper paragraphs, & by private letter; yet after 7 months of darkness & filth you will all as usual talk about the 'climate of England' as the 'best in the world'. So God tempereth the wind to the shorn lamb: so the Esquimaux believes that train oil is before all food the most excellent. . . .

You ask about the state of public feeling here, a question not easy to answer. The decree about the non-destruction of the forts of course was soothing, but (I judge only by Lady Wolff's talk, as she seems to me ever to hold a brief of hatred for [on behalf of] the Greeks) they say, 'No thanks to the English for that: you *wished* to leave the place in ruin, but the King of Greece threatened to go if you did, & you were *forced* to give way' — which I suppose is bosh. Lady W. denies we have ever done *any* good here, but when I stop this nonsense by saying, 'Well, well, at all events then if we have been as bad as you say, the ground will soon be cleared of us', she instantly turns round & says, 'But nobody wants you to go — your going will occasion great misery etc. etc.' — 'Then why did the Ionian Parliament continually vote for annexation?' 'Parliament indeed!' she answers. 'Do you call 42 or 50 democrats public opinion?' 'Then why', say I, 'if that is so trifling, why did not the Ionians prevent its eternal repetition by electing other *deputati*?' On which she says, 'But do take some coffee', & twists the converse all awry.

Meanwhile the cannon are all taken down from the Fort Neuf etc. etc., & as soon as the 6th go (under orders for Jamaica) Vido will be emptied & blown up — or down. There are however many who have *no belief* at all in our ultimate departure. The Turk Albanian Beys opposite go into strong convulsions of laughter at the idea (so officers tell me who come from Parga, Delvino, etc.) & a mass of the lower orders here also do not credit it, but believe some dodges will turn up & keep us in the islands — or at all events in this island. On the other hand, dismay & distress pervade whole classes. Domestic servants, yatchtsmen, innkeepers, small shops, etc. etc., see before them simply blank new beginnings of life — how or where they know not. My man's whole family think of migrating to Patras, or the Piraeus. The war-like Danish–German news of the last few days complicates matters still more. It will be funny if war with Austria arises, & a fleet come down from Cattaro & chaw us up suddenly, when the guns are gone.

As for poor Sir Henry Storks, you say well, he *will* be glad to go indeed. I know of no position much sadder than his — for nearly 5 years working hard always, with a self-negation & conscientiousness not to be surpassed, yet as it were wholly alone, barring the 2 good aides-de-camp who help him. Just think of this. His Secretary — you know what *he* is, & how *he* helps him. Of the 2 judges, one (Colquhoun) bitterly writing against him & doing all the harm he can; the other (Sargent), though now reconciled to him in public, yet a man of no brains, & wholly controlled by H. D. Wolff. And the 2 priests hate him because he keeps a woman, & don't believe in Noah's ark, though he attends church regularly. All the rest are so far below the Lord High in position, & it may be truly said that he lives a life of most painful loneliness, all the more dreary that his efforts to do right as a public man have been met with such small appreciation by the British fool, not to say by abuse from those who should have known better than to make grave matters of right & wrong handles for mere party violence. The A.D.C.s (Baring & Strahan) are valuable to Sir H. S., but, tho' very clever, they are young. *I think that any letter you write to him now he will be pleased with*: the Duke's* illness affects him, & he seems to me to feel any kindness coming from England; & I think too that much which has been said & written of him by people, or with the knowledge of people who were once his friends, has hurt him at times a good deal. So *Q.E.D.* — as you say — Storks *will* be glad to get away...

My life here (barring blowing my nose & lying in bed ill) has been of the most regular order, & it is a grim fact that never more when I go hence can I look for similar — 'there is no joy but calm'.... Having 'put by' £300, £9 a year for life is the result of my labour — but *quâ* ready money, & the necessity of getting it by work, things are as they were before the Fathers fell asleep....

The new Italian Consul's wife or sister plays in the most bean-like & beneficial manner. By April or May at furthest, I shall hope to be fixed as to fixing or unfixing: perhaps I may go about in an unfixed mode continually & evermore. What's the odds?... The 2 or 3 months of hard writing before I left England have sickened me of pen & ink, & I shall henceforth write MUCH LESS than formerly. *Please to accept this as a nintimation or warning.* Have you read Abbé Michaud's *Maudit*? Burton's *Abeokuta*? Speke's *Nile*? Froude's *Elizabeth*? Kingsley's *Water Babies*? I aive.... Catch then O catch the transient owr, improve each momient as it flies, man's a short summer, life's a flower, he dize alas! how soon e dize. Goodbye. [C.F.]

14 FEBRUARY	Most perfect climate all day: sun, but not too hot. Big Italian steamer — & saluting-fuss.... Went to De Vere's & lunched, & walked with De Vere by Virós to the plane tree fountain below Kalafatiónes: most lovely. Those immense olives, light-trunked, dark-stemmed against the background, & the gleamingness & sparkle of the lemon or orange beyond & through. A wonderful world is this Corfu, but — we leave it! [J.]
17. FEBRUARY	Wonderful lovely calm brightness all day. But it is better to try not to regret this place — tho' if Sanders or d'Everton was coming as Consul, I could half try to live on. Painted at Jameson's Florence till 12, & also penned out a little. At 12.30 — or 12.45 — called on Lady Wolff, & later on Mrs Boyd — both out. Came home.... Unhingy am I, undecided: where to go & what to do — to go from here at once or later. At 2 went to the hill beyond Mandoúki — looking to the city — & finished a drawing begun in 1857. Seeing Craven pass, I walked a bit with him, but he does not enliven nor is enlivenable. So I returned & drew again till 5.15 & then walked back by 6.15. They say Vido & Fort Abraham are all ready to '*saltar in aria*' [to be blown up] — Dizagreeable.... [J.]
18 FEBRUARY	... Unwell. Distressed as to present & future, but not as to the past.... [J.]
23 FEBRUARY	Gray — fine. The 21st steamer, & the yesterday's regular came in, bringing the other 3 papers. No letters. I sent no letters to post. Dim & dreary life. Worked at Turin trees, & somewhat at Florence, mainly withal I looked out of window, watching the 'dismantling' of Fort Neuf.... [J.]
29 FEBRUARY	Violent rains at times all day: dark & light by fits. Early, unwell, & could work not at

Corfu from beyond Mandoúki, 17 February 1864, 5 p.m. – 8 March 1864, 5 p.m.

all. . . . I walked out at 5, the rain having ceased, by the Prison round, & back by the Kokáli houses. Walks soon to be forever discontinued. . . . [J.]

2 MARCH

Fine — north wind. Went at 8.30 to Taylor's, to ask about leaving with them various things in case I go to England & do not keep on this house. But they say: 'Send them to the Custom house.' Back to breakfast, & then painted sky of Argostóli, distance of Turin, & trees, & sky of Florence, putting all by at 12. Lunch. Paramythiótti came, & says I may have this house on month by month if I like. Wade Brown came at 2.30, & we walked to Alepoú, Afra, Kourkouméli, & back by Gouvia road, coming to the gate at 6.10. What can be lovelier than these village scenes about Afra? — or the olive woods beyond, the bright gray & pale yellow lichen'd trunx showing out from the dark glens of foliage, here & there broken by bright green, with long streams of shadow. And the silver-edged — as it were — ever-moving sheep. The anemones, & myrtle. Ahi! So we walked back — a round of 14 miles? . . . [J.]

3 MARCH

. . . All things suffer change. At 2.30 I walked slowly to Kanóni, & drew there from 4

211

to 5.30, possibly for the last time — yet one thought the same in 1849 & 1858! Walked back all along the Análipsis peninsula. What wonderful effects: dark blue gray filmy dells, with bright bits of gray light in olive branches here & there. After such evenings in Corfu, what is left as to beauty of outer life? . . . [J.]

5 MARCH   Fine — light showery clouds about . . . From 1 to 2 the bugles were sounding, & the 6th collecting. At 2.30 crowds began to pass, & at 2.30 the 6th marched by. Phillipps saw me & I him. I shall now go — & I begin to pack. I could not stay to the end for any money.

    Begin to pack up. [J.]

Corfu, 6 March 1864 — 'all over anemones'.

6 MARCH   O bad day!
  O bad boy!
  O bad!
  Did nothing, & went no whither . . . [J.]

... Revoked plans, & suddenly unpacked my oils, as, if it is only possible to finish these paintings & send all 6 to England, a great matter is gained. Finished the small Olympus & the Turin. Hurray! ... [J.]

7 MARCH

My house here is till 7th April: & before then I shall have come to — at least — half decision. Palestine I cannot manage I fear: I incline to going to Athens, in the end to Crete, & perhaps Poros, Hydra & other islands, returning to Athens, & then *possibly* to England –– late. But that will depend on events. This double annual journey I can bear no longer, & it is possible I may send my books & furniture to Athens, & sit down there for 2 years or so. If matters do not seem to allow of this, I must send all my things to England, & possibly winter at Nice or Genoa. It is very disagreeable for me to leave this place at all, & if it were possible to avoid doing so, I would. The 6th went on Saturday & all things tend to dissolution. The people in great crowds behaved well. The demolition of any part of the Fort has been a most singular folly, done one would think simply to aggravate & vex an impressible people — for military men say it could be built up in no time (Vido & Abraham are a different matter). But anyhow the more you can please, & the less you can irritate the people here by little silly ways, the better it will be. There is no sense in allowing a handle to the violent opposers of England to abuse us more, if we can easily leave the place in good odour. ... I see a good deal of Sir Henry — always dining there on Sundays, he is immensely kind, tho' bothered out of his life. [C.F.]

7 MARCH

9 MARCH   Paradise calm weather all day — & sunset glorious, with a new moon. But I never moved out. Yet it was one of those strange happy days all through (barring one hour) which I never knew elsewhere than here, except in very long ago days. . . . [J.]

10 MARCH   . . . It is difficult to fancy any place where one could be happier than here; but if war became general, or if these people are restless & boring, it would not be a bed of roses. [J.]

12 MARCH   Warm, cloudy at times, but mostly bright & lovely. Unwell all night more or less. And because of this all the day. Worked at the 'Florence', but ill — & now I hardly know if I have done well or badly to keep on working at them. 3 papers, no letters. At 6 walked round by Kastrádes. Dined solo. George made a lot of orange marmalade this summer, as a '*regalo*' [gift] for me, & it makes good puddings, which I call 'Boudini Tzikarátou'. Penned out, namely the last of the Cerigo drawings. [J.]

14 MARCH   Quite fine — but over warm — all day. Fires left off totally some time ago. Began to work on 'Florence', but got the colour worse; so, having done somewhat also to Argostóli, I resolved to do no more. Whereon I cleaned off & shut up all my oils & colours, & placed the pictures against tables for anyone to see who chose — in the next 2 days . . . [J.]

15 MARCH   Same calm, semi-cloudy sunny weather. Packed more boxes of books — 4 in all — & a few over. . . . At 3.30 I walked to Análipsis, & to the heights at the end of the promontory, drawing till 6. The green & gold, & the shadows! — the light-catching myriad arm-branches of the olives — the sheep & goats! Returning saw a drunken sailor by the roadside sleeping, & wished I could do something for him, but did not know how . . . [J.]

17 MARCH   Rose & after breakfast came Luigi the Zincaro, & we packed & zinced a large case, containing the Argostóli, Turin, & Florence, & much else. After that I packed & camphored the carpets, & arranged towards more packing till 3. . . . [J.]

18 MARCH   Rose before 8, & packed winter clothing; breakfast, & then packed at times all day long. Saddish weary work. Did not go out. The day was fine & blue cloudy, with the port full of incident, cattle landing, & porpoises to wit. But *cui bono?* — all is passing. How to arrange, as to taking or sending or leaving things, I know not. . . . [J.]

23 MARCH   Bad days. And the weather is all milky cloudy gray — mountains invisible. I sit, open window, penning out Zantë drawings, with a fire: dim gloom, sorrow, hesitation & uncertainty abound. . . . At 4.30 ἀναχώρισα [I set out], & meeting the Elmhirsts, they told me a big explosion was to happen at Fort Abraham at 5.30. Whereby I sat on a wall till it occurred. These things are a bore: for a great people we are singular

bunglers. Walked partly to Análipsis. Gray the olives are, yet minutely clear & wonderful in dark gray. Certainly no place on earth is so lovely.

So I came back by 7. George had a good dinner for me, to last 3 days — a turkey & baked potatoes, & 'Tzikarátou' pudding. At 9 I sent him home: it is better that old Vasilía should not be quite alone with her dying son Christos. '*Ha sofferto molto in questi 3 anni, la madre*' ['my mother has greatly suffered these last 3 years'] — διὰ τὴν ἀρρώστειαν τοῦ Χρήστου [on account of Christos's illness]. It is a pity that Spiro has become so little a part of the family.

I have resolved to send off 2 other cases to England, & they go tomorrow. What a thoroughly gray muggy day. Yet I'm glad of fires at night. [J.]

Same muggy calm weather — dim. Sent off 2 more cases for England, one with books & a case of drawings, & the other with 'Yannina' & canvasses. Penned out till 1. Close muggy dim weather — all distance obliterated. Set out by 2.15 intending to go with George to finish drawing at Evrópoulos, but the Italian steamer being signalled I went alone. But I never got further than Potamós bridge, dogs bothering me, & disinclination & apathy abounding. Having 'sate upon' the bridge for an hour & a half, I returned, meeting George about 5.30. . . . Returned to dine at 7, on cold turkey, & read papers. George has gone to his mother's: Christos, poor fellow, was the same today. [J.]

24 MARCH

Very dark & cloudy — storm & pouring rain till 10 or 11. Christos was the same all last night, only weaker. But at noon George returns & says Nikóla has the smallpox! He thinks it is so at least. Finished penning out of last year's Seven Islands sketches — Kefaloniá, Cerigo & Zantë having been done here.

25 MARCH

At 4.30 walked out, gloomy & dirty but not at the moment raining. I went up by the Fort Neuf steps; some 2 or 3 people — peasants — look at Fort Abraham & talk of it; but others, earnestly discussing, turn out on nearing them to be speaking of domestic matters & other things. Went up, by the *moulin à vent*, & the reedy cactus donkey-habited lane, to Análipsis. How beautiful are the dark modelled olive trunks in this gray light! At the village it began to pour with rain, & Paraskevoúla asking me to go into her house, I did so, & we talked — ἐλαλήσαμεν — about Christos, & the rest of our mutual acquaintance. She is a good nice girl, & I wonder she was never married. Returned, pretty wettish, by 7. Dined — cold turkey, eggs & spinach, Tzikarátou pudding & olives. George has gone to his mother's. I saw poor old Vasilía today. She said of Christos: «Εἶναι πολὺ πολὺ ἀδύνατος» ['he is very very weak'] & of Nikóla: «τὸ ἴδιον εἶναι» ['he is the same'] . . . [J.]

At 7 George returns. Christos grows weaker. Nikóla I don't think has the smallpox, for he has no eruption on his face. After breakfast, George got a *carro*, & all the better part of the furniture was taken away, to a room in a house Spiro lives in now, & I am to pay $2^1/_2$ dollars a month for it. (In the evening I came to know that the large & next

26 MARCH

sized tables would not go up the stairs, & that Spiro & George had had those taken to their mother's as well as my iron beds & mattresses. . . . Then I walked slowly to Potamós: the annoyance of dogs from the many wayside gardens & houses has much increased. The day was fine, not clear, but with large unsettled clouds, & Akrokerávnia in a haze of gray mists & gleams. Above Potamós was poor Dionýsios, to whom I gave 8 pence, telling him it would be the last. His sister — a pretty little girl, Sophia — brought me some flowers — stocks, white & purple, & said: «Δὲν θὰ σοῦ εἴδωμεν ποτέ; ποτέ; — ἴσως ἀπάνω.» ['Shall we never see you? — perhaps above.'] How strange & beautiful is faith. So I went on sadly, looking at the loveliness of the landscape, & saying «ὥρα καλή» ['may your time be good'] to all the peasants, up to the hill & then to Potamós flats, & all among them & to the 'Condi' road. At the old Fort cliff, looking over Mandoúki, I sate from 5.15 to 6.15, supposing Vido would be blown up. Then I came away, but a thunderstorm came on suddenly, & I only ran home to save a great wetting. Huge claps of thunder. George gave his last dinner of curry-turkey, eggs & spinach, & Tzikarátou pudding. He went at 8.15 to his mother. Another violent but short burst of storm happened at 9. I read Kinglake. [J.]

28 MARCH   Dark — violent wind, & pouring rain. Christos is the same, weaker only. At 12 called on Mrs Boyd, then on Baring, & on Loughman, where I lunched. If the Loughmans want 'the interesting', they are at least full of 'the amiable'. Returned home at 2 — violent wind. (But the Loughmans *are* interesting to those who find that the fulfilling of duty claims an interest. Old Mr Loughman sets off tomorrow in hope to be at the deathbed of his mother, 92 years old, he having been telegraphed for today. It is not all men would do this. My hour there was pleasant in some ways — they are kindly good people, & we may never meet again.) Returned, & sate, & thinking: no boox, no nothing; so, after long observing the 6 little geese just hatched today, I lay down & slept till 4.30. Then I walked out . . . Home by 7. Gaspipe-upset streets. At 7.30 dinner at Carter's & home by 8.30. Sent George to Kastrádes, a weary sad duty for him, poor fellow. O dear, this leaving Corfu! . . . [J.]

29 MARCH   Finer day, but cloudy, & towards 5–6 rain & thunder, then clear again, but violent gusts of hailstorms later. Rose at 8. After breakfast came Paramythiótti, who is already enragious about England, & says we do this fortress destruction of our own proper ugly will. Man looks at the last act — you have done us good first, lastly evil: on the evil we now judge you. . . . At 3 walked to the hill beyond Mandoúki, where — cloudy & rainier — I watched from 4 to 5.20 when the lunette was blown up. Returned hastily when there were more explosions. Captain Deverill's gander, 2 geese & 10 goslings are lovely to see. . . . Sad night of violent winds. Sad poor Kokáli family — poor Christos still suffers. [J.]

30 MARCH   Cloudy, & gleamy, but with very violent gusts of west wind all day at times, & storms of rain — indeed a truly odious day. Packed my lamps & various smallnesses, & did

nothing all day but look at Captain Deverill's beloved geese. The conduct of that exemplary gander is indeed beautiful. Poor Christos was the same all last night. . . . Dined at Boyd's, 6.30. The Martello tower fell at 5.30. The gas pipes laid down everywhere impede the Line Wall passengers. Evening far from unpleasant. But the wind is dreadful, & great rain has fallen. A very sad day. [J.]

Wind perpetual, but shiftier towards N.W. Rose before 7. Zinc & nail for last 3 boxes. . . . At 4 walked with Wright & Dunn to Análipsis. O ever-loved olives! gray solemn, & delicate-twinkling, dark-branched. Never more shall I see you – – – . Heavy storms of rain & wind when I got home. At 7 to Citadel. Very pleasant. Stayed till 10.30. Walked home by the narrow *calle* of St Spirídon. The 'university' boys had a row this last week, & attacked Baker — δὲν θέλομεν Ἄγγλον διδάσκαλον [we don't want an English professor]. They pelted him with slates & books, & Mrs Baker fainted. Police came. [J.] 31 MARCH

I have been more or less unwell internally all the winter, & bothered by the state of the place, by packing, & in many other things. Easels, frames, oil & water materials, paper, canvasses, etc., are surprisingly cumbrous, & books etc. etc. have to be arranged & moved. As it is an absolute condition of my remaining life that I have some winter home, the question has been, & is still, where that is to be — & finally I have thus disposed matters. My finished pictures of Turin, Bassae & nearly complete Argostóli & some drawings in one case, books & sketches in a 2nd, Yannina & other canvasses in a 3rd — these have all gone off already to Liverpool & will await my coming to England on July 2nd. All my furniture — of which some is good & not easily replaced in these parts — has gone into a single room hired for $2^1/_2$ dollars a month until I decide on its fate — sale here, or conveyance to Athens. 3rdly, 7 large cases containing the easels, books, etc. etc., go tomorrow to the Bonded Customs warehouse, there also to wait my future decisions. And 4thly, 7 trunks & other objects take my clothing & my numerous sketches, all of which will go on board with me, I trust, on Monday the 4th — in the Syra boat. I am thus cleared out. My beautiful rooms are already taken by others, so there is an end of Corfu life, & this is the last letter you will most probably ever receive from the island. 31 MARCH

I am not yet certain I shall go straight to Athens, & then, leaving heavy luggage there, return to Syra & go to Crete, or whether I shall go on to Crete from Syra in the first place: but Crete it seems is on the list of destinies & being part of my polygraphic Hellenic proclivities, is one of the things necessary to be done. After some 6 or 7 weeks in Crete, I should in any case return to Athens, & there look about for a possible winter home. I know well that Athens would have great drawbacks — dust, climate in summer, remoteness, liability to rows & riots etc., but on the other hand it seems to me the most analogous place to my pursuits, & one where possibly improvement & quiet may be combined, being as it is, too, not wholly out of the route of drawing-buying tourists. To make a better winter settlement nearer England is difficult. Nice is crowded & Anglo-vulgar; Rome & its priests, as well as its forced art quackery atmosphere, I detest. I shall therefore make an effort about Attica: & it would grieve me to give up all further chance of Greek learning & landscape. You see therefore that as the little fish said in the Pacific, I am at sea, nor will much more be assured till I have been to visit the owls of Minerva.

And indeed glad shall I be to go. The place is all altered & sad, & there is no pleasure to me in seeing the daily explosions & ruins of fine masonry & picturesque lines. Moreover, the angry & violent feeling against everything English is disagreeable tho' it is not so general as it seems. You know I dare say that the Bishop (always the prime agitator for the Union) is now the head of a very ferocious Club, who are publishing a paper of the utmost virulence against us, calculated to stir up all the idle & intriguing in our disfavour. Such 'facts' as the open insulting of 'Greek' women on the Esplanade by 'parties of brutal English sailors' might excite your astonishment, as they do mine, but in the present state of things the assertion of good old Vasilía Kokáli (my servant's mother) that in 50 years of English rule she has never known one female insulted by soldiers or sailors, goes for nothing.

The truth seems to me this: a great party, naturally regretting the English going — & moreover, another party who desired it but yet justly appreciated our actions — would all have united to make public demonstrations of respect & friendliness etc. on our leaving the island. This I know to be the case from various people who declare they are grieved that they cannot now make any manifestation in our favour. The handle given by the fortress-dismantling to the democratic party is therefore one I believe they are delighted to get. It is of course of great importance to the annexation party that no demonstration in an opposite sense, or such as could by any possibility be construed, should be made — & now I do not expect anyone will dare openly wish us 'Godspeed'.

For myself I avoid as much as I can speaking on the subject at all, but I cannot avoid making allowance for those who are constantly having the irritating sight of the forts being blown up — now for many weeks the almost daily object — nor can I wonder at their vexation when they hear of parties going over 'to see the beautiful blow up' etc. etc. When I am forced into talking, I do all I can (as Mr Gregory didn't) to show them how far better it would be to weigh this fortress wrong — if wrong it be — against the benefits England has given them — a useless task, however, in their present mood. 'Do you think', said one to me, 'that if you give me a thousand pounds, & then box my ears, that the last act would not outweigh the first, although in itself the last is trifling?' But the very addition to this which a second speaker instantly gave convinced me that I am right in believing the 'Fortress Question' is a godsend to the violent party. The speaker was an amiable man & desirous of softening down his friend's observations. '*In somma*', said he, '*la politica esige che si alza la voce contro l'Inghilterra.*' ['In short, politics demands that one raises one's voice against England.'] It is I think much to be regretted that this '*alzando la voce*' was so supplied them by ourselves.

Meanwhile the mass of the people behave quite well, & individually nothing uncourteous is said or done to anyone. Sir Henry walks about everywhere, & is treated with the same respect as ever. He is a splendid fellow, & has a most difficult part to play, for Colquhoun & others nameless who should work with him are against him. I suppose you will make him a 'Barnet' as Lady Young used to say, or a peer if he goes to any higher post. If ever he goes to Ceylon I will certainly then go out to India, Attic Greek & Attic furniture notwithstanding. The reports here of all possible sorts are endless; Woodhouse, Taylor, Sanders are named as to be the Consul. 'The church is to be turned into a theatre as a mark of *disprezzo* [scorn]' etc. Don't you think that would be a just judgement on a place where they have read the blasphemies of [the] Athanasian creed? So you see, the place is all breaking up & blowing up & bebothered & boshed.

What is really a serious vexation to me is that the equallynoxious gales have come late after two weeks of hot but dim weather wherein the mountains were unseen & undrawable, & all my hopes of getting some 10 or 12 favourite & long-postponed drawings are gone. And as bothers never come alone, poor Christos Kokáli, my man's brother, ill of consumption for four years, has now it seems really taken to die. And George has therefore a double journey to his mother's daily, & to sit up all night, besides the lots of rough extra work all this 'exodus' begets. Thunderstorms & violent squalls make life disgusting; add also that a gas company has turned up all the streets for pipes, & as I fall into the beastly trenches, I can say truly 'you have piped unto me, but I have not danced'. You perceive we are in the midst of bores therefore . . . Meanwhile, Captain Deverill's gander's two eldest wives have brought out a brood of lovely queer puffy fluffy goslings, & my whole pleasure in life is to watch them. Goodbye, my last furniture is going. I shall sit upon an eggcup & eat my breakfast with a pen. . . . [C.F.]

1 APRIL

Quite clear early — the Albanian snow as if in January — I fear all my ten little geese are lost . . . & wind N.W., but altogether a fine day, colder towards sunset & half an hour after, bitter & violent cold wind, almost north. Christos was worse all yesterday & last night. Rose at 7, & concentrated all my unpacked belongings into the studio — bed & all. George went out to arrange about the cases, & at 9 brought men. All 7 cases were removed to the *Dogana* before 11 — George works like 20 men when at it. Mr Woodley wrote a receipt for all. At 12 went to various places to get in bills. Mrs Carter, poor old lady, cried on shaking hands with me. She goes to Scotland, she says. Page's people say *all* the Maltese will go by degrees, &, I fancy, *all* the English shopkeepers. Sate a bit with Mrs Boyd, & lunched . . . By this time it was 2, & then I sat talking with Baring & Bowden, & Baring solo, playing, singing & talking, till 3.30 — alack for the oranges & flowers in a garden of light! Then, alone, I walked to Análipsis, but a vastly cold high N.W. wind blew, & made all things cold & sad. Yet went I on to the Kanóni, & perhaps see that too for the last time. 'Thou seest all things — thou wilt see my grave.' [J.]

2 APRIL   Very clear, & cold all day, wind high, N. by W. Rose at 6. George comes about 6.30. Poor Christos still lingers, but is more suffering, & weaker. The terrible trouble for the good Kokáli family. Breakfast. Spiro came — he seems not to know if he stays or goes . . . Writing & bothering endless — bill-paying etc. etc. till 11, when I went for a carriage ride to Pantaleóne. . . . Pantaleóne by 1.30. . . . A vast gray gray gray delicate myriads landscape, but immensely inferior to the more central views. Drew for an hour, & afterwards by stopping degrees as I walked down till 3.15. Then, the carriage overtaking us, we got into town by 5.20. O asphodels! O olives! O shadows! [J.]

3 APRIL   Everybody here is packed up & going away, & we are all everyone of us cross & disagreeable & sorry & in a fuss & bothered. . . . I am going to start tomorrow, having sent my luggage away, & intending myself to go by sea as it is cheaper than going by the steamer. I therefore join Capt. Deverill's 3 geese & we are going to swim all the way round Cape Matapan & so to the Piraeus as fast as we can. [N.D.]

3 APRIL   Awful north wind all morning, with tremendous storms of rain, beginning at 5 or 6 a.m. with a huge thunderstorm. Poor Christos still lingers, poor fellow, but is nearer his end hourly. All the morning I wrote notes to heaps of people . . . But the outside was like one long continued tempest, I never saw the seas more violent nor heard the wind more horridly here. At 1 I went out, but was nearly thrown down by the wind, & had to go by the Ghetto to De Vere's. All is sad; but it is a pleasure to see Mrs De Vere's real honest face. I stayed till 3, but had not courage to say goodbye. Went to the A.D.C.s rooms, & sate for 2½ hours with Strahan, afterwards walking in garden with him, Bowden & His Excellency. (I forgot — I went to Wolff's after De Vere's, & was disgusted at his praising a most atrocious pamphlet of Dandolo's just out: a viler production is not possible; but Wolff is vile.) 2 steamers coming in made an alarm of Mexican majesty, but falsely. Returned by the *calle* to dress — the Line Wall being all

up for gas. Evening [at Palace], as ever, pleasant. I grieve to leave good kind Sir Henry. Sate till 11 singing with the A.D.C.s & Bowden. Home by 11.15. Still the storm rages frightfully. [J.]

4 APRIL

Weather fine, but strongish north wind. Everything was ready as early as I could manage, & George took the last things away to Spiro's room. So only the 11 packages for the voyage remained. Wandered about miserably, & had to get 1 or 2 little things at Courage's & Taylor's. Walking up the Ghetto, spoke to Políti, who thinks all the Jews will go sooner or later. At 12.40 to De Vere's, & lunched with them for the *last* time. Came away at 2, & came off at 3 with George & Spiro in a boat to the Austrian Lloyd's *Stadium*. (Saw Captain Deverill, & heard that all the 10 little geese were dead or stolen.) Sad enough I am, but in better spirits than when I went last year, for Evelyn Baring joined me soon after & at 5 we left Corfu. Once more I left the loveliest place in the world, with a pang, though less this time through not being alone. Dinner, & afterwards Baring & I walked, talked, smoked & sat till eight, when there was tea, & then we sat star-gazing till 9, when we went to bed. Slept till 10.30, but the rolling & cracking of the ship when we got out into full sea beyond Paxos bored & worried me terribly: later it grew calmer, & I slept from 12.45 to 6.15, when George woke me.

> She sits upon her Bulbul
>   Through the long long hours of night,
> And o'er the dark horizon gleams
>   The Yashmack's fitful light.
> The lone Yaourt sails slowly down
>   The deep & craggy dell,
> And from his lofty nest, loud screams
>   The white plumed Asphodel... [J.]

ENVOI: 1877

15 SEPTEMBER Slept well, some 5 hours or so — absolutely *no* movement in the vessel. Rose at 5 or 6 & was on deck to see all bright & lovely, with a dazzling low sun just above the vast Akrokerávnian hills. So far, I have indeed cause to be thankful. Go on, & trust. Talk with Mr G. Arthur Vansittart, going to Athens as attaché, with dispatches; & drawing those Akrokerávnian hills just once more. Violent discussion among Greeks as to 'moving' or not moving in this war*... Breakfast at 10 or 10.30 — good enough. Sat next to Vansittart. Later, sitting on deck, looking at that *wonderful* lilac coast & all those islands where Frank & I used to be — Fano . . . etc. etc. At 12.15 the Citadel & canal, all the old Frank Lushington memories . . . By 1.30 we anchored below Fort Neuf & lo! — in a boat — George Kokáli! Lambi! & Dimítri! Immense pleasure & thankfulness! Poor George is very thin & altered, & feeble — yet not so much so as I had feared. He walked with me to the [Hotel] Bella Venezia, complaining dreadfully of the room he is living in. No trouble at Custom House. At Hotel, a long talk & I again determine to buy him a house, & pay a sum monthly while he is ill: if he recovers, he may yet come back to me. Thank God that I can see my way even to this hope — the bettering of his life while it lasts. At 2.30, he goes to Courage's & I wait luncheon. At 3, George comes again & we go to Courage's, where Swan was & says more time is wanted to arrange about any house. But he will do all he can. Then George & I walk to Kastrádes (where [suffering from diarrhoea] I am only just able to get to a hedge!).... When I came back, George said, '*Ho qualche cosa bisogna farsi vedere*' ['I have something I need to show you'] — & he took me to the corner of the railing, & said, '*Quella croce di ferro marca dove giace la mia Tatianí*' ['that iron cross marks the grave of my Tatianí'] — & this he said trembling like a leaf in the wind. I said to him, '*Ma voi la vedrete pui tardi.*' ['But you will see her hereafter.'] On which he replied, '*So bene che qui stanno osse soltanto, ma il cuore ed il spirito di essa non sono perduti; en Paradiso c' incontraremo. Si quella non e in Paradiso, chi puo andarci?*' ['I well know that here there are only bones, and that her heart and spirit are not lost, and that we will meet in Paradise. If she is not in Paradise, who can go there?'] I asked him if he would like me to put up a stone, but he said, '*No, basta questo ferro per memoria.*' ['No, this iron is memorial enough.'] We then called on Dr Koskino . . . he rather comforts me about George's health. He says George has had some great internal shock & cannot come right at once (he spoke of dysentery), but by care he may come quite round again. We left & went to see a corner house (none it seems is for sale) but one I fear much too large for them to move into, if we can hear of no others. Tomorrow we are to know 'particulars'.

We walked across to the Strada Reale; never did I see such a heap of ill-conditioned destruction! Called at Baron d'Everton's — out. And so to the Hotel Bella Venezia — by half round the Esplanade.

Nikóla has just been drawn for the army & comes on Monday; this poor George, with great good sense, is pleased with. He allows he *must* do one of 2 things — 1st, stay here always with his 3 sons, or 2nd, come with them all 3 to San Remo. I know not what to advise as to the future; all I can do at present is to get him out of that dreadful hole.

George left me at the Hotel & at 7.30 I dined there — well as to food, but the people were nasty. Came up & wrote this. The heat is very great, but I am thankful things are no worse than they are. It is 9 p.m.

16 SEPTEMBER

Thank God, slept well & wrote a lot of journal from 5 a.m. Grant that now I have done half of this sad journey, the rest & its chief errand may be as happily carried out. *No sacrifice* of money will be too great if I can get rid of the feeling that George has not been as well cared for as he merits. He came at 7, & he now thinks — & it seems to me not without reason — that for him to live at Kastrádes would be too far, & lonely, & cold in winter, so we agree that it will be better to find *rooms*, & he goes to enquire. Then I [go] off to Paramýthia & see Giovanni Paramythiótti who says there *may be* a floor vacant in the old uncle's little house, & is to let me know tomorrow: it would be £1 10s. a month — £18 a year. Back, & went with one George Riechi, a courier, to see another house near Condi Terrace: price unknown. Back to breakfast 8.15 — very good breakfast. German travellers to Greece. At 9 called on Mr Swan who is very kind & helpful . . . & quite approves of the apartment theory, & is also to look out for rooms. Call again at the Baron's — not up yet. Back [to] Hotel — 10. Later called on Baron d'E. who is much the same, & very little aged: to dine there αὔριον [tomorrow] at 7. He is quite as *anti-Russ* as anybody, & wholly anti-Greek — & is, moreover, sure the Turks will win. The man Riechi has seen other houses, but all £48 or £50 a year. 11.30 comes Filippo Bohaja, J. B. Edwards' old servant; he has one daughter a governess here, one a nun, & one well married to a clerk in India! (What a contrast to G.'s life & family!) Also a son, a shoemaker at Malta, to whom I send an English half-crown. Then came George, who has seen a little house at San Rocco, the upper part of which he seems to have set his heart on. The rooms would be only £1 a month, & there is a bit of garden, where he might keep fowls. Perhaps, dear good old fellow, this may be after all the best for him? Ποιός ἠξεύρει; [Who knows?]

Slept & read till 1.30. *Great heat.* Lunch. At 3 came George & at 3.30 went with him to see the 'Palazzo'. It is really well-placed, but not yet complete. There must be a W.C., & a wall to separate the 2 gardens. There are 5 rooms — kitchen, eating room, a double-bedded room & one for me if I ever come there & one for George. The owner is a Souliote, & below is to be a shop. I don't see that any better affair can be taken up — either as to my own ability for payment, or as to George's benefit, for it is very near the town, & yet in a healthy & high position. The man wanted 27½ francs a month, but will take 25 — so tomorrow we are to close the matter. We then walked up to the lovely Análipsis & 'called' on Paraskeví, who is a real nice good woman & nearly as good-looking as ever. She gave us some coffee & then we came slowly down to the

Hotel, along the dirty crowded Esplanade, by 6. I am feeling happy at having been able to do somewhat what I ought to do & what I believed it my duty to do; & old George seems happier & better. Dinner 7.30. Very good. Talked German abstrusely.

17 SEPTEMBER Slept well, thank God. Rose at 6. Weather the same. . . . George came at 7.30 & left to get house agreement drawn up. Later at 9, I went to Courage's & to Beale's, 3 beds £6 — also tables. Breakfast at 9.30 . . . After 10, went with George to the notary, where the agreement was drawn up, & then to Courage's, where Mr Swan suggested some alterations. George then went away, expecting Nikóla to come down. Then I called on Mrs Barr, & saw her, but not Barr, who I take it sees no one now. J. W. Taylor, I was sorry to hear, has had a slight paralysis. Hotel by noon. Filippo Bohaja comes & volunteers to be my servant if I get no other, wages £3 pounds a month, & 'rations'. Read Dicken's *Mystery of Edwin Drood*. At 2.30 went with Mr Arthur G. Harrison in a carriage, first to Análipsis. Walked up to the little church, & to the plateau, & down to the old temple ruin: all lovely, though day not clear & hardly any distance visible. Then drove to the One Gun Battery & back, & across to the Potamós road, & up through Potamós & along the ridge, & down to the Gouvia road, so finishing the *giro*; actually reached the Hotel by 6.10. Throughout all this, the extreme delight with & appreciation of the Corfu scenery on Harrison's part quite pleased & immediately interested me. It is so long since I fell in with so nice a fellow. At Hotel found dear old George; Nikóla had just come so at all counts he had his 3 sons with him. George's quiet sadness I should feel more deeply, but I have vowed against all tendency to the 'morbid'. Changed dress & went to Baron d'Everton's. Dinner at 7. Very nice dinner & pleasant evening; & I don't think I made any very foolish blunders. The Baron walked home with us all. Clouds & some rain. A change of weather ahead — possibly. But we have come on a duty. [J.]

18 SEPTEMBER Slept well, thank God, after a loud thundering & rattle of rain from 11 to 12. Rose before 6 finding myself less depressed & better in health. At 7.30 came George, certainly looking better, with Nikóla, grown into a fine tall fellow of over 6 feet! He went off to the Citadel, & George with me to the New House. Its only objection seems that it is so new — yet it was begun in April last & the walls seem thoroughly dry with the summer baking sun's heat. Anyhow, one cannot have all one's own way, & the place is certainly very suitable — quite so indeed — in all respects except that it is new. And they are working at the inner wall, & the garden wall also. Afterwards, I bought a sketchbook, & left the agreement to be copied; also called at the fat tinman of old days . . . (Changed £10.) . . . Hotel by 9. Breakfast, 10 to 11, slowly reading English papers. Breakfast, *trigli* [mullet] wonderfully good, also omelette. Afterwards, slept a bit & finished the unfinished story of Edwin Drood. Lunch. Sleep — reading — but now, 3 p.m., it is all cloudy & begins to rain, so I don't see how my plan of going out to draw can be finalized. Perhaps it may hold up. At 3.30, George came, seeming somewhat more cheerful. I gave him £10 for his doctor & medicine, the latter very

nearly £8. We went out then, but I alone to Courage's, where I left a letter from R. J. Bush for Mr Swan, ordering Corsica & 3 Nonsense books to be sent to him. Rain holding off, I went to the new house of San Rocco & drew it twice. The Souliote owner is evidently hurrying on the finishing of it. While I was drawing, Nikóla Kokáli came up; he is undoubtedly improved by adversity & seems a likeable chap, with a good countenance.

Afterwards I came across to the Kastrádes side, & drew the inconceivable Citadel twice. Surely nowhere have art & nature so combined to make beautiful landscape as here. All the distance, however, was clouded. Hotel by 6.30. Dinner at 7. Much excitement about recent telegrams — are they true or not. A vastly horrid man opposite spat so disgustingly that I nearly 'vomited' & at last had actually to leave the table. Two boys also were highly odious. Landlord's sorrow about spitting man. Wrote to Courage's enclosing an order on Drummond's for £20 & to themselves to advance £3 monthly to George. All this makes my conscience lighter. [J.]

Rose before 6. Cloudy & soft morning — having rained & more rain probable. So our outdoor picnic must be given up. George came 7.30 — & I to Courage's: the house settlement to be signed this morning. (George wants me to take a monster melon to H. & A. Congreve.*) Back to Hotel — 8.30, breakfast. At 10, poked about for books, but found slender encouragement. Got, however, *Villette*, & Cowper's poems! . . . Got 4 ink stands for George & his 3 boys. At 11 came Notary, & I signed my name in grisogenous Greek & had my agreement for Casa Zitso, for 2 years. At 11.45 the table is laid — funny idea! — for my old servant, his 3 sons & myself. The dinner or lunch went off very nicely; the *ragazzi* being at first φοβισμένοι [frightened], but afterwards more conversible, & always absolutely well-behaved. George flies out when Lambi hands plates on the wrong side, or when Nikóla won't speak out, or when Dimítri won't take grapes when adjured so to do. But on the whole I think the party was happy; & most certainly I was greatly pleased, & very thankful at being able to see my dear good servant in the midst of his sons & in somewhat better health.

19 SEPTEMBER

Slept till 3 & woke to find sky all overcast & a rather sharp heavy rain falling. Wrote address-envelopes to myself for the Souliote. Then called on Baron d'Everton. He still persists in believing that the Russi will be utterly defeated. His account of Lord Palmerston & the cession of the islands is interesting. Also, when the celebrated 'suggestion dispatch'* — afterwards stolen & published — was hatched in Corfu, it was sent to Sir J. Young (at Venice) who signed it unread. Baron d'E. says he thinks G. F. Bowen had no hand in that particular theft, though he confesses that he constantly intrigued with the Romas, & [?]Russina. Afterwards called on Lady Emily Kozzíris, who is bird-like & lively as ever. Then tried to call on Woodley, but his place was shut. So I walked up the well-remembered Ghetto, & to the new house. Close by, fell in with poor George, wandering sadly — alas! he is so feeble! Let me however be thankful that I may have added some comfort to his later days! Hotel by 6.15. Dined at 7, sitting at the further end of the table — the *sputatore* [spitter] being 'too much' for me. Dinner vastly good. Came to room & worked till 9.30 — a long letter to Frank Lushington. Pouring rain always. [J.]

20 SEPTEMBER   Disturbed night & wretched morning. Torrents of pouring rain, & somewhat more wind. Yet, as it was my duty to come, so it is my duty to go, & go I must. George comes at 8, & I have persuaded him to let me take the 2 rooms downstairs for him, Lambi, & Dimítri, so that they need not be a day longer in the horrid hole. Then, 8.30, comes Dionýsios Gazzi, & says 10 francs a day shall do for all 3 — rooms & food included. Next comes Mr Thomson, to say Bank is shut, *festa*, but Swan will be there at 11. Weather rather horrid; more wind. Came Nikóla, to whom I spoke of the 10 fr. a day arrangement for his father & 2 brothers. Went at 9 to the Austrian Lloyd Office, & took a ticket for Brindisi, 35 fr. Rain still. Called on Mr Woodley — out; *pouring rain*: wait in office till it holds up: but the prospix is not very encouraging. Hotel by 10. George comes, so I persuade him to go & get his trunks, so as to sleep here tonight. Then I go to Loughman's & see young Loughman who really seems a nice amicable gentle chap — but I can conceive he may not be a tip-top professional. I am very glad I wrote that letter to Loughman Senior. Next to Willi Swan, where I changed 2 of Drummond's credit notes of £10 for £10 worth of Greek paper & £10 of mixed gold & dollars. Swan seems to me a really good-hearted active man. Came back with my tin to Hotel, & breakfast at 11.30 very pleasantly, & thank God again that the dark cloud of last night & early morning seems lightening. Read papers. Then saw the brother Gazzi's little cripple child, reminding me of poor Masciarelli, *anni fa*. My God! when I look at him, & when I think of the sorrow of my poor good Souliote, & when I reflect on endless other miseries, what am I to complain or grieve? — when rather I ought to be always thanking the power under whom my life has been what it is, & through whom I can even slightly relieve others. More shame to me that I have done so little. . . .

I give George £10 in paper for various furniture. Various cautions to George about money etc., & walked out at 12.40 to the New House, but today being a *festa* all was shut. Paid my bill, 103 fr. Back by 1.30 — George at Hotel. He brings me a pair of slippers for Hubert [Congreve] & one for myself. Take George to see his *mezzanino* rooms here. Hoja plant in bloom. Pay for a dozen of Ithaka wine: 20 fr. Take leave once more of my dear old George, who goes to get his traps. Talk with Dionýsios Gazzi. Lunch at 3. Man brings a parcel of Cerigo work — a baby sack — sent over by H. Bulwer in 1863!* This is supremely ridiculous! Dionýsios Gazzi gives me a pot of good olives. The sun shines, & one has yet once more to be thankful. Come upstairs, & write this. All things considered, *how much* have I to be thankful for through all this sad & difficult task!

At 3.30 George comes, & his 3 boys. By 4 — on our way — all. By 4.15, on board the Austrian Lloyd *Oreste*, & once more I am *alone*. For all now are gone, waving handkerchiefs to the last. God be thanked that I have been able to arrange as I have for some extra comfort to one of the best human beings, & may I henceforth lose sight of no opportunity to do good to him & his! Compared with last March 2nd,* what comfort! The sun is bright, & the loveliness of Corfu greater than ever. So I set to work & draw & draw till 5, when dinner. At dinner was a Cerigo man, also one 'Sanders', son of a banker at Kefaloniá, knowing me by name through the Baron & Loughman; a pleasant sort of Scotch fellow. We talked again. Afterwards, I drew, drew, drew the sadly receding Corfu. Walked about deck till nearly 9. Sea quite calm. [J.]

APPENDIX ONE
LEAR AS LANDSCAPE PAINTER

'I'm a landscape painter, and I desire you like me as sich, or not at all', Lear had written to a friend in 1851. Becoming a landscape painter had been his concern during the years he had spent in Rome and southern Italy after he had left Knowsley Hall in 1837 and had abandoned his earlier career as a painter of birds and animals. In a sense he had little or no formal training for his new vocation. On the other hand the way had been prepared for him by a long line of antecedents, English and continental.[1]

This line had already begun to emerge in the early 17th century when painters like Inigo Jones (1573–1652) — though he was primarily a designer not of landscapes but rather of architecture and fête scenery and costumes — had visited Rome, and painters like van Dyck (1599–1641) and Wenceslaus Haller (1607–1677) had painted romantic water-colours and topographical views. But it really came into its own subsequent to the rediscovery of Herculanaeum, near Naples, in 1738; for it was then that artists began to exploit the 'picturesque' that Italy provided in such abundance: classical ruins, distant mountains, the blue waters of the Mediterranean and the Adriatic, lakes, stone pines and cypresses, the graphic appearance of peasants and their villages.

The mould into which it was the growing fashion to pour this love for the picturesque was largely shaped by the classical tradition of the great 17th century continental painters, Claude Lorrain, Nicholas Poussin and Salvator Rosa. It was they who provided the canons of what was to become the ideal of High Art in the Grand Manner, reduced to absurdity in those large, infinitely dreary Victorian pictures with classical trappings, allegorical significance and landscapes literalized to death. Already in the middle of the 18th century Richard Wilson (1714–1762) — who spent the years between 1749 and 1756 in Rome — was introducing these canons into the mainstream of English painting, and half a century later even Samuel Palmer could speak of enjoying in Claude 'that Golden *Age* into which poetic minds are thrown back, on first sight of one of his genuine *Uncleaned* pictures'.

The spate of artists intent on capturing intimations of this golden age at their source — above all, it was thought, in Italy, although by now Greece itself and even the Levant were beginning to encroach on this priority — continued unabated in the years preceding Lear's own initiation into the world of topographical painting. It included artists such as Cotman (1782–1842), Prout (1783–1852), Boys (1803–1874), David Roberts (1796–1864), James Duffield Harding (1798–1863) — possibly in some respects closest to Lear in purpose and achievement — and of course the most important Grand Tour artist of them all, the great Joseph Turner (1775–1851), who

---

[1] See Philip Hofer, *Edward Lear as a Landscape Draughtsman* (Cambridge, Mass., 1967).

made his first visit to the continent in 1802 and went again and again until 1845. It was within this perspective — the perspective of transitional, neo-classical romantic coventions applied to 'dramatic' or 'picturesque' landscape — that Lear shaped his aspiration and style to create grand and timeless works in his own topographical speciality.

If we are to understand why in spite of this aspiration and style Lear was able to produce works of art which do possess living qualities, we have to perceive what might be called his artistic predicament more clearly. This requires a brief preamble, mental rather than historical, though couched in historical terms. The Renaissance, it will be recalled, had promoted the idea that the purpose of art was *imitare la natura* as well as possible, and this idea had penetrated into Germany in the 16th century — it was appropriated, for instance, by Dürer — and above all into France in the 17th century, where painters such as Claude and Poussin sought to exemplify it in their works. But side by side with this idea went another: that imitation must be not directly of nature but of those who had best *imitated nature*. And those who had best imitated nature were the Ancients. Hence the greatest revolution in the history of the idea of *mimisis*: the displacement, from the 15th century to the end of the 17th century, of *imitation of nature* by *imitation of antiquity*. Artists had to imitate nature, but to imitate it in the way that the ancients had imitated it. The traditional theory was changed into an academic neo-classical theory. Direct vision and experience of nature were inadequate unless robed in the garb of antiquity.

Such an attitude was re-affirmed in the 18th century by artists and writers like Winckelmann and Menge, Adam and Flaxman. As Schelling, in his lecture 'Concerning the Relation of the Plastic Arts to Nature' (1807), was to point out, although for Winckelmann the idea of imitation remained, the object that had to be imitated had changed. The place of nature was taken by the exalted works of antiquity — or at least by the outward forms of these works, without the spirit that imbued them. Winckelmann had been deeply moved by the forms of the plastic arts of antiquity and he taught that the production of an ideal form, more noble than any natural form, was the highest purpose of art. Yet such ideal forms — imitations of those of antiquity — must in fact be deader and colder than the forms of nature unless they are envisaged by the spiritual eye that penetrates their husk and feels the force at work within them. In short, the whole neo-classical theory of art was a recipe for death: nature was a mere product of things lifelessly existent, not living and creating; while the ideal forms of antiquity that the artist was supposed to imitate were in reality dead forms, incapable, like nature itself in this view, of self-active procreation.

The neo-classical view of nature was of course very much akin to what was fast becoming the all-pervading view of modern science or of what Goethe was to call the 'empirico-mechanico-dogmatic torture chamber' of quantitative knowledge. What one might describe as the vitalist or hermetic view of nature, according to which nature is seen as the theatre of vitally operative forces, divine in essence, had been abandoned in the 17th century — though not without a struggle, as the works of the

Cambridge Platonists and of poets like Traherne evince. What took its place was the non-vitalist view in which nature is seen as so much dead matter, inanimate, and lacking all innate living and creative powers. This non-vitalist view was magnificently competent to explain natural phenomena in terms of mechanical laws, but was incompetent to explore man himself. Still more incompetent was it to take account of the reciprocity that can — and should — exist between man and nature when man looks on nature with the eyes of the imagination and not simply with his cold mechanical reason and when consequently he sees nature not as an abstract world of lifeless objects but as the landscape of the soul, as the living, richly varied but scattered 'portions of Man's immortal body', a form of wordless music. Once you begin to explain nature in mechanical terms, it is but a short step to trying to explain man and his inner life in mechanical terms. In the end everything becomes non-vital, all qualitative distinctions are obliterated, and everything is reduced to the kind of simplicity which expression in non-vital terms makes possible. The lowest common denominator has a perennial attraction for the systematic scientific mind.

By the end of the 18th century, however, and in the opening years of the 19th century, there was a growing ill-defined dissatisfaction with the 'universe of death' offered by followers of Descartes, Locke and Newton. It is expressed in Goethe's treatises *The Metamorphosis of Plants* and *A Theory of Colour,* as it is in his remark that 'a man born and bred in the so-called exact sciences will, on the height of his analytical reason, not easily comprehend that there is also something like an exact concrete imagination'. It is expressed in that lecture by Schelling to which reference has already been made, where Schelling pleads for a rejection of neo-classical theory with its insistence on the imitation of the antique and its concomitant idea that the task of the artist is to impose ideal forms on a nature that in itself is regarded as dead and abstract. He asks for a return to a vitalist view of things, calling on the artist to imitate nature, not in an external, literal way, but by becoming aware of the living essences that animate it from within. Art should be the vision and expression of the indwelling spirit of nature. In such a meeting of man and nature, the spirit of nature is liberated from its bonds and feels its kinship with the human soul. At the same time, it is only in so far as the artist has apprehended in living imitation the spirit of nature, which is at work in the core of things and in whose speech form and shape are merely symbols, that he is capable of creating a living work of art.

In England, Coleridge was to speak in much the same strain: 'The artist must imitate that which is within the thing, that which is active through form and figure... the *Naturgeist*, or spirit of nature, as we unconsciously imitate those whom we love; for only so can he hope to produce any work truly natural in the object and truly human in the effect.' For Coleridge, too, there is a reciprocity between man and nature: the substance of all we see, hear, feel and touch is in ourselves; to know is to resemble. Our task is to acquire not lifeless technical rules, cold notions, but living and life-producing ideas, with the certainty that such ideas are essentially at one with the germinal causes of nature, for man's consciousness is the focus and mirror of both, and it is this conjunction of inner and outer which the artist should try to express in his work.

To be sure, there is a kind of idealistic dualism in Coleridge's vision of things. Nature and natural forms constitute a kind of symbolic alphabet; they are a code of lost wisdom which it is man's task to decipher. Hence the beautiful in nature is necessarily regarded as symbolical of a spiritual reality; it is not regarded as co-existent with this reality or as an essential medium of its fruition. It is at best a reflection by which we are aided to a deeper knowledge of reality, which is also a deeper knowledge of ourselves. At the same time it is a vision, like that of Goethe and Schelling, which affirms that the reality of nature is something that can be perceived and experienced, not by the analytical reason, but only by the imagination, which sees nature as animated by living forces akin to those that animate the innermost reality of man himself. Thus the task of the artist is to imitate, not the external forms of nature, still less the idealized natural forms as represented by the artists of antiquity, but the beauty and harmony that constitute the non-material essence of nature, just as they constitute the non-material essence of the human soul. It is a vision consequently that is at odds with the neo-classical vision which through painters such as Claude, Poussin, Salvator Rosa and their numerous imitators, had established itself as the prerequisite and hallmark of all great art.

Thus — to speak in a general and somewhat oversimplified manner — during the first half of the 19th century two views of the artist's function, each with its corresponding view of nature, began to confront one another in the English art-world. The first is what we have called the neo-classical view, deriving from the great French masters of the 17th century but amplified beyond all expectation in the 18th century by the ever-inflating waves of idolatry for the ancient world which swept over the sophisticated north-European mind. In this view, art was above all the imitation of antiquity, and nature not a reality to be confronted and experienced through direct personal contact and intercourse, but rather a non-vital, passive background for figures and monuments on which the artist might impose corresponding prefabricated ideal forms. The artists who appropriated this view are legion: we have already mentioned some of them as among Lear's precursors, but there are countless others, including all those — names like Thomas Hope, Gell, Dodwell, Cockerell, John Linton, Joseph Cartwright and Hugh Williams spring to mind — who managed to kill the Greek landscape stone dead in the name of the artistic ideals they had accepted.

The second view is related to the attempt to revive the vitalist sense of nature about which we have been speaking. In this view, art is the imitation of nature, but nature itself is regarded not as inanimate or simply material, the mere function of mechanical laws susceptible to the abstract analytical mind. On the contrary, it is regarded as the revelation of an immaterial beauty and harmony that themselves correspond to the deepest realities of the human soul. It is this view — though it should not be labelled romantic in the literary sense of the word, since its pedigree, in the European world at least, is hermetic and Christian — that found expression in the era of which we are speaking above all in the works of the romantic poets, particularly perhaps of Wordsworth and Keats. But it also found expression in the paintings of Samuel Palmer and the group of painters connected with him, as well as in the works of Constable and Turner. In addition, the call, 'return to nature', 'render nature as she is', was to become the *leitmotif* of the greatest English art critic of the 19th century, John Ruskin, who as early as 1843, in the first volume of his *Modern Painters*, could exhort artists to 'go to nature in all singleness of heart, and work with her laboriously, having no other thought but how best to penetrate her meaning; rejecting nothing, selecting nothing, and scorning nothing.'

The confrontation of these two views is not unconnected with a change in the attitude to colour in painting which emerges in the latter half of the 18th century and in the first half of the 19th century. According to the neo-classical view, colour in painting is regarded as an element that is separable from form and even opposed to form, a kind of adjunct to it. It tends therefore to be applied in flat, horizontal areas, extrinsically, or exteriorly, without an inner life of its own apart from the form to which it is subordinate. This accords with the Lockeian distinction between the primary quality of form and the secondary quality of colour. Indeed, it accords with the prevailing 'scientific' way of looking at the world as if it were an object exterior to man, flattened and neutralized, and spread out before him like a chart whose features he passively reflects.

The shift in the attitude to colour in painting is related to the vitalist view of nature of which we have been speaking. According to this view nature is regarded not as an object exterior to man but as intimately connected with his own inner being, a kind of mirror in which what he sees, and how he sees it, is an image of the state of his own soul. This makes the determining factor of what man sees in the so-called outer world, and how he sees it, not the outer world itself as an object extrinsic or exterior to man which he passively reflects, but the activity and state of his own subjective being. The emphasis shifts from object to subject. Correspondingly, colour is not something objectively given to the eye by the outer world; it pertains first of all to the subject, to the organ of sight, to the eye whose changing vision — which changes all that it sees — is the reflection of the changing inner states of the being whose organ it is. The perception of colour is therefore an action and reaction of the soul itself. Indeed, colour is the very condition of the act of seeing, an energy which engages and is communicated to the whole being.

This means that the Lockeian distinction between form as primary and colour as secondary is reversed. In fact, it is displaced altogether, for, according to Berkeley, who is here re-affirming the mediaeval view, the eye sees 'only diversity of colours' and no form at all. Goethe made this proposition the whole basis of painting. 'The colours we see in bodies', he writes, 'do not effect the eye as if they were something foreign to it, as if it were a matter of an impression received purely from outside. No, this organ is always so situated as to produce colours itself, to enjoy a pleasant sensation if something homogeneous to its nature is presented to it from the outside.'

Colour is not a passive impression, but the language of the soul itself.

Consequently, colour in painting by itself produces in the spectator a reaction akin to the action — the imaginative action — of the artist who paints it. Particular colours produce particular and definite mental and psychic reactions. This means that increasingly painting is conceived of in terms not of form but of colour. Ultimately a painting could be not a depiction of objects in the outside world but a self-subsistent colour harmony. As Ruskin was to remark of the later paintings of Turner, colour becomes the principal element of decision: what is important is 'the almost instantaneous record of an *effect* of colour or atmosphere ... the drawing and the details of every subject being comparatively subordinate, and the colour nearly as principal as the light and shade had been before.' One is even approaching the idea — present for instance in Orthodox iconography and closely allied to if not identical with alchemical colour symbolism — of the symbolic use of colour, where colours are used because they express not a chromatic harmony but rather a metaphysical or spiritual significance, the conflict of light and dark in the human soul itself.

This brief analysis of the two opposing currents of thought and feeling which were competing for ascendancy in the consciousness of painters and poets in the early decades of the 19th century has been necessary in order to situate Lear's own work in a perspective, less historical than mental, which explains a dichotomy that runs through it and enables us to understand why his most ambitious paintings are by and large academic and lifeless, while only in his water-colours does he affirm his gifts unshackled. As we noted, as a young man Lear had no formal training in painting beyond that which he received from his sister Ann. It was only in later life, when he was approaching middle age, that he put himself to school to 'study art', first at the Royal Academy in London, and then under the direct tuition of Holman Hunt; and by that time his aspiration and capabilities had already developed along lines too definite to be modified fundamentally. As a self-conscious artist whose ambition was to produce works in oil in the grand manner, Lear placed himself within the tradition of painting exemplified by Claude Lorrain and his peers and successors — that neo-classical tradition some of whose features and developments we have specified.

The result was what one might have expected. Lear's oil paintings lack practically all the qualities that go to make a work of art — vitality, rhythm, subtlety of line and colour, the imprint of an active and richly endowed imagination. Instead they are characterized by all the opposite traits: ossification, crudity, and a literalness so unimaginative and static that it could be excelled only by the camera. And the same might be said in general about Lear's other self-conscious and 'worked-up' paintings: to the degree to which he tried to make his work conform to the canons which he accepted as those of great art, it exhibits that lack of creative qualities and that deadness which typify his oil paintings, just as they typify the works of those other neo-classical artists who effectively killed off Italian and Greek landscapes and monuments in their moribund paintings.

Fortunately, however, not all Lear's painting was crippled in this manner: some of it escaped the Procrustean operation that we have been describing. There was, as he himself affirmed to Holman Hunt, a vein of poetry in him, and in manifesting it, as he does in many of his unelaborated, non-selfconscious water-colours, he breaks free from his neo-classical fetters and comes far closer to expressing the vision of the opposing current of thought and feeling implicit in the vitalist view of nature, with all that means in terms of the use of colour. I am not suggesting by this that Lear had studied the writings of such people as Schelling or Coleridge, in which the vitalist, non-scientific view of nature was being re-affirmed, still less that he was familiar with Goethe's theory of physiological colours. But he was nourished in his youth on the romantic poets in whom this vitalist view was seeking and often finding expression, and he was a lifelong reader of Tennyson's poetry, in which some of its undercurrents are certainly present.

Moreover, of contemporary artists his great idol was Turner, and we have already noted how Ruskin was able to discern in Turner's later works an attitude to colour that makes colour the decisive element in a way that accords, knowingly or unknowingly, with the views of Berkeley and Goethe. And when we recall that Turner, in his 1811 lectures at the Royal Academy, repeats Dryden's statement that 'art reflecting upon Nature endeavours to represent it as it was first created without fault', we are at least given a hint that Turner himself was aware of a perception of nature quite other than the non-vitalist scientific perception. In addition, Lear was a faithful reader of Ruskin, as he acknowledges in a letter he wrote in old age thanking Ruskin 'for having, by your books, caused me to use my own eyes in looking at landscape from a period dating long back'; and Ruskin, whatever else he may have been, was certainly a liberating influence from the desiccating conventions of neo-classical art. Finally, it must not be forgotten that Lear read and deeply admired Plato and, himself a self-confessed lover of the beautiful, he can hardly have been unaffected by Plato's understanding of beauty and the status he accords to beauty as the principal attribute of the divine world.

All this being the case, it is not surprising that there was another side to the painter in Lear. In fact, there is a curious parallel between Lear in his private and public life and Lear as a painter. Just as Lear lived within a social world whose conventions and attitudes were radically at odds with and largely stifled his own temperament, so as a painter he strove officiously to make paintings according to conventions and attitudes that were at odds with and largely stifled his true gifts. The result was that these gifts find expression only in paintings that Lear did not subsequently attempt to work up into what he considered to be art in the proper sense of the word. They find expression, that is to say, in the water-colours he painted without regard for the conventions to which he sought to subjugate most of his work. And although these water-colours are still in the picturesque mode, in them Lear nevertheless manifests an inner freedom and spontaneity that transcend the hackneyed neo-classical formulas and make it clear that he possesses a feeling for nature and a capacity for expressing that feeling which set him in another class altogether.

Lear here is not just passively reflecting nature in terms of impressions coming from outside and which he then proceeds to formulate according to preconceived notions. On the contrary, he is actively participating in what he sees. There is a vital interplay between inner and outer, between his creative imagination and the scene which it confronts. The scene, that is to say, becomes informed, even transformed, by the activity of his own soul.

That is why these water-colours possess a poetic, even musical quality totally lacking in his other work. This is nowhere more evident than in the fact that in them colour, as in Turner's later works, is the decisive factor — colour again not as a passive impression but as the language of the artist's own soul. The best of the water-colours are indeed self-subsistent harmonies of colour. It is not that Lear distorts, falsifies or invents the landscape he is painting. He actually sees it in that way — sees it in that way because he is experiencing it in the light of a poetic imagination and not simply as a draughtsman wanting to produce an exact literal record. That is why the drawing and the details are relatively unimportant, and it is not form but colour, as an expression of the activity and state of Lear's own imaginative being, that operates as the determining principle. If Lear's water colours of, say, the Greek landscape often possess a freshness and warmth, a vitality and rhythm, which one may look for in vain in other 19th century renderings of the same landscape, this is not because he paints it more accurately or more in accordance with what the ordinary eye or the eye of the camera would perceive to be its natural features and coloration. It is because in it and through it he recognized something that corresponded to his own innermost identity, something that evoked and galvanized into activity the vein of poetry which he knew he possessed and which, once activated, enabled him to express in paint intimations of those aspects of the non-material beauty and essence of this landscape with which he felt such affinity. It is in this way that the best of Lear's water-colours help to awaken in us an imaginative vision of things which in our scientific and materialist age is too often overlaid and eclipsed. It is his triumph, modest yet authentic, and his vindication as the landscape painter that he so earnestly claimed to be.

APPENDIX TWO
THE NEW BARBARISM

I add this second appendix because it seems unfair not to warn the reader of Lear's Corfiote letters and journals that the island of whose beauty they speak so feelingly — 'it really is a Paradise', 'assuredly, there is no place in the world more beautiful than Corfu' — has in recent years been cruelly disfigured. I don't know how far the total coastline of Corfu extends in terms of miles; but whatever its length every stretch of it accessible by road or track has been so butchered and bartered, drawn and quartered, and so immersed and desolated beneath the ferro-concrete hideosity of hotel and boarding-house, discotheque, bar, cafeteria and chop-house, and the wave after wave of pink-faced, white-bodied neo-Visigoths that summer-long blotch and bespatter its beaches, with all the accompanying raucousness of motorcar, motorbike, motorscooter, transistor, radio, motorboat, and the other gimcrackery and detritus (plastic and mineral) of mass tourism, that one searches in vain, across the wreckage of this dishallowed world, for the virginal loveliness that confronted Lear at virtually every footstep. His beloved Palaiokastrítsa, for example, is a total disaster, but it is absolutely no exception. And this contagion is gradually creeping inland and up the hills... In one of his last poems the Greek poet George Seferis wrote:

> Years ago you said:
> 'Essentially I'm a matter of light.'
> And still today when you lean
> on the broad shoulders of sleep...
> you look for crannies where the blackness
> has worn thin and has no resistance...

Alas, the blackness that has submerged the Corfu landscape has not yet worn thin, nor does its resistance show any sign of weakening. And in any terms other than those of economics, the damage is irreparable. That this should make the testimony of Lear's paintings even more precious may be cold comfort; yet if art does not give us at least a glimpse, an image, of things as they are in their original purity — in their flowering — why do we value it at all?

NOTES

A.L. 13 April 1848

George Ferguson Bowen was Rector of the Ionian Academy (see Introduction) when Lear first arrived in Corfu in 1848. He was later to become Secretary to the Lord High Commissioner, and was duly knighted. It was during his term of office as Secretary that Lear's opinion of him changed drastically, as is only too apparent in a later part of this Chronicle. He married a Greek, the Countess Diamantína Roma, whose father was appointed Vice-Governor of Ithaka in 1858. Her brother married a sister of the Queen of Montenegro. In 1860 Bowen was appointed Governor of Queensland.

Chichester Fortescue (later Lord Carlingford), whom Lear had first met in Rome in 1845, was one of Lear's closest friends, and he followed his career as a Liberal politician with affectionate interest. Many of the passages in the present text are taken from letters Lear wrote to Fortescue while in Corfu, and two passages are from letters to Countess Waldegrave, Fortescue's wife.

See Introduction, p. 13.

Knowsley Hall had been the home of the Stanley family since the fourteenth century when John de Stanley, grandfather of the 1st Earl of Derby, married the heiress Isabel Lathom; and it was to Knowsley that Lord Stanley, heir to the 12th Earl of Derby (founder of the Derby stakes), invited Lear in 1832 to make drawings of the animals in his private menagerie. See Introduction, p. 22.

The Palace referred to is the Palace of St Michael and St George, the residency of the Lord High Commissioner. During the first years of the British Protectorate, the Commissioner and his retinue had been housed in a small and unimpressive building in the Old Fortress; and it was on account of this that Sir Thomas Maitland, the first Lord High Commissioner, sought leave to build a new residency at the north end of the Esplanade. The Ionian Senate approved the erection of the building in November 1818. It was also in 1818 that the Order of St Michael and St George had been founded in England 'for natives of the Ionian Islands and of the Island of Malta'; and this event was associated with the new building by naming the latter after the Order, whose headquarters it was to be.

    The plan of the building, as well as the overseeing of its construction, was entrusted to a colonel of the Royal Engineers, Sir George Whitmore; and the foundation-stone was laid on the 23rd of April 1819 — the day which coincides with the feast of St George. After various changes of plan, it was officially inaugurated in April 1823. Built of white stone imported from Malta, and of wood from Italy, and by workers who spoke nine different languages, it is perhaps the finest Regency-style building to be found outside the British Isles. The ground floor consisted of administrative offices and housed the Ionian Parliament (until a separate building was built for it) and the Ionian Senate. On the first floor were the state rooms, in which the official receptions and state balls took place (there were two state balls each year, one on the anniversary of the granting of the Ionian constitution, and the other on the birthday of the reigning English sovereign), not to mention the various other social events to which Lear's journals and letters frequently refer. In spite of war and other damage the town has suffered since the British left, the Palace, although in need of maintenance, has survived intact. Its first floor now houses a fine collection of Asiatic art. For further details, see Stelio Hourmoúzios, 'The English Palace' (*Country Life*, April 26, 1962), and Maria Aspióti, *The Palace of St Michael and St George* (Corfu, 1964, in Greek).

A.L. 4 December 1855

Franklin Lushington, a lawyer and classical scholar, had toured Greece with Lear in 1849, and it was with him, now appointed Judge to the Supreme Court in the Ionian Islands, that Lear returned to Corfu in 1855. As is clear from several of Lear's comments in the present text, their friendship hardly flourished as Lear would have liked, though it lasted throughout his life. Indeed, it is possible, if not probable, that Lushington, although he had helped Lear to prepare some of his work for publication, was actually responsible, in his capacity of legatee and literary executor, for destroying a considerable number of Lear's papers — notably much of his diary — after his death.

Kourkouméli is the name of one of Corfu's most distinguished families. Sir Demétrius Kourkouméli, K.C.M.G., head of the family during Lear's sojourn on the island and his first landlord in Corfu, was Regent of Corfu in 1864, and presented the parting British garrison with the Municipal Council's farewell tribute. Lear often visited the Kourkoumélis at their country house at Afra, and appears to have been on most friendly terms with Effrosíni, known as Frosso or Foffy, one of the daughters of Demétrius Kourkouméli.

A.L. 13 December 1855

The Crimean War.

A.L. 18 December 1855

Khimára was a town on the coastal plain of Albania opposite the northern coast of Corfu which lent its name to the whole district and the mountains that hemmed it in. Lear had visited the area in 1848, and it — and particularly the beauty of the Khimariote women — had made a deep impression on him. See *Edward Lear in Greece* (London, 1965), pp. 131 ff.

Wife of Sir John Young, who had been appointed Lord High Commissioner in 1855.

A.L. Christmas Day 1855

Bishop Heber had been Bishop of Calcutta.

E.T. 15 February 1856

Kastrádes was the name of the suburb now known as Garítsa. It extends along the Bay of Garítsa and the promenade is still a favourite strolling-ground of Corfiotes.

A.L. 18 April 1856

Lear took rooms at 65 Oxford Terrace, London, in February 1853, and retained them until early December in the same year, when he left England for Alexandria.

For information about St Spirídon, see Introduction, pp. 10–11.

A.L. 24 May 1856

The domestic Julus to which Lear refers is a species of millepede, one of the Iulus genus.

A.L. 19 June 1856

Smith O'Brien was the famous Irish revolutionary. He was tried for high treason in 1848 and sentenced to be hanged, drawn and quartered; he was, however, only transported to Tasmania, receiving a pardon in 1854.

A.L. 20 July 1856

James Uwins, a painter whom Lear had met in Rome in 1838, and with whom he had walked from Rome to Naples in May of that year.

Mrs Warner, who lived in Bath, and was apparently a friend of the Lear family, as well as being very wealthy, left Lear £500 in her will when she died in 1849. The rest of her fortune of nearly £50,000 she had bequeathed to perpetual widows. 'I thought directly I heard of this matter that I would instantly marry one of the 30 viddies', Lear told Fortescue, 'only then it occurred to me that she would not be a viddy any more if I married her.'

A.L. 15 December 1856

Edward Gage was the brother of Viscount Gage and a colonel in the Royal Horse Artillery. He was married to a cousin, Arabella.

Viscount Kirkwall was the author of *Four Years in the Ionian Islands* (1864).

Charles Church was a nephew of the veteran of the Greek War of Independence, Sir Richard Church. He had been Lear's companion on his travels in Boeotia and Evia (Euboea) in 1848.

A.L. 4 January 1857

Butrínto Lake takes its name from the ancient Buthrotum (now Butrínto, uninhabited), which traditionally was built by the Trojan Helenus on a low hill at the seaward end of a narrow channel leading from the lake. The town possessed fine harbours and fisheries and was a port of call on the coasting route along the Epiros. It has pre-historic remains, a fine theatre, and strong Hellenistic fortifications. The centre of a tribal union, it later became a Roman colony.

A.L. 18 January 1857

F. Clowes was a friend of Lear's from Knowsley days.

C.F. 1 May 1857

Henry Labouchere, at this time Colonial Secretary, became Lord Taunton in 1859. The doctor appointed to Mauritius in place of Bowen was Humphrey Sandwith, C.B., who had acted as staff-surgeon during the Crimean War. Prior to that — in 1853 — he had been correspondent to the *Times* at Constantinople.

C.F. 27 December 1857

Theodore Bunsen was the son of Baron and Baronness Bunsen. Baron Bunsen had been German Ambassador in London from 1841 to 1854.

A.L. 28 December 1857

The Marchioness of Headfort, wife of the second Marquis, was the widow of Sir William Hay McNaughten, Bart., of the Bengal Civil Service, assassinated at Cabul in 1841. Lear writes in a letter to Fortescue (27 December 1857): 'Lord H. is described to me as a well got up blasé old boy; milady not to be perceived clearly, along of Indian shawls & diamonds, of which jewels & her concealment of them, during a flight from some Afghan place when she was Lady M(cNaughten), wonderful tales are about.'

Lord Clermont was Chichester Fortescue's elder brother. He married a daughter of the Marquis of Ormond.

C.F. 10 January 1858

The General in question was Sir George Buller who, after serving in the Crimean War and the first and second Kaffir Wars, commanded a division in the Ionian Islands.

Sir Henry Holland was physician to William IV, Queen Victoria and Prince Albert. In 1815 he had published his *Travels in the Ionian Islands, Albania, Thessaly, Macedonia*.

Dandolo and Zambelli were extreme radicals in the Ionian Assembly and both lived in Condi Terrace. Scarpe was probably Lear's landlord.

J. 19 November 1861

Mr (afterwards Sir) Henry Drummond Wolff was appointed Secretary to Sir Henry Storks, the Lord High Commissioner, in May 1860, after the departure of Sir George Bowen. He was the son of the Rev. Joseph Wolff, of Hebrew origin, who in the 1820s had preached to the Jews in Corfu and Kefaloniá. Joseph Wolff was also the first modern missionary to preach to the Jews at Jerusalem, styling himself 'Apostle of our Lord Jesus Christ for Palestine, Persia, Bokhara and Balkh'. See his *Travels and Adventures* (1861 ed.).

C.F. 1 December 1861

Sir Patrick Colquhoun was appointed Chief Justice of the Ionian Islands in 1860, in the place of Franklin Lushington.

As noted in the Introduction, the Jews constituted one of the major elements in the population of Corfu during the time of the British Protectorate; and their number substantially increased over this period. On the whole they appear to have kept a remarkably low profile until the 1850s, when they were responsible for some slight agitation in an attempt to secure a modicum of political rights. Both Sir John Young and Sir Henry Storks took up their cause, but — given the hostility of the rest of the population, and the indifference or worse of Senate and Assembly — they could achieve but little. As Young wrote in 1858, 'I have not been fortunate enough to gain for them, though I have repeatedly attempted it, ought but the scantiest measure of toleration, and some assistance for their schools; but they remain excluded from the exercise of the Elective Franchise and from practice at the bar'; and a few years later, in 1861, Storks was to write in the same strain: 'The position of the Jews in these States is very unsatisfactory.... Public feeling is very strong against them. Were it not for the Protectorate they would be constantly exposed to insult and even danger . . . they are public creditors for no small amount, and they are consequently unpopular on this account as well as on religious grounds.' It might also be added that, along with the Orthodox Christians, the Jews of Corfu were the object of almost continual missionary activity during the Protectorate, one mission (the *English Presbyterian Mission to the Jews of Corfu*) being formed specifically for Jewish evangelization.

Essays and Reviews was a collection of essays on religious subjects written from a Broad Church standpoint and published in 1860. A meeting of bishops denounced the book for its liberalism in 1861 and the *Essays* were finally synodically banned in 1864.

Lady Emily Kozzíris was daughter of the second Earl of Clancarty. Her husband, Giovanni Kozzíris, was Keeper of the Prisons.

J. 8 December 1861

Baron d'Everton was Resident of Kefaloniá and subsequently of Lefkáda (St Maura). The Resident, appointed by the High Commissioner, had the right to suspend the power of the local authorities and to approve the proceedings of the Regents (nominated local functionaries who formed part of the Judicial Bench) and their municipal councils.

The Casino was the name given by the Lord High Commissioner Sir Frederick Adam and Lady Adam to a summer palace they built for themselves above the coast beyond the Bay of Garítsa — the idea of such a palace being instigated possibly by Lady Adam, the Corfiote Nina Palatianoú, anxious to extend the settings for her social activities. Its official name was the House of St Pandeléimon, for it was built on the site of a church — then in ruins — dedicated to that saint. The building, in the neo-classical Regency style, was started in 1828 — its architect may have been Sir George Whitmore, also responsible for the Palace of St Michael and St George — and was ready for occupation in 1831. After Adam's departure in 1832, his successor, Lord Nugent, proposed that the building should be used for some public purpose, and in the event, after much procrastination, in 1840 it was adapted to serve as a seminary, a role it occupied, however, for only two years. During the subsequent years of the British Protectorate it was used from time to time either by the Lord High Commissioner himself or by members of his staff, civil or military. After the cession of Corfu to Greece in 1864 it passed to the Royal House of Greece, one of whose members rechristened it *Mon Repos*. It was there that Prince Philip, Duke of Edinburgh, was born in 1921.

E.T. 15 December 1861

The Great International Exhibition opened at South Kensington on 1 May 1862.

The 'American Outrage' probably denotes the American civil war or some incident in it. The war had begun on 12 April 1861 when Confederate guns in Charleston opened fire on Fort Sumter, South Carolina.

J. 24 December 1861

The clown and circus at Highgate were connected with one of the earliest of Lear's attacks of acute depression which he called 'the Morbids'. In his journal entry for 24 March 1877, Lear writes: 'The earliest of all the morbidnesses I can recollect must have been somewhere about 1819, when my father took me to a field near Highgate, where was a rural performance of gymnastic clowns etc. & a band. The music was good — at least it attracted me — & the sunset & twilight I remember as yesterday. And I can recollect crying half the night after all the small gaiety broke up, & also suffering for days at the memory of the past scene.'

J. 30 December 1861

Julia Goldsmid, who arrived in Corfu on 27 January 1862, was the daughter of Sir Francis Goldsmid, the first Jew called to the English Bar and the first Jewish Q.C. and Bencher. He was President of the Senate of University College, London.

J. 10 February 1862

Geoffrey Hornby was the second son of Lear's old friend, Admiral Sir Phipps Hornby.

J. 15 April 1862

Casa Kandóni is the handsome villa built by Antónios Kandónis on a hill (Kandóni Hill) about 2 miles south-west of the town of Corfu. The villa — now called Mamalous — still stands. D'Annuncio and Eleanora Dusa lived there for some months towards the end of the last century, and D'Annuncio's *Il Fuoco* was written there and dedicated to the cypresses of Mamalous. Kandónis himself was of Epirote origin. He was a merchant, the richest Corfiote in urban property, very astute and hardworking, and apparently extremely honest. In 1822 he and his wife adopted Mariétta, a refugee girl from Souli, from the Boggari clan, and made her their sole heiress. In 1840 she married Angelos Kogerínas. The villa of Mamalous is still owned by a Kogerínas (a nephew of the painter Lykoúrgos Kogerínas).

J. 21 April 1862

The monastery of St Sabas near Jerusalem.

J. 29 April 1862

Sir George Markoran was one of the two Ionian members of the Supreme Council of Justice who were summarily dismissed by Sir Henry Storks.

C.F. 7 May 1862

The 'medium' Forster, to whom all London was flocking at this time, so much so that the *Times* devoted a leading article to the matter.

Kinglake was the author of the celebrated history of the Crimean War.

J. 14 May 1862

Count John Capodístrias, born in Corfu in 1776, became first President of the newly-founded Greek state in 1827, and was assassinated at Nafplion in 1831 by two members of the famous Mavromikhális clan of the Greek Mani. This assassination is possibly the 'murder affair' to which reference is made here.

J. 22 November 1862

Why Mr Baillie was called the 'extinct Duke' Lear does not explain, although he added a footnote to the diary entry for this day, the first part of which reads: 'The "extinct Duke" Mr Baillie has a wife which her name is Lady Pigott.'

C.F. 30 November 1862

John William Colenso (1814–1883) was appointed first bishop of the newly constituted see of Natal in 1853, and provoked criticism by not insisting on the divorce of the wives of polygamists on their baptism, and violent opposition when, in a commentary on St Paul's Epistle to the Romans issued in 1861, he denied eternal punishment and rejected much traditional sacramental theology. In spite of being formally deposed by his metropolitan, he contrived to retain his position and the affection of his diocese until his death.

See Introduction, p. 19.

C.F. 3 December 1862

Evelyn Baring (later Lord Cromer) was aide to Sir Henry Storks, the Lord High Commissioner. It was with Baring that Lear left Corfu on 4 April 1864, and their friendship lasted until Lear's death.

C.F. 1 January 1863

Lear did in fact publish his *Views in the Seven Ionian Islands* in 1863.

C.F. 11 January 1863

The Judges that Sir Henry Storks dismissed were the two Ionian members of the Supreme Council of Justice.

J. 4 February 1863

George Finlay (1799–1875), initially a Philhellene but subsequently increasingly critical of modern Greece's political and social developments, wrote a monumental *History of Greece from its conquest by the Romans to the present time, B.C. 146 to A.D. 1864* in 7 volumes. Although the whole work was finally published in 1877, individual volumes had been appearing over the previous decades, and it was probably one of these that Lear was reading.

J. 24 February 1863

D. T. Ansted, a well-known geologist, was author of a book entitled *The Ionian Islands in the Year 1863* (London, 1863).

C.F. 1 March 1863

Lord Seymour was the son of the Duke of Somerset.

J. 6 March 1863

Spirídon Valaorítis was a member of the distinguished Ionian family of that name, cousin of the poet Aristotélis Valaorítis. He studied Law at the Ionian Academy and in 1849 was elected to the Ionian Parliament.

J. 7 March 1863

Sir Percy Florence Shelley, only son of the poet, succeeded his grandfather as third baronet in 1844. He married the widow of the Hon. C. R. St John.

C.F. 23 March 1863

Lear's sentiments here are prompted by the fact that Fortescue had recently (20 January 1863) married Lady Waldegrave.

C.F. 7 February 1864

The Duke of Newcastle, Secretary of State for the Colonies.

J. 15 September 1877

The Russo-Turkish war that broke out in April 1877. The arrival of the Tsar's army within striking distance of Constantinople so aroused hopes of liberation among Greeks still under Turkish domination that uprisings broke out in Epiros, Thessaly and Crete. The 'discussion' about Greeks moving or not moving here mentioned probably concerned the advisability of sending the Greek army to the support of these risings. In the event the Treaty of San Stefano, signed by Russia and Turkey in March 1878, ended the war before the Greek army could march.

J. 19 September 1877

Hubert and Arnold Congreve were the sons of Walter Congreve, Undermaster at Rugby and second master at Malborough, whom Lear found already living at San Remo when he moved there in 1870. Lear became a close friend of the family, and developed a particular affection for Hubert, whom he had hoped might become an artist under his tuition and indeed might fulfil the role of spiritual companionship that Lushington had failed to fulfil. It was the shattering of this hope in the summer of 1877 — Hubert decided to leave San Remo for England, to take up a university course — that produced what was perhaps the last major emotional crisis of Lear's life. See Vivien Noakes, *The Life of a Wanderer*, op. cit., pp. 276–277.

The dispatch in question was one that Sir John Young (Lord High Commissioner 1855–1859) sent in the autumn of 1858 to the Secretary of State recommending that the islands of Corfu and Naxos should be annexed by Britain, while the other five Ionian islands should be ceded to Greece. The dispatch was leaked, and was published in the *Daily News*. The suggestion that Corfu should be thus annexed naturally incensed the Corfiotes and reinforced their already strong aspirations for union with Greece.

J. 20 September 1877

Henry Bulwer was Lear's host in Cerigo (Kythera) when he visited the island in 1863.

2nd March 1877 was the date on which George had returned from San Remo to Corfu — he had not been well and was anxious to be with his three remaining children. George actually stayed in Corfu through the winter and spring following Lear's final visit there, and then returned to San Remo in the summer of 1878. He was with Lear at San Remo until his death in 1883.

There was an Old Man of Corfu,
   Who never knew what he should do...

ALBANIA

Butrínto

Kassiópi

Mon. Pantokrátora
Mount San Salvador

Panteleímona

Barbáti

Vido

The Citadel
Fort Neuf
Bay of Garítsa
Fort Abraham
The Casino
Lazareto (Gouvíno)
Mandoúki
(Mon Rep
Análipsis
Kanóni
Vlakher
Pondik

Smakierás

Nimfes

Alepoú

Sokráki

Potamós
Evrópouli

Agrafí

Gouvia

Afra

Mon. Kombítsi
Virós
Aghios Yiórgios
Kinopi
Psorarí
Kalafatiónes
Aghii

Skriperó

Horoepískopi

Kastellános

Doukádes
Gardelládes

Pelekas
Garoún

Spargus [Pagus]

Mount San Giorgio

Lakónes
Mon. Myrtiótissa

Makrádes
Palaiokastrítsa
Kastro St Angelo

Kravia

MAP SHOWING THE PLACES LEAR VISITED IN CORFU

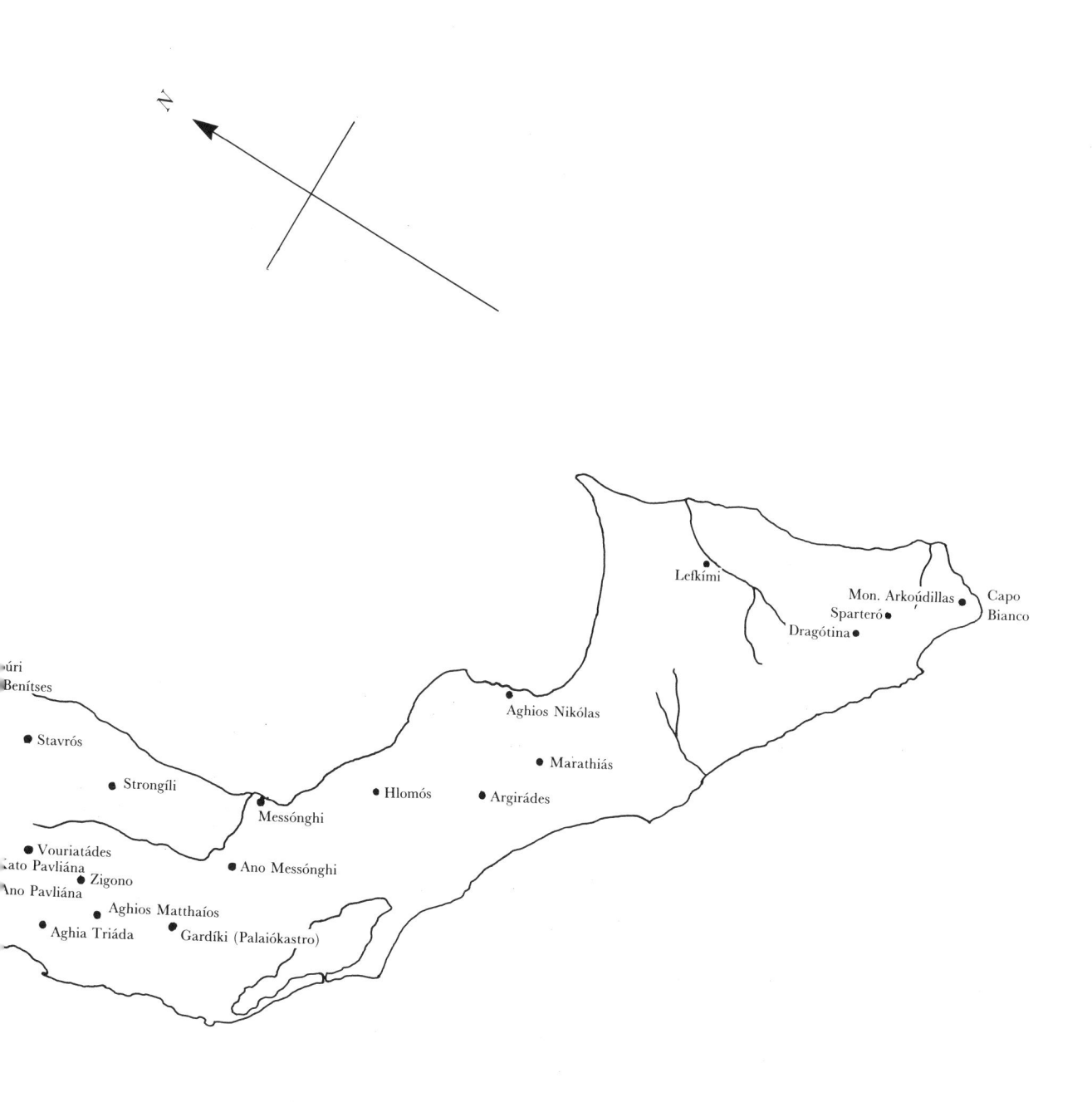